The Satisfaction Factor

A diet that gets results for us must work with our female bodies, not against them:

- It must include foods that help us deal with what I believe is the number-one fat-fighting problem for women: not hunger, per se, but *cravings*.
- A diet that works for women must give us enough food in the right proportions to prevent intense hunger, help protect against muscle loss and flab, keep our bodies energized and purring along at peak efficiency.
- A diet that works for women should satisfy our need for variety and be composed of foods that are good-tasting and easy to prepare, or order (if we're eating away from home), so that we're not led into temptation by boredom or inconvenience.

In short, a diet that really works for women has to satisfy us hormonewise, moodwise, nutritionwise, and tastewise. Otherwise, we won't stay with it long enough to see it through to success.

The beauty of this plan is that it *does* meet all our special requirements. It has made a major difference in my life, and in the lives of other women who have tried it.

D1115949

THE WOMEN'S BODYRHYTHM DIET

DIET

with the 28-Day Antistress and Craving Program that Can Change the Way You Lose Weight ... and Keep it Off

HENRIETTA SPENCER, Ph.D.
and Margaret Danbrot

BANTAM BOOKS
NEW YORK · TORONTO · LONDON · SYDNEY · AUCKLAND

NOTE

Fitness, diet, and health are matters which necessarily vary from individual to individual. Readers should speak with their own doctor about their individual needs before starting any diet program. Consulting one's physician is especially important if one is on any medication or is already under medical care for any illness.

THE WOMEN'S BODYRHYTHM DIET

A Bantam Book / July 1990

ISBN 0-553-28470-3

Published simultaneously in the United States and Canada

Bantam Books are published by Bantam Books, a division of Bantam Doubleday Dell Publishing Group, Inc. Its trademark, consisting of the words ''Bantam Books'' and the portrayal of a rooster, is Registered in U.S. Patent and Trademark Office and in other countries. Marca Registrada. Bantam Books, 666 Fifth Avenue, New York, New York 10103.

PRINTED IN THE UNITED STATES OF AMERICA

OPM   0 9 8 7 6 5 4 3 2 1

Contents

Acknowledgments

Without the help, support and patience of many, no one would have ever seen this book. The first note of thanks goes to my family who always cheered me on and put up with me when I got bogged down under pressure.

Of course, this book would never have made it to the bookstore without Alison Acker, former editor at Bantam now at Villard Books, who reviewed my original proposal and brought it to Bantam's attention, or Barbara Alpert, Bantam's editor, who inherited the project and helped me through many revisions.

Much appreciation goes to my agent, Connie Clausen, who maneuvered this book through the publishing maze and to my co-author, Margaret Danbrot who helped coordinate my stacks of notes and translated a collection of journal references into a coherent and readable form. Roberta Lamb, registered dietician, provided nutritional advice and reviewed some of the more nutritionally oriented chapters. Many other dietary facts and tips came from Tina Botnick, registered dietician, and some psychological input came from Los Angeles psychologist Linda Trozzolino, Ph.D.

Finally, I want to thank my female clients. You women told me of your nagging food cravings and gave me feedback of how my anti-craving plan helped you. Thank you ladies, THE WOMEN'S BODYRHYTHM DIET would never have been possible without you.

1 | A Different Diet for Women Only

You are about to learn some facts that can change the way you think about yourself, change your way of eating, change your shape . . . and change your life.

You'll learn how to succeed where countless others have failed. How to win the war that has defeated millions of other women. How to lose pounds of fat, safely and surely. And how to keep them off.

In short, you're going to learn all about the Women's Bodyrhythm Diet and how to make it work for you.

I'm also going to explain why you, *as a woman*, have had trouble losing weight in the past. Why the fat goes straight to your hips, rear, and thighs, and once there, why it's so difficult to budge. Why you get food cravings that can lead to wild eating binges. Why it's harder for you to stick to a diet at certain times of the month. And how, with the Bodyrhythm Diet, you can finally overcome these biological obstacles to slimness and have a trimmer body.

The Women's Bodyrhythm Diet is a new and different approach to female fat-fighting. It's a unique program that helps promote weight loss in even the most diet-resistant women because it works in harmony with—not against—the physiological and psychological rhythms of a woman's body.

- The Women's Bodyrhythm Diet will help you trim away excess fat. You'll feel better, look better. But that's not all.
- It will help you control the food cravings that interfere with healthy eating, on a diet or off. Now you can defuse diet-destroying binges and curb body-bloating, guilt-inducing pig-outs!
- It will help you minimize the mood swings that make you feel down, depressed, defeated, or mean and irritable— negative emotional states that can lead to overeating and interfere with your ability to function your best in all areas of your life.

From Desperation, Success

I developed the Women's Bodyrhythm Diet out of desperation. It grew out of my own feelings of frustration in attempting to lose fat and to control binges, and later on, out of the difficulty I experienced in maintaining my weight loss. It's the result as well of my professional concern for the overweight women I counsel—women who had tried and failed countless times to lose the fat that made them miserable and who, like me, were often haunted by food cravings that led to overeating followed by feelings of discouragement and self-hate. Not to mention weight gain or re-gain.

Over the years of fighting my own fat problem, and later helping other women fight theirs, it became clear: Ordinary diets—even the "super-diets" devised by celebrity doctors and other weight-loss specialists—rarely lived up to the extravagant claims made for them. When they did work, those diets were most effective for men; women didn't get the same good results. Something, obviously, was wrong. Was it the fault of the diets? Or were we, as women, to blame for our fat-fighting failures?

Desperation spurred me to take a closer look at the mechanisms of fat absorption and storage in women. Listening to my clients criticize themselves for giving in to food cravings, and experiencing those same food cravings myself, led me to study the role played by "mysterious" insistent desires for food in women. The distress of these women (and my own) led me ultimately to investigate the way hormones—the female hormones estrogen and progesterone, along with insulin—changes in brain chemicals, biological factors, and societal pressures work against women to make us fatter than men, and keep us fatter than men.

The Women's Bodyrhythm Diet is the end product of that investigation.

Later on I'll explain more about fat, cravings, hormones, biology, and other factors that influence our eating behaviors and our bodies. I'll tell you why it's easier for women than for men to put on excess pounds. Why we have a harder time losing weight than they do. And how to fight fat and win, despite these roadblocks to success.

But before I do, a few words of encouragement: It doesn't matter how many diets you've tried and given up on in the past. It doesn't matter how down on yourself you may feel at this very moment, or how low your opinion of your own willpower. I, too, experienced umpteen diet failures and frustrations in the past. I, too, was down on myself, felt totally lacking in willpower. A wimp in the face of food. Yet Bodyrhythm Diet eating principles worked for me and continue to work. Those same principles have helped many, many women lose weight and keep it off. Once you understand and apply them, Bodyrhythm Diet principles will help you, too.

The Bodyrhythm Diet Difference

Think about it a moment and you'll realize that almost every diet you ever tried or even heard of gives a single food plan for both sexes, with the only difference being, in some cases, that women are advised to eat smaller portions or consume fewer calories than men.

But my investigation of studies on fat absorption, food

cravings, and mood swings as they relate to women, made one thing abundantly clear: when these all-important factors are ignored, simply eating less is often not enough to cause the female body to give up or keep off its stores of fat.

I came to several conclusions.

A superior weight-loss plan for women must—like any safe and sensible diet—supply ample amounts of all the nutrients necessary for vibrant good health.

It must include a variety of good-tasting foods that are easy to prepare at home, and readily available in restaurants, since so many of us now eat at least one meal a day away from home.

Most important, it must help defuse food cravings, promote a good balance of certain mood-moderating brain chemicals, and deactivate specific hormonal mechanisms that encourage fat storage in the female body. Unless it does, losing weight and keeping it lost is, for women, almost always a hopeless battle.

Working with dieticians, psychologists, and the clinical research into fat absorption and food cravings, I developed a diet that fits the needs of women, a diet I would later call the Women's Bodyrhythm Diet. It's based on a balance of foods that influence fat storage, appetite, even mood in the female dieter's favor.

And if all the talk about fat absorption, hormones, and brain chemicals makes it sound complicated, believe me, it isn't. The key to it all is to eat more of certain foods at certain times and less of them at others. It's as simple and basic as that.

This unique program is a two-part approach to losing pounds and keeping them off. As you'll see when you turn to the diet itself, it consists of Stage I eating, for times of reduced cravings, and Stage II eating, for those days when changes in hormone levels, moods, and even weight loss itself can result in food cravings and you need all the help you can get to stay on track.

Throughout, you'll be eating increased amounts of those foods that tend to discourage fat storage, as well as

foods that help prevent the brain-chemical changes that
make you feel down, edgy, and less motivated to stick to a
diet.

The Bodyrhythm Diet gives you appealing and good-
for-you breakfasts, lunches, dinners, and snacks. And
because the plan is nutritionally sound, you can repeat the
eating cycles again and again—as often as you need to, in
fact, to get down to your best weight. With a few additions, you can use the plan for a lifetime to *stay* at that best
weight.

Because of the two-part approach, you'll find that this
plan is easy to follow and stick to. Indeed, many of my
clients tell me it's one of the simplest—and most effective—
weight-loss programs they've ever tried. That's because all
the details have been worked out in advance. You'll see.
You'll always know just how much to eat, when, and in
what order. Your body and the food do all the rest.

You can start the Bodyrhythm Diet anytime you like—
I'll tell you how—and start to lose pounds and inches
immediately.

As you do, you may also begin to experience a new
vitality and the benefits of living on a more even emotional
keel. That's how it's been for me, and for many other
women as well.

No Willpower? No Problem!

In my work with dieters, I've seen over and over
again how women tend to blame their lack of diet success
on a lack of "willpower." (I used to do it, too!)

The tragedy, of course, is that when a woman sees
herself as the kind of person who can't lose weight, the
feelings of being a failure often carry over into other areas
of her life. Even women who are high achievers often say
to themselves, "What a weak-willed quitter I must be if I
can't control what I eat and get rid of a few pounds!"
(Sound familiar?)

But what most women don't fully understand is that

the overwhelming cravings for fat-making foods are often promoted by certain hormones, brain chemicals, and other physiological influences that men don't have to deal with. And that when a woman—especially an overweight woman—gives in to her urge for certain foods, or even goes on a binge, it's not just because she can't "control" herself. Rather, she's obeying the demands of her own psychobiology. In short, even a successful, creative, disciplined woman has to be almost twice as strong, twice as determined, twice as motivated as a man in order to lose weight on an ordinary diet. Why? Because on ordinary diets, she must fight her own biology.

But with the Bodyrhythm Diet, you'll be eating foods that help to ease and appease the cravings created by hormones, female biology, and brain chemicals—"safe" foods, that keep you losing weight at a steady pace. This diet asks less of you in the way of willpower. In fact, I think you'll be surprised at all the willpower you discover in yourself when you start the Bodyrhythm Diet, because the balance of foods you'll be eating works *with* you, not against you. No matter what your age, or how much you need to lose.

In case you still need convincing, let me tell you about my own diet experiences, and later on, about a few of my friends and clients. (Of course, I've changed their real names and some of their characteristics to protect their anonymity.)

At five feet, eight inches tall, I weigh between 130 and 135 pounds. New friends can hardly believe I was ever fat. People who knew me in my "fat days" can hardly believe that I've "shaped up."

My weight problem began at the age of twelve. By the time I was twenty-eight, I was a tubby 185 pounds. By that time I was frantic to get rid of 55 pounds and tried every new diet "breakthrough." The pattern was always the same: I started each diet determined to succeed. The first few days were easy and usually resulted in a three- or four-pound weight loss. That chunk was enough to keep me motivated. For a while. But sooner or later—usually sooner—food cravings got the better of me, and I always ended my diet-of-the-moment with a binge that put me right back where I started. Or fatter.

Finally, I joined a diet group, and after two years of meetings, I achieved my weight goal.

I'd always imagined that if I could just get down to my ideal weight, my problems would be over. Fat chance! Food cravings continued to plague me, and my weight bounced up and down repeatedly as I alternately binged and fasted. Almost without realizing it, I was back on the diet trail again, looking for the right diet that would help me control the cravings and stop the binges. Nothing worked. Not the liberal diets that allowed me to eat 1200–1500 calories a day. And not the stricter, fad-type diets, which, I'm sorry to say, I eagerly tried, despite realizing that most of them were unhealthy and some even dangerous.

I remember, for example, one very strict low-calorie regimen. After following it for a week, I was seized in the middle of the night with such an overwhelming urge for Sara Lee Cheesecake that I jumped out of bed and into my sweats and drove frantically to the nearest twenty-four-hour food store. My intention was to eat a single slice and dump the rest into the garbage. Ha! I ate the whole thing—still frozen.

I chalked it up to being "just too weak" for the moment and told myself, "Better luck next time."

Next time was a low-carbohydrate diet that allowed me to eat my fill of fish, meat, chicken, eggs, and certain cheeses. At first, no food cravings, no problems. Not until a few days before the onset of my period. Then, suddenly, I was a woman possessed. By doughnut demons, of all things. That day at lunchtime I screeched off in my car to a doughnut shop and bought a dozen, along with an assortment of coffees "to go"—black, black with sugar, cream no sugar, etc.—because I didn't want the counterman to think all the doughnuts were for me. Of course they were. Another binge, and more feelings of failure.

A few weeks into a revolutionary, nearly no-fat, high-carbohydrate diet, I went off on a chocolate orgy. At an elegant shop specializing in imported chocolates, I directed the clerk to make up a two-pound assortment—nuts, chews, creams, hard centers—and to "Gift-wrap it, please." That way, I imagined, neither he nor the other customers would suspect that the candy was for me alone. Back in my car, I tore off the gift wrap. Then with one hand I popped chocolate after chocolate into my mouth, while with the other I maneuvered through the traffic out of Beverly Hills.

Worse than the binges was my sense of being a fraud. Here I was, already working with overweight women, explaining to them how to modify their behavior and control their eating, and I couldn't practice what I preached. It was a classic case of do as I say, not as I do.

It took years of trying and failing and failing and trying and going on and off diets for the truth to penetrate. It wasn't just plain hunger that made me eat, I wasn't totally weak-willed, and it certainly was never that I didn't care about my weight. No, I was responding to biology!

When I asked female friends about their attempts to diet, I discovered that though the details of their stories varied, the plots were remarkably similar.

Ruth, a doctor in her middle forties, told me that Chinese food was her downfall. She was forever trying to lose fifteen pounds. But after a few weeks or so on every diet, she found herself irresistibly drawn to fried rice, egg rolls, and platters of chow fun. As a result, she considered herself a failure.

A failure! Here was a woman who mustered the strength and determination to put herself through college and medical school and later to become a well-known and respected practitioner in her field, and she imagined herself a failure because she couldn't withstand her body's demands for certain foods at certain times.

And then there was Clare, who battled her way up the public-relations ladder to become the head of her own successful agency. Obviously, it wasn't an accident that she landed at the top. It took discipline and lots of headstrong perseverance. Nevertheless, like Ruth, and like me, she was convinced that she lacked the willpower to lose weight—in her case, thirty pounds that made her so self-conscious she never wore shorts or a bathing suit. For Clare, bread-and-butter pig-outs were the problem. After each one of her binges, it took days of constant reassurance from her friends to convince her that she wasn't a "hopeless failure."

For me, for my friends Ruth and Clare, and many of my clients, fear of fat is a thing of the past. Not because we all suddenly found new ways to bolster our willpower. Willpower, or the lack of it, was never the whole problem. It was food cravings resulting from hormone fluctuations and poor eating habits, along with other physiological and psychological factors, that made us, *as women,* fat-prone and diet-resistant. A new way of eating changed all that.

Now think hard about your own diet experiences. Was it really hunger that cause you to rush off to the kitchen, the grocery store, or the candy stand and fill up on the foods you craved? Was it hunger that made you continue to eat even after you felt comfortably full . . . even stuffed? Probably not. I'd be willing to bet you did it because the diets you tried didn't satisfy your cravings for certain foods. They allowed your hormones, biology, and brain chemicals to take control. They didn't take into consideration your distinctly female physiology.

But the Women's Bodyrhythm Diet gives you the ammunition you need to ease cravings even as it promotes fat loss and a slimmer, shapelier body. Don't worry about willpower. Bodyrhythm Diet principles will help you take control and stay in control even on the dangerous, high-craving days when you're most likely to slip up.

As women, more fat-prone and diet-resistant than men, we need to take a different approach to losing weight. The Women's Bodyrhythm Diet is it.

2 | Your Female Fat Handicap

My client, Sally, sat across from me. A competent, highly paid, thirty-five-year-old sales representative, she felt successful and in control—except for her weight. Sally leaned forward and, eyes filling with tears, confided that sometimes she almost believed there was a "conspiracy" working to make her fat and keep her fat. "Paranoid, right?" she added with a weak, wry smile

No, I didn't think Sally was paranoid. In fact, there is more than a grain of truth to this particular "conspiracy theory." Many elements—biological, psychological, and societal—combine in ways that can frustrate women in their efforts at weight control. Elements that don't affect men. Which is why we often have such difficulty losing pounds on the very same diets that quickly trim excess weight from men.

I'm going to tell you more about some of these fat facts of life, facts that are not included in other weight-control programs. Much of this information will be new to you, and initially discouraging, perhaps. But chin up. Knowing how and why women tend to get fat should take a lot of the mystery out of achieving slimness. Gaining a better understanding of your female fat handicap will, I'm convinced, reinforce your efforts to switch to antifat eating, and increase your chances for success on the Women's Bodyrhythm Diet.

Fat Fact #1. Where fat is concerned, men and women are not created equal!

Men are less fat-prone than women. They don't gain weight as easily as we do, and they lose weight more quickly.

The body of a lean, fit man who exercises regularly and vigorously, is made up of about 10-percent fat; the body of a comparably well-exercised woman, however, is about 20-percent fat. As for the average, healthy Americans, men are still less fat at 15 percent to our 25 percent.

The difference has to do with the fact that men are more muscular, and muscle tissue burns more calories than fat. In fact, it has been estimated that muscle tissue burns five more calories per pound than sluggish fat tissue.

What does this mean for us? Well, since women—even slim women—are fatter and less muscular than men, we burn calories at a slower rate during the same activity—whether it be exercise, talking on the telephone, sleeping, etc. As a result, what men eat is more likely to be used as fuel. What we eat is more likely to stay sitting around in our fat cells.

In a sense, the female body, with its higher percentage of slow-burning fat tissue, is a fat trap.

Nature's dirty trick? Yes, when considered from the perspective of twentieth-century America, where food is shoved at us from all sides yet slimness is the ideal and a mark of higher social status. But nature has her reasons. The female affinity for fat was built into our bodies thousands of years ago to ensure the preservation of the species.

When our early ancestors roamed the earth, remember, there was no guarantee as to where or when the next meal would appear—no drive-throughs, no all-night markets. In prehistoric times, feast or famine was the rule.

By endowing the female with a supply of extra fat, nature helped prehistoric woman sustain a pregnancy during the lean times. It's the same today. A reserve fuel supply of extra fat can be used to feed the unborn baby if the mother goes hungry, acts as insulation by keeping the fetus at an even temperature, and functions as a built-in shock absorber, protecting against sudden jarring.

Female fat is so linked to survival of the species that a woman whose total body fat falls below 17 percent of her weight may stop ovulating—nature's way of helping ensure that the female who isn't fat enough to bear a healthy baby won't conceive.

Natural selection appears to be the reason our bodies became fat traps. Anthropologists speculate that during the early migrations out of the warmer "Garden of Eden" —most likely somewhere in Africa—to the colder continents of Europe and Asia, fatter people survived longer and bore more children. Fat women were probably looked on by men as being more appealing, sexier, better mate material than thinner women. Treasured and admired, these fatter, more fertile women no doubt got more of their fair share of food in times of scarcity, which gave them an additional edge over their thinner counterparts. As a result, fewer thin women survived and reproduced, while fat women flourished (relatively speaking), passing on to their daughters their own genetic traits for female obesity. And now we're stuck with fat-prone genes.

Man's greater muscularity is also thought to be the result of natural selection. After all, strength and endurance were assets in hunting, a primary occupation of our caveman forefathers. Those who were too weak to bring home the bacon, or the wild boar, must have been viewed as poor potential husbands and sired few offspring, while the gene pool overflowed with contributions from the more muscular, macho males.

Now it should be clear why most of the men you know—your coworkers, friends, father, husband, or lover— are more muscular and leaner than most of the women you know. Both sexes are products of their own somewhat different genetic makeups.

And now you know why most men, when they need or

want to lose a few pounds, can do so quickly and easily—especially when they combine calorie reduction with exercise. (It's estimated that during the same physical activity, a man's body "naturally" expends almost twice the number of calories as a woman's body!) And why, when you and a male partner start on the same diet as the same time, your body is tenacious about holding on to fat, while his gives it up relatively quickly.

You can't totally change biology. But you *can* change to a way of eating that takes your special female physiology into account and gently coaxes your body to give up its stores of fat while it also encourages your body to store less fat. That's what the Women's Bodyrhythm Diet was designed to do.

Fat Fact #2. You are literally "shaped" by your sex hormones and your genes.

Natural selection favors fatness in women; hormones are the tools nature uses to ensure that fatness. There is more than one female sex hormone, and more than one way these and other substances work to turn our bodies into fat traps. But for now, I want to focus on estrogen, the hormone that has the most direct bearing on the female *shape*.

Produced primarily within the ovaries, estrogen (and other hormones) triggers changes in a young girl's body as she approaches puberty. The rapid growth spurt occurring just before puberty slows to a near halt (by the time of her first period she will have reached about 90 percent of her adult height). Her pelvis bones grow and widen. Her breasts develop. Total body fat increases, much of it accumulating on her rear, hips, and thighs, resulting in a rounder, fuller, more "feminine" shape.

Increasing levels of estrogen encourage fat cells already in place in a young woman's breasts, hips, and thighs to produce more of an enzyme called lipoprotein lipase—LPL, for short. LPL acts as fat-padder, "pulling" fat from the bloodstream and directing that fat into the fat cells LPL inhabits.

Heredity is another factor influencing individual body configuration. To a large degree, genes determine breast size, how much the pelvis will widen during puberty, and whether hips and thighs become voluptuous or remain relatively streamlined. Like mother, like daughter, in other words. Or, if not like mother, then look to maternal or paternal grandmas for a clue to why you're shaped the way you are.

Nevertheless, without denying the importance of heredity, I want to stress that estrogen governs the *pattern* of female fat, directing most of it to breasts and lower body. The fat pattern of large hips and thighs is typically female, although women can also have accumulations of fat concentrated around their abdomen or above.

The male body also produces fat-depositing LPL, but, of course, not enough estrogen to stimulate high levels of LPL and result in the female pattern of (lower-body) fat distribution. On the contrary, male hormones may help steer fat in the overweight man to his midsection, forming a "spare tire" or a "beer belly," and he tends to stay lean in just those places where most women are well padded.

(Abdominal, middle- and upper-body fat is much more lethal than lower-body fat. Anyone—male or female—fatter through the middle or on the abdomen is several times more likely to have diabetes. And more fat in any upper-body region—waistline, trunk, arms, back, neck, chin— puts a person at greater risk of developing heart disease than someone fat in the rear, hips, and thighs.)

Actually, it's the male hormone testosterone that gives men a major fat-fighting advantage, since it encourages muscle growth. And muscle tissue, as I explained, is "active," in that it burns more calories than fat tissue. So, while *their* sex hormones build fat-fighting muscle, *ours* promote fat storage. *Vive la différence?*

No diet will totally alter your pattern of fat distribution. Whether the extra padding is concentrated in your lower regions or above depends partly on your hormones. (Relatively more "apple-shaped," than "peared," could be the result of a woman's higher-than-average level of male hormones, but in no way makes her less feminine.) Weight loss plus exercise will slim and tone you all over. And because the Bodyrhythm Diet was developed to counter excessive hormone-directed fat storage, it should work for you, as a woman, better than any unisex diet.

Fat Fact #3. "Female fat" can be harder to get rid of, and stay rid of, than "male fat."

All fat is not the same. Researchers now distinguish between two different kinds of obesity:

Fatter fat cells (hypertrophic obesity). In this type of obesity, fat cells are filled to bursting, but their *numbers* are near normal. Upper-body fat, common in men, tends to fall into this category. Fewer, but fuller, fat cells is the easiest kind of fat to diet away. And once gone, it tends to stay gone, unless the dieter goes back to old, fat-making eating habits.

More fat cells (hyperplastic obesity). Here, fat cells are not yet filled to capacity, but there are too *many* of them. Unlike the simpler condition of fatter fat cells that can be dieted down, the condition of more fat cells is harder to control. That's because these fat cells are already at near-normal size and can't shrink much more. There are just too many. Lower-body fat—the kind that is typically female, remember—is usually hyperplastic in that it is characterized by greater-than-normal numbers of normal-sized fat cells.

Concentrated on hips, rear, and thighs, this type of fat has been compared to a "stocked pantry" that is difficult to be unlocked and raided, or depleted, except in certain circumstances, such as an emergency food source for the fetus or when a new mother breast-feeds her infant. No wonder hyperplastic obesity (more fat cells) is so stubborn. Nature, it appears, lays in a supply of extra fat cells in the lower body for the sake of the baby-to-be and has taken special precautions to see that it is not easily dieted away. (Never mind that a woman may not plan on having children! Never mind that a mother gets more than enough to eat and doesn't need this extra larder on her hips. This fat is stored there from puberty on, just in case.)

You may have heard that the *number* of fat cells doesn't increase much after puberty. That's diet oldthink. New research indicates that fat cells can and do "multiply" at any age if there is significant rapid weight gain. In other words, when existing fat cells are all filled up and can't accommodate more fat, the body will, if necessary, create new fat cells—as might happen, for example, when a pregnant woman gains too much weight too quickly. (Note: This is *not* to be taken as a warning to gain as little weight as possible if you become pregnant. Most obstetricians, pediatricians, and dieticians, in fact, now recommend a weight gain of about twenty-five pounds over the course of a pregnancy, even for overweight women. But no matter what you weigh, you should follow your doctor's advice when you are pregnant.)

More fat cells, I suspect, may also be the result of yo-yo dieting when there is not only a quick gainback of pounds after a weight loss (where old fat cells are refilled), but often a rapid regain *plus,* where new fat cells could be in the making. For women, postdiet weight gain is most likely to occur after an ordinary diet, one that doesn't pacify food cravings related to hormone swings and changes in brain chemistry. That's because cravings ignored too long can gain the upper hand and lead to bingeing, which puts the dieter right back where she started. Or worse, leaves her with a net higher gain and, perhaps, a batch of brand-new fat cells.

Unfortunately, once these new, greasy fat cells are in place, they can't be removed. Though proper diet and weight loss will shrink them, they stay with you, always ready and waiting to swell up again with more fat. So, as yo-yoing continues, and additional, stubborn fat cells could be in the making, each new attempt to lose weight becomes more difficult than the last.

No, the situation is not hopeless. You can help yourself no matter what your fat pattern and type, and even if you've been a yo-yo dieter in the past. The first step is to follow Bodyrhythm Diet antifat eating principles, which work to modify fat absorption and defuse cravings. Once you reach your goal, the very same principles that make the diet effective should help you keep your weight down where you want it.

You probably can't do anything about the fat cells you already have. But you can do the next best thing: eat in ways that reduce fat-storing, help shrink to near invisibility existing fat cells, and prevent the formation of new ones.

Fat Fact #4. Estrogen is profat and can switch on the "female fat cycle."

The female hormone estrogen is sometimes described as being "profat," and for good reason: it promotes the conversion of food into fat, encouraging the body to store it rather than burn it.

As I explained earlier, estrogen triggers the production of ultrahigh levels of the enzyme LPL in the fat cells of your breasts, hips, rear, and thighs. LPL in turn pulls fat out of the bloodstream and shoves it into those same fat cells, increasing their size and, in certain conditions, their numbers.

In premenopausal women, the ovaries are the primary source of estrogen. Women taking synthetic hormones (the Pill), get an additional dose of estrogen as well as the hormone progesterone. (New oral contraceptives, of course, supply smaller amounts of both hormones than ever before.)

And (here's the kicker!) women with large stores of body fat get still more estrogen from another source: their own fat.

As it turns out, our fatty tissue converts androgen—a biologically inactive male hormone present in all women—into estrogen.

Thus, we can get caught up in what I call the female fat cycle: Estrogen promotes fat storage. More estrogen is produced in fatty tissue. Increased amounts of estrogen result in more fat storage, which leads to more estrogen production, more fat storage . . . and so on, and on.

Ordinary diets do not address this specifically female fat cycle. The Bodyrhythm Diet does. On it, you will be eating foods that help modify estrogen production and encourage your body to excrete excessive amounts of the profat hormone, as well as foods that discourage the formation of fat tissue. In short, it gives you what you need to break out of the fat cycle.

Fat Fact #5. Cyclical swings in progesterone production can add to your problems.

On or about the fourteenth day of your menstrual cycle (if your cycle is the average twenty-eight days in length, and you count the first day of your period as day one), your body begins to produce greater amounts of another hormone, progesterone. When progesterone levels escalate, your tissues tend to retain more water, which explains why you sometimes feel bloated and look puffy in the days before your period.

Bloating and puffiness are a nuisance. Worse, however, from a weight point of view, is that water retention, along with other hormonal factors that come into play at this time of the month, can cause changes in brain chemistry that result in sagging spirits, fatigue, bouts of moodiness, and food cravings. That's when it hits, the impulse to reach for favorite feel-good foods.

Now, it wouldn't be too awful if, as a result of rising progesterone production, you felt an urge to splurge on low-cal, high-nutrition vegetables and salads. But that's probably not the case. I've never met a women in my work as a weight-loss counselor nor anyone socially who told me she went on cabbage binges, or raw broccoli pig-outs. Instead, when progesterone goes up, most women want rich sweets, such as chocolate, cookies, ice cream. Or bread and butter, potato chips, french fries, and other fatty and perhaps salty starches. A few go overboard for hot, spicy, highly seasoned ethnic foods. All of these foods are notorious fat makers and diet destroyers.

Men don't have to be concerned with cyclical variations in progesterone and other hormones, or the cravings they cause. You do. That's why the Bodyrhythm Diet is designed to supply foods that aid in the release of water from the body, help ease premenstrual discomfort, and satisfy cravings without sabotaging the weight-loss process.

Fat Fact #6. Insulin can trip you up.

A primary function of insulin, the important fuel-regulating hormone produced by the pancreas, is to clear sugar out of the bloodstream and stow excess calories—or fuel—into fat cells.

Problems can arise, however, when insulin does its job too well, making blood sugar levels plummet. And when blood sugar dips down below a certain point, the brain and body send out hunger signals. For obvious reasons, that's bad for the dieter.

Unfortunately, many diets—perhaps some of the diets you've tried in the past—were planned without regard to this insulin/blood sugar/hunger response. These are the diets that are "unbalanced," either too high or too low in carbohydrates.

When carbohydrate intake is too high, the pancreas releases a gush of insulin that quickly removes sugar from the bloodstream. Result: low blood sugar, and hunger, soon after eating. When carbohydrate intake is too low, the end result is the same: low blood sugar, and hunger.

Much better, and easier on you when you're trying to lose pounds of fat, is a diet that doesn't include foods that stimulate the pancreas to overreact with a flood of insulin, but does include foods that keep blood sugar levels high enough to prevent hunger from getting the better of you. A diet that "prescribes" those foods in just the right, balanced amounts. The Women's Bodyrhythm Diet in other words.

Fat Fact #7. Our environment can be "fattening."

Besides the body reasons that tend to make females fatter and keep us fatter than men, the way we live still favors fat for us, leanness for men.

Just one for instance: despite all our gains in educational

and employment opportunities, despite the move toward equal partnership with men on all fronts, women continue to be more involved with food than men. We're the ones who do most of the shopping, putting away, cooking, and cleaning up. And of course, the more contact we have with food, the greater the temptation to nibble, or overeat.

In addition, we're less likely to be physically active. Though the fitness boom is real, it's fueled by younger, in-shape women. By and large, fat-prone females who are most in need of exercise don't get in on the action. I suppose this is partly because so many of us grew up with the notion that exertion and sweat weren't "feminine." And partly because, young or old, we're more self-conscious about our bodies, more reluctant to display ourselves in bathing suits or shorts or revealing exercise gear than men, who generally seem to think less about "letting it all hang out."

A good weight-loss program is more than just a diet. To be truly effective it must also offer guidelines for setting up an antifat environment and developing antifat attitudes and habits—especially exercise. These guidelines are an important part of the Women's Bodyrhythm Diet.

Now you have some of the fat facts. You know that nature arranged it so that to be born female is almost by definition to be born with a greater potential for over-weight than the other half of the human race. You know that food cravings are not "all in your head." They're real, and a result of your female physiology, which sends periodic demands for gooey sweets, greasy starches, or highly spiced dishes. You know that your hormones play a major role in making you fat, and keeping you that way. And you know why diets that pretend that the female fat handicap doesn't exist are so often confusing, frustrating and ineffective, for *women*.

In the next few chapters, I'm going to explain how Bodyrhythm Diet principles can help you overcome your female fat handicap and enable you to lose the pounds and inches that stand between you and better looks, better health, a better feeling about yourself.

No matter how tempted you may be to skip these chapters and go straight to the diet itself, please take the time to read them. They'll arm you with more of the information and know-how you need to achieve the diet results you've always wanted.

3 | Breaking the Female Fat Cycle

Don't get me wrong: for most women, the main reason for overweight is overeating. But it's important to recognize that it's *not* the only reason. Many other elements—hormones definitely included—are involved.

To reiterate, the female hormones estrogen and progesterone help make your body a fat trap. Estrogen encourages fat storage. Progesterone can trigger monthly food cravings for rich sweets, too many starches, and a variety of other foods that produce a pileup of unwanted pounds.

But don't hate your hormones. Without them you wouldn't be the woman you are.

Estrogen is responsible for much of what is distinctly female and sexy about you: your smooth skin, your ability to conceive, your feminine contours. It even helps protect you from heart disease. When estrogen levels drop too low, your skin becomes drier and wrinkle-prone. You may lose some of the hair on your head, while at the same time hair on your face and body may become more profuse. Vaginal secretions diminish, making sex difficult. Breasts can lose their fullness, and hot flashes are a possibility. Too little estrogen even affects bones, causing a loss of the calcium that is so necessary to keep them strong. To top it all off, researchers now have evidence that drastically diminished estrogen production can result in insomnia and short-term memory loss!

As for progesterone, it's often called the "hormone of the mother" because it helps turn the uterus into a soft, spongy, nourishing "nest," in which the fertilized egg can grow and develop into a full-term baby. It also acts to prevent an excessive buildup of cells in the lining of the uterus and thus helps protect against uterine cancer.

Nevertheless, estrogen and progesterone are the hormones that make us the fatter sex and interfere with our efforts to lose weight, even when we count every single little calorie.

The Women's Bodyrhythm Diet will help you moderate your body's fat-making, fat-storing, food-craving mechanisms. It will give you the nutritional information and food plans that allow you to keep hormones in line and avoid the fat-promoting hormone highs as well as the unhealthy lows.

The Bodyrhythm Diet and Excess Estrogen

In the previous chapter, I discussed how estrogen produced by your ovaries encourages the rapid conversion of the food you eat into fat; remember? Estrogen does this by stimulating existing fat cells in breasts, hips, thighs, and rear to make more LPL, the enzyme that moves fat out of the bloodstream and shoves it into those same cells for storage.

That's not the end of it, though. If you are overweight, fatty tissue can be a significant source of additional, "manufactured" estrogen. And the fatter you are, the more estrogen and estrogen-related substances your body will produce. More estrogen means more LPL and more fat stored. And more body fat equals more fat-storing estrogen.

It's a vicious cycle men don't have to contend with. In fact, the relative absence of fat-storing estrogen and the presence of muscle-making testosterone (which results in the male's higher percentage of fat-burning muscle tissue), helps explain why it's easier for men to lose excess pounds simply by cutting back on calories.

For you, as a woman, *eating less* probably isn't enough. To break the fat-making, fat-storing cycle and achieve your goal of a slimmer, fitter body, you need to *eat differently*. In particular, you need to learn how to eat to help decrease excessive amounts of the female fat-storing hormone, estrogen.

One way to lose excess fat is to get your body to make less estrogen. But as we've seen, body fat tends to encourage estrogen production, and if you're already overfat, your body will continue to manufacture large amounts of the hormone. Sounds like a hopeless, catch-22 situation, but there is a way out. It requires that you begin to eat larger amounts of certain foods that act to curb excessive, potentially hazardous-to-your-health estrogen production. And to restrict your intake of other foods that tend to make estrogen levels soar.

Keep in mind that there are other, very powerful fat-making mechanisms that work against you in your efforts to get slim and stay slim. The Bodyrhythm Diet will help put you in control of them, too. For now, however, we're going to focus on defusing estrogen, the fat-storing hormone.

Fiber Up, Estrogen Down

When you follow the Bodyrhythm Diet, you're going to be eating high-fiber foods in abundance.

Of course, you've known for years that fiber is good for you. You've read it in magazines and books and heard it on radio and TV: a diet too low in fiber and too high in fat puts you at a greater risk for heart disease or cancers of the breast, uterus, and colon, while the diet rich in fiber and low in fat appears to protect against these killer diseases and also appears to help control diabetes. The American Heart Association, the American Cancer Society, the American Dietetic Association, and almost every major public-health organization continue to urge everyone to increase fiber intake by consuming more whole grains, fresh whole fruits and vegetables, and to reduce fat intake from the average whopping 37 percent of total calories down to a more moderate 30 percent.

But perhaps you didn't know, because it's less publicized, that fiber has an effect on estrogen production.

In short, getting more fiber into your diet can reduce estrogen levels in your body.

Precisely how fiber works to modify estrogen levels is not clear. Some experts believe that fiber may serve as a "trap" for the estrogen that is normally stored in bile (a digestive juice that is released into the intestines after eating), binding to this estrogen, pulling it out of the body with food wastes, and preventing it from being reabsorbed into the system.

The theory may be superseded by others, but why wait until we understand exactly *how* fiber influences estrogen? (After all, we still don't know precisely *how* smoking causes lung cancer!) The important point researchers are now making is that fiber *does* reduce estrogen levels.

For instance, in one fascinating study carried out by researchers in Hawaii, a group of breast-cancer patients volunteered to eat more fiber and much less fat. Within a year, these woman showed a significant decrease in estrogen levels! Not only that, they also lost an average 7 percent of their body weight—even though they were not asked to cut back on calories.

Fiber helps the weight-loss process in many ways: because fiber absorbs water and provides bulk, high-fiber foods are more filling than calorie-dense, high-fat foods. And because fibrous foods are crunchy and chewy, they provide lots of oral satisfaction. Fiber also binds with and carries out of the body small amounts of the fat contained in food, preventing that fat from entering the bloodstream and being transported to those ever-ready-and-waiting fat cells.

Fiber is one of the essential tools you'll be using to

break the female fat cycle on the Women's Bodyrhythm Diet.

Fat Down, Estrogen Down

In the Hawaiian study just mentioned, the women cut back on fatty foods as they increased their fiber intake. Many researchers believe—and I'm with them all the way—that when the goal is to reduce estrogen levels, eating less fat is at least as important as boosting fiber intake. Maybe more so.

Much of the evidence that fat reduction coaxes the body to make less estrogen has come out of cancer research. For years, scientific investigators have been aware of the link between high estrogen levels and breast cancer. There is evidence of a fat connection, too—that is, a high-fat diet tends to elevate estrogen levels, and that, in turn, leads to an increased risk of breast cancer.

The cancer rate is lower, and so are estrogen levels, in women who typically eat a "fat-poor" diet. Japanese women, for example, who consume less fat than American women, are at less risk for breast cancer, *and* have lower levels of estrogen. They're also on the average much thinner!

The Japanese findings aren't new. More recently, however, a study of American women, conducted under a contract with the National Cancer Institute, found that women who consumed high amounts of fat also had high levels of estrogen in their blood.

Even more than a simple excess of calories, *an excess of fatty foods* appears to stimulate the female body to produce more fat-making, fat-storing estrogen. Even more than simple calorie cutting, a reduction in dietary fat appears significantly to reduce the amount of fat-making, fat-storing—and cancer-causing—estrogen.

Because of the relationship between a high-fat diet and estrogen levels, eating less fat is another key to breaking out of the female fat cycle on the Women's Bodyrhythm Diet.

A Calorie Is a Calorie...or Is It?

I'll bet you've read and heard many times, as I have, that all excess calories, whether they come from fats, sugars, protein, or fiber, have the same basic effect on the body in terms of storage.

According to the calorie-is-a-calorie school of thought, the source is unimportant—all you have to do to lose pounds is restrict yourself to fewer calories. In order to shed one pound a week, they say, just cut back 500 calories a day from those you need to maintain your weight (500 calories, times seven, the number of days in a week, equals 3500, the number of calories in a pound). It will work no matter what you eat, say the all-calories-are-equal proponents. The calories could come from french fries or chocolate, broiled fish or celery, as long as the daily total is 500 calories less than before, you can expect to lose a pound every seven days.

Most female dieters have suspected that something was wrong with the theory. Now many members of the scientific community are confirming what so many of us have known all along through intuition and experience: the calorie-is-a-calorie theory isn't entirely false, but it's only partially true. Case in point: over a two-week period, women in a recent study who were given a high-fat diet (40 to 50 percent of total calories) gained weight, but on low- and medium-fat diets (15 to 35 percent) the women lost weight, even with no calorie restrictions. The all-calorie-equal idea, it seems to me, is even less true for women than for men, because our bodies are so much more efficient at absorbing and storing fat.

The new fact of the matter is that calories supplied by different foods are indeed absorbed in different ways. *For women especially, 100 calories' worth of food that is high in fiber is literally less fattening than 100 calories supplied by sugar, processed starches or a fatty food*.

This is so in part because of the beneficial, estrogen-lowering effects of fiber. Add to that the fact that fiber binds to some of the fat in food, preventing it from being absorbed into the body; that it takes up space in the stomach, contributing to feelings of "fullness"; and that crunchy, chewy high-fiber foods help satisfy the dieter's need for oral gratification; and it begins to look as if every little fiber calorie consumed is a fat fighter!

Conversely, because fatty foods appear to pump up estrogen levels, which tunes up the body's fat-making and fat-storing capabilities, *and* because fat is more easily absorbed and less easily burned once it is stashed away in fat cells, *100 calories' worth of high-fat food is literally more fattening than 100 calories' worth of high-fiber food, low-fat protein, or even starchy food*.

Every calorie you eat in the form of fat is a fat maker.

In the chapters to come, I'll tell you about some of the other revolutionary diet findings that disprove the all-calories-are-equal theory. I'll tell you why fats are more fattening than carbohydrates. Why sugar is more fattening than many starches. Why eating more often is less fattening than eating the same number of calories at only a couple of meals. And more. This is new and valuable information, vital to you as a woman and a dieter, information that will help make your goal of slimness for a lifetime more attainable. You'll learn how and why to put the new research to work for you later on.

For now, the message of the moment is this: Eating more fiber helps reduce levels of fat-storing estrogen within your body. Eating less fat allows fiber to work more efficiently. On the Bodyrhythm Diet, it's up with fiber, down with fat.

Diet Oldthink vs. Diet Newthink

Counting calories without regard to where those calories came from is diet oldthink. Perhaps you've tried to lose weight on a reducing plan that allowed you to eat anything, or almost anything, you wanted—as long as you didn't exceed a certain number of calories each day. Unless you included in your diet plenty of high-fiber foods and cut back on fats, it probably didn't work very well. Now you know why. Fiber calories are antifat, in part, because they appear to bring down levels of estrogen. Fat calories do the opposite.

Many of the women I counsel resist the idea that some calories are antifat and some are profat. No wonder. For years we were told that a calorie is a calorie, no matter what its source. Magazine articles said so. Diet books said so. Doctors said so. Especially *male* doctors, who, of course, never had to struggle with the consequences to their weight of elevated estrogen. (Haven't you ever visited your doctor and had to report that despite the fact that you stuck to the calorie-counted diet he gave you, you didn't lose an ounce—may even have gained? And didn't you get the feeling he thought you cheated? Or were lying? It happened to me so many times that I began to think I was sleep-eating!)

Another problem with diet newthink: Once you accept the idea that fat calories are more *fattening,* you have to face the fact that eating smaller portions of all your favorite foods isn't quite enough to get you the body you want. You're going to have to adopt a new way of eating in which all calories are *not* equal. The Bodyrhythm Diet is designed to help you do it.

Calorie awareness is good, but fat awareness is critical to weight-loss success for women.

Special to Diet-Resistant Women

Losing weight is almost never as quick and easy as we'd like it to be. But there's a certain kind of woman, with a certain physical makeup, who seems to run into more trouble on a diet than others. Who is this woman?

She's full-figured, with large breasts and voluptuous hips and thighs. As a schoolgirl, she "developed" sooner than most of her friends. And she began to menstruate at an earlier-than-average age. (The average age for menarche is 12½; menstruation that begins any time from nine to seventeen is considered "normal.")

Estrogen, menstruation, and body fat are linked, remember. Fat must account for almost one quarter of total weight before estrogen levels are high enough for menstruation to begin. However, for the girl who menstruates well before her peers, it's not clear which comes first: "prematurely" high estrogen levels resulting in an early accumulation of body fat, or more body fat at a younger age, leading to an early elevation in estrogen and the early onset of menstruation. Whatever the scenario, I've often noted a relationship between early menstruation, a hyper–female-accumulation of fat, and the body's resistance to weight loss.

What about you? Did you begin to menstruate before most of your friends? Did your breasts and hips develop before theirs did? Do you have more lower-body fat—the shape that signals more and fatter fat cells, not just normal numbers of easier-to-shrink full fat cells? In short, are you an ultrafemale pear, not a banana or an apple? If so, you may be more than normally diet-resistant, partly as a result of higher-than-average estrogen levels.

The Bodyrhythm Diet with its emphasis on high-fiber, low-fat foods, was planned to help you, too, break out of the female fat cycle by moderating estrogen production and encouraging your body to give up its stores of fat. It will help pare pounds and inches all over—arms, trunk, tummy, and even hips and thighs.

But the Bodyrhythm Diet won't give you brand-new proportions, or make you lean and lanky where your genes have programmed you for curves. No safe, healthy diet will do that. In short, learn to love your female contours. (Men do!) The time is certainly right—firm, fit, and softly rounded is in; scrawny is out.

It may sound as if I'm advising you to settle for less than your dream of a sleeker, slimmer shape, but that's not the point at all. I *am* urging you to be realistic and avoid the built-in frustrations of trying to be someone you're not.

Go for the very best body *you* can have. Bodyrhythm Diet eating will help you get it.

The Bodyrhythm Diet Health Advantage

As we've seen, the female fat cycle is insidious. Estrogen, one of the hormones that determine our very femaleness, also helps make us the fatter sex. And when fat accumulates, it encourages the manufacture of even more estrogen.

To break the cycle, you need to do more than simply lower your calorie intake. You need to eat more of the foods that interfere with your body's propensity to make and store fat. These foods, high in fiber, low in fat, will help you regain control of your weight.

As you lose pounds and inches on the diet you'll also be following the recommendations of virtually every nutritional expert and major health organization, and thereby lowering your risk of developing heart disease, stroke, diabetes, and some forms of cancer. More and more, it appears that there is only one right way to eat: the way you'll be eating on the Women's Bodyrhythm Diet.

There's more to the Bodyrhythm Diet than increasing your intake of high-fiber, low-fat foods, of course. In the next chapter, I'll tell you how other foods, eaten at key times, can help minimize another major female fat problem: monthly food cravings.

4 | Beating the Binge Syndrome

It's an old familiar story. You're out running errands. Or getting some of the paperwork cleared off your desk. Or heading home at rush hour. Suddenly, almost against your will, you're drawn to the nearest candy counter, where you buy a chocolate bar, or a pack of peanut-butter cookies, or a bag of potato chips, which you proceed to devour as quickly as possible.

Afterward, you wonder what possessed you to do it. And then, maybe you make the connection: your period is due in a few days.

Though it's not clear whether *all* women have premenstrual food cravings, it's a known fact that many *do*. Certainly, a majority of women in my weight-loss groups have told me they experience overwhelming desires for certain foods before menstruation. Some want sweets or starches, especially fatty kinds, such as chocolate or french fries. Others want salty or spicy food. Some will settle for any—or all—of the above.

But even if you're sure you've never had a premenstrual food craving in your life, this is a must-read chapter. Why? Because similar food cravings (perhaps stemming from similar hormonal changes) can be activated when you lose pounds on a diet. Researchers suspect that since nature programmed us to be fat to help in species survival, if our female fat stores are threatened, internal alarms, in the form of cravings, are set off to urge us into eating and re-storing lost fat.

Cravings vs. Hunger

I'm not talking here about simple hunger, the pangs you feel when your stomach demands filling up. These are not special to women. Men obviously get hungry, too.

No, the cravings we're concerned with now have little to do with an empty stomach. In fact, you can experience hormone-activated cravings even when your stomach is relatively full! These mysterious, nagging food "itches" are, rather, a consequence of having a fertile female body, capable of conceiving and bearing a child.

Of course, men don't need to know how to cope with female-hormone-related cravings. We do. So any diet planned to address our specifically female weight-loss problems needs to be reinforced with what I call "binge insurance"—foods that can help satisfy these special cravings without sabotaging the slimming process.

On the Women's Bodyrhythm Diet, you will be eating a little more and a little differently at certain times of the month, or anytime you sense a craving in the making. The binge insurance extras built into the plan aren't meant to satisfy hunger (there's enough good food on the diet to keep you feeling pleasantly full most of the time) but to help you deal harmlessly and healthfully with cravings before they have a chance to take over and derail your efforts to lose pounds and inches.

Progesterone, the Binge Hormone

The villain in the food-craving story appears to be the hormone progesterone. For years, researchers have been aware of a correlation between monthly elevations in progesterone production—which for most women starts to occur about halfway through the menstrual cycle—and an increased appetite for certain foods. A cause-and-effect relationship was assumed. In other words, it was believed that food cravings were a result of the rise in progesterone. But the how's, why's, and what-to-do's were never fully understood.

However, recent work by research endocrinologists focusing on pregnancy, has shed some light on the phenomenon. During pregnancy, progesterone production soars and remains high for nine full months—and food cravings are notoriously strong and persistent.

To simplify, progesterone is known as a "catabolic" hormone. Catabolic refers to the breaking down of complex materials in the body into simpler ones, and in this particular case, progesterone is thought to break down (catabolize) more protein than usual into its component parts—the amino acids. Broken-down proteins are then used for fuel and the leftovers are excreted with the urine.

But wait a minute. Protein has a vital role. It's not supposed to be used for fuel. And protein definitely shouldn't be wasted. Protein is essential for the developing life; protein provides the building blocks of the body and also plays a vital role in repairing and maintaining cells. In being used up as fuel and then being excreted, protein is "wasted," not being retained by the body to fulfill its function as cell builder and repairer.

What seems to be going wrong? After all, plenty of protein is crucial for cell formation in the unborn child. Yet those high levels of progesterone seem to *decrease* the amount of available protein in the pregnant woman's body. But why not eat additional protein then? Load up on chicken, fish, or beef, in other words.

Strangely enough, say researchers, eating *more* protein doesn't help either. Rather, with more protein the breakdown process just increases and the extra supplies are excreted with even more urine.

So here we have a mystery: protein is essential for cell building, yet protein is wasted when it is broken down, used up as fuel and excreted; and eating more protein only causes more wasting.

Does this mean that nature has goofed? No. There's more to the story. Mother Nature has planned a nifty way around this protein breakdown and protein loss. Researchers suspect that when levels of certain proteins drop down low enough, the hypothalamus—a small, glandlike organ in the brain that masterminds hormone activity and food cravings—quickly gets the message of protein drop.

But instead of stimulating an increased need to eat more protein (which would only be wasted), the brain sets off a craving for more fats and carbohydrates which are easier to break down and use for fuel than proteins.

Voilà! Now, with more of these foods—carbohydrates and fats—the body can then turn to them as energy sources, and leave the protein alone, more or less, to do its critical job of developing the cells of the newborn.

So, with a diet that is protein rich, but low in fats and carbs, the body just breaks down, uses up, and gets rid of the plentiful protein—it's wasted, in other words—and not used for its necessary functions of repairing and maintaining the body cells. But protein is *spared*—and available to fulfill its primary function as builder and repairer of cells—when carbs and fat intake are increased.

During pregnancy, a high level of progesterone indirectly triggers an appetite for more carbohydrates and fats—ice cream, candy bars, cake, or even oranges and melons—so that protein can be spared for the important job of "making" the fetus.

The scenario, I think, would seem to apply as well to other hormone-related cravings for carbohydrates and fats. In the days before a period, progesterone production rises, just as it does during pregnancy—although not to the same level and, of course, not for as long a time. More protein than usual is broken down, used as fuel, and wasted. The hypothalamus, sensing a decrease in amino acids in your blood, *demands* that you eat more carbs and fats so that protein will be spared.

Never mind that you are *not* pregnant. At this time of

the month, progesterone rises to prepare your body for the possibility of pregnancy. And your premenstrual cravings may be your body's way of getting ready for a baby... just in case.

To complicate matters, metabolism—the process by which the body burns, or uses, fuel—increases during the days when progesterone levels rise and conception is possible. The result is a slight elevation in temperature. (That's why women who want to become pregnant are instructed to take their temperature.)

Usually, a metabolic rise is a good thing for dieters, since it causes speedier calorie burn-off. But when a juiced-up metabolism accompanies the rise in progesterone, it's often accompanied by hunger.

It's a double whammy. When progesterone climbs, it turns on cravings for carbohydrates and fats, and at the same time, a turned-up metabolism increases your desire for food.

It has been found that the average woman just naturally needs about 150 extra calories a day during the two weeks prior to a period. (Of course, with higher levels of progesterone and other nutritional needs, a pregnant woman, following her instincts, will eat about twice that amount— about 300 more calories a day than the nonpregnant woman.)

Overweight women seem to be hit even harder. When we're not dieting, we tend to eat more than 150 extra calories at this time of the month!

My thin friends always seemed able to satisfy preperiod cravings in controlled, guilt-free ways. One would nibble part of a candy bar, and that was that. Another ordered french fries when she felt the itch, then ate as usual for the rest of the day. Me? I sat and suffered for days with sliced turkey breast and a dry green salad and other diet foods until the double whammy finally got to me and I'd go off on a wildcat binge of carton after carton of ice cream.

Perhaps you've had similar experiences. If so, you know that successful dieting during the danger days before a period is more than just a simple matter of "controlling yourself," as so many diet-book writers, male doctors, and thin friends and family seem to imply. You need extra help.

Why Other Diets Don't/Can't Break the Binge Syndrome

High-protein diets only exacerbate cravings, and practically invite you to binge. Remember, stoking up on protein at certain times of the month promotes the use of more protein as fuel, when what your body *really* wants to burn are carbohydrates and fats. Because it's not getting what it wants, your body becomes more and more insistent. It nags and nags until your resistance breaks down. And when it does, the stage is set for an eating jag.

One of the women I counsel told me about being on various high-protein diets and wanting peanut-butter sandwiches more than she ever wanted any man. She remembers taking a loaf of bread and a big jar of peanut butter to bed with her one night a few days before a period. "Before I was able to regain control," she said, "I'd put back every single pound I lost in the previous month."

Despite their continuing popularity, high-protein diets are not the answer for women and they never were. Filling up on proteins and skimping on carbs can intensify monthly cravings and set us up for self-defeating bingeing.

Newer but just as ineffective are high-carbohydrate, low-fat diets. Some of these are so low in fat they're fat-free for all intents and purposes. Low fat is good. Fat-free, however, is risky for women who are subject to food cravings. It's like an accident waiting to happen. Your body needs *some* fat in order to help keep cravings pacified and hunger turned down. When that fat is not forthcoming, both hunger and cravings can become more intense and, finally, send you off on a wild foray among the super-fattening foods that are most destructive to the weight-loss process.

Remember, you are dealing with nature. She doesn't know or care that you are restricting carbs and fats in order to slim down. When progesterone rises, Mother Nature assumes that pregnancy is possible and begins rehearsing the body. Nature's concerned with maintaining a proper, adequate fuel supply—and that means more energy-providing carbohydrates and fats in order to spare vital, cell-building protein. And nature will torture you with food cravings if that's what it takes to get what she wants.

Defusing Cravings

Much better for women than high-protein diets that discriminate against carbohydrates, and high-carbohydrate diets that skimp too much on fats, is a food plan that eases us through the danger days—one that helps us control the cravings rather than allowing the cravings to control us.

The Women's Bodyrhythm Diet was developed, with the help of dieticians, to fulfill this requirement. It's a diet that works along with nature to give your body *some* of the foods it wants when it wants them.

Of course, you won't find candy, doughnuts, cheesecake, or pepperoni pizza on this diet. Eating high-sugar, fat-drenched junk would be self-defeating. Might as well go ahead and binge!

What you will find in Stage II—the danger-days section of the diet—are slightly larger portions of nutritious, fiber-rich, complex carbohydrates and slightly more fat. These few additional calories of high-fiber complex carbohydrates and fats will give your body enough of what nature has programmed it to want, but in amounts that won't interfere with sure, steady weight loss.

For example, an extra slice of bread in the Stage II lunch or dinner should supply enough complex carbohydrates to blunt cravings that could prompt you to gorge on cookies or ice cream later on. Proteins with a slightly higher fat content than those called for in Stage I of the diet should provide enough fat to tone down the urge to splurge on greasy chips, ribs, and fried foods that will put you back on the road to overweight.

For a close-up look at binge insurance in action, consider how it worked for one woman, a thirty-five-year-old advertising copy writer I'll call Ricky. On joining one of my diet groups, Ricky told me that for months she had been on and off one of the well-known high-protein diets. These diets, by the way, are not just high protein; they're loaded with fat, as well, since some allow slabs of high-fat red meats and gobs of rich dairy products.

"Although I never feel starved [not with all those fatty steaks and cheeses, she wouldn't] I sometimes have these incredible cravings. Mostly, I deal with them by pushing thoughts of food out of my head," she said.

"But then," Ricky went on, "something seems to hit me and all my willpower evaporates. I don't understand it. Suddenly I'm obsessed with Mars Bars. I'm embarrassed to admit it, but I've eaten as many as a six-pack at a time."

Just as I suspected, when I asked Ricky to try to be specific about the times when her Mars Bars monster got the better of her, she realized that the cravings were strongest on the days before her period. The lunches on her high-protein diet—a small salad with either a huge hamburger patty, a ham omelette, or half a fried chicken—supplied practically no carbohydrates, but lots of protein and fat. That mysterious "something" that hit Ricky was the frantic signaling of her brain, calling out for food that her body could most easily use as fuel: carbohydrates, in other words.

I suggested that Ricky cut back on protein and add complex carbohydrates to each meal—perhaps a slice of whole-grain bread with a dab of margarine. On those days when she felt her cravings mounting, I suggested that she double her intake of complex carbohydrates. Example: I suggested she add an *extra* roll with her dinner.

She looked at me as though I'd taken leave of my

senses. "Bread? Margarine? Rolls? They're not diet foods."

"Well, neither are Mars Bars," I responded. Ricky thought it over for a moment and then decided to give my way a try.

Eating small amounts of foods she'd never thought of as "diet" helped put Ricky back in control of her eating during the danger days. It allowed her to find the solid middle ground between feeling tortured by cravings and stuffing herself in order to satisfy them. Most important, it helped her to keep losing weight at a sure and steady rate.

Binge insurance has been valuable to many women who, like Ricky (and perhaps like you), are vulnerable to hormone-related food cravings and tend to lose control for a few days each month. It's also worked for women who are hit with strong food urges when their bodies have given up some amount of weight—and then signal cravings, designed to get them to resist more weight loss.

Binge-control techniques won't work miracles, of course. The small increases in carbohydrates and fats in Stage II eating may not do away entirely with those cravings— though for some women it seems to work that way. But by defusing them, binge insurance can make the difference between diet success and failure.

A Few Words on the Carb Controversy

My advice about getting more carbohydrates into your system in the days before a period may be diametrically opposed to everything you've heard so far about premenstrual eating and about weight loss.

For instance, you have probably been told that preperiod bloating, fatigue, and irritability, not to mention temporary weight gain, are a result of water retention. That's true. You may also have heard that your body's tendency to hold on to water at this time of month can be exaggerated by overeating carbohydrates. Also true. The same book, magazine article, or TV talk-show guest suggesting a *reduction* in carbohydrate consumption in the days before a period might also recommend an *increase* in protein, since a diet high in protein seems to promote the release of water from the cells.

This is not bad advice for the nondieter, especially if she's in the habit of consuming large amounts of sugary junk foods but not very much in the way of protein. Eating less sugar and more fish, chicken, and lean red meat might indeed minimize her premenstrual bloating or discomfort.

But based on my experience with hundreds of overweight females, all of them desperately trying to get rid of excess fat, I believe it's different for the dieter.

Because of calorie considerations, the dieter's carbohydrate and fat intake is already relatively low. Keeping fats and carbs low, or reducing them even further, while at the same time boosting protein consumption, can intensify preperiod food cravings and lead to eventual *overdosing* on sugar- and fat-rich foods. This in turn may worsen the very premenstrual symptoms she had hoped to avoid, and result in an additional problem: the piling back on again of pounds it took her weeks to lose.

It's worth repeating. A *slight* increase in complex carbohydrates and fats, before a period, should make you less vulnerable to premenstrual cravings and make you less likely to load up on the sweets and/or greasy foods that will *really* get you into worse trouble.

Binge insurance has worked for others. It should work for you, too.

Preperiod Salt Cravings

Maybe the foods that turn you on in the danger days are salty nibbles such as corn chips, salted nuts, salt-studded french fries. Or cuisines with a high-salt content, such as Mexican or Chinese food.

It's not unusual. Many, many women experience a powerful desire for salt before the onset of menstruation.

And believe me, this particular preperiod lust can be just as damaging to the cause as more common cravings for sweets or fatty starches.

There are several possible explanations of why a woman on a diet might go salt mad. For one thing, traditional "diet" food is boring. So when she starts to feel low and down in the dumps as a result of preperiod progesterone highs (or just feeling the blahs for other reasons), she longs for something exciting. And what's quick, relatively cheap, not "sinful," and always available? Right. Tastier food. Add to that the fact that most low-cal fare—dry salads, steamed vegetables, plain, lean chicken, and fish, etc.—is so lacking in taste-enhancing fats, it's natural to turn to salty food with high-impact flavor.

My hunch, however, is that preperiod salt cravings are another "gift" of nature and are instinctual, relating back to the possibility of pregnancy at this time. As it turns out, research backs me up.

For one, dietitians and obstetricians are now doing, if not a complete about-face, at least a partial look at the benefits of some sodium for the mother-to-be. Salt may be needed during pregnancy for the increases in blood, fluid, and tissues. When you are pregnant, or before your period, when your body "thinks" you might be, salt cravings could be your body's signal to eat more of what it needs—an extra sodium supply for the fetus. (However, when and if you become pregnant, you must follow your doctor's recommendations with regard to sodium and the use of salt.)

For another, some brand-new research indicates that salt seems to aid in making carbohydrates more available to the body. Salt either ups digestion of starch so more sugar is liberated from it, or salt urges the intestines to absorb the carbohydrates more efficiently, or both. However it does it, given the same food in the same amount, when it's salted, more carbohydrates may be freed up and ready for use.

What has this got to do with preperiod cravings for salt? Well, remember that the food-craving hormone, progesterone, stimulates a desire for carbohydrates (in order to spare protein). Salty foods that deliver more "extractable" carbs help satisfy that desire. In a sense, a salt craving just might be a sugar or starch craving in disguise!

But why does one woman respond to the preperiod rise in progesterone with a mad desire for sweets, while another woman becomes a salt maniac? I can only speculate. Maybe a preference for salt over sweet is a simple matter of accustomed or cultural-induced taste. We all know people who'd rather have cheese, caviar, or potato chips than ice cream or chocolate cake any day.

One thing is certain. Almost never have I heard of a premenstrual craving for salty foods that are not also high in carbohydrates or fats. In all my years of counseling overweight women, not one has confessed an overpowering urge for, say, *just* pickles or sauerkraut on danger days. Even those cartoons depicting the wacky cravings of the pregnant woman most often have her reaching for the pickle jar with one hand and for the ice cream with the other.

Obviously, allowing a salt craving to get out of hand can be just as bad as giving in to the desire for sugar or fat. Maybe even more so. Loading up on salty foods usually means loading up on fats and carbohydrates, too, and can cause a pile-on of pounds. And as you know, these salty foods can exaggerate the tendency to retain water before a period. The water is usually eliminated soon after menstruation begins, but the fat stays put.

The Salt Solution

The question now is how to pacify a rage for salt and prevent it from undoing the results of weeks of healthy, low-cal eating. You already know most of the answer: when your body wants more protein-sparing carbs and signals its desire in a roundabout way by sending an SOS for salt, small amounts of additional carbohydrates can help. It's the binge insurance all over again.

Does it really work? It does for some women, though I can't guarantee that it will for you. But if a craving for salt is indeed one of nature's ways of prodding you to eat more carbohydrates, it can't hurt and might very well help to bypass the salt and give your body more of what it *really* seems to want. Bodyrhythm Diet Stage II eating should do it.

As for feeding a salt craving with salt, I urge you not to do it. There's no evidence that consuming showers of salt satisfies these cravings. On the contrary, eating more and more salt only builds up tolerance for the taste. And the more tolerant and accustomed to salt you become, the more you may want.

In fact, since most of us already consume a lot more salt than our bodies need—indeed, much more than is good for us—I've purposely designed Bodyrhythm Diet menus to supply less salt and sodium than the typical American diet. Even during the Stage II part of the diet, in which food choices and recipes include slightly larger amounts of food with a slightly higher sodium content, total salt and sodium are still relatively low.

In following Stage I and Stage II of the diet, you'll be consuming less salt. This in turn should minimize bloating, water retention, fatigue, and the irritable feelings that often result. And if you use my seasoning suggestions, I can almost promise that you'll hardly miss that salt.

Spice Attacks

For some few women, danger days bring cravings not for sugar, fat, or salt, but for spicy hot foods. Once again, the source seems to be the mother hormone, progesterone, as it attempts to fulfill nature's best-laid plans for you, should conception take place.

Think about what happens when you eat something very hot and spicy. You reach for water or some other liquid to put out the fire. Spiced-up dishes induce you to get more fluids into your system, fluids that will help prepare your body to carry the developing fetus if you become pregnant.

More to the point, perhaps, is the fact that spicy food is almost invariably mixed with something fatty and starchy. This makes taste sense: fats help neutralize "capsaicin," the chemical compound that creates the kickback, hot sensation, and starches also take some of the heat off far better than plain water can. So when you think you want red-hot and spicy, it could be that you are actually lusting after the *fat and starch* that accompany it—the corn chips that come with the chili sauce, for example. The rich lamb and buttery rice pilaf nestled in sinus-opening curry. The fried rice and the oily sauces drizzled over taste-tingling, spicy Szechuan and Hunan Chinese cuisines.

So we're back once again to fat and starch, prime fuel sources for the body, ones that help spare protein for its main job of cell building and repair.

If zesty, hot foods are what you yearn for on danger days, try to imagine eating them without the high-fat ingredients or starchy side dishes they're served with. I'll bet spice suddenly loses much of its appeal. If it does, you can be pretty sure that your craving for red-hot foods is just a variation on the more common desire for fat and carbs that hits so many women when progesterone levels escalate.

Spice Solution

Recognizing that a spice craving could be a cover-up for something else doesn't necessarily make the craving less intense. To reach your goal of a slimmer, fitter body, you're going to have to face up to this hormone-related food "itch" and learn how to scratch it without jeopardizing your chances for weight-loss success.

Here again, Bodyrhythm Diet Stage II eating can be a diet-saver. In providing you with slightly increased amounts of fats and carbohydrates on the danger days, it should help take the edge off progesterone-related cravings, making them more manageable, less likely to trigger wild bingeing.

When you're in the throes of a spice attack, it might also help to boost your fluid intake. (Remember, these attacks could be your body's way of signaling a need for more fluids.) Water is best. For a change of pace try mineral water with a squeeze of lemon or lime. Coffee shouldn't be used for this purpose, as it tends to be too dehydrating.

It wouldn't hurt either to add some low- or no-cal zest to Bodyrhythm Diet meals, provided you don't overdo. Salt-containing condiments such as mustard, salsa, or soy sauce are provided in specific amounts in the Bodyrhythm Diet. And "free" items like chili powder, fresh garlic, and herbs perk up food with the flavors you crave without making it more fattening.

For many of us, hormone-related cravings are the biggest pitfalls on the road to diet success. As you know if you've experienced these cravings, they're almost impossible to ignore, and they tend to get worse before they get better. Giving in can lead to an all-out binge, unless the giving in is controlled and preplanned. That's the kind of giving in you will be doing when you switch to Stage II of the Bodyrhythm Diet. By supplying your body with a *little* of what it wants and needs, Stage II eating should help pacify the cravings and get you through the danger days, month after month.

5 | Modifying Your Fat-making Mechanism

As you now know, losing fat is more than just a matter of cutting back on calories. And being fat is determined by more than just how much you eat. In fact, the shape of your shape has almost as much to do with what goes on inside your body as with what you put in your mouth!

A quick recap:

As I've explained, the hormone estrogen tends to fuel the female fat cycle, keeping it spinning on itself. Estrogen stimulates high levels of the enzyme LPL, which piles pound after pound into your fat cells, especially on your hips, rear, thighs, and breasts. Stored fat "makes" and pumps out more estrogen. And so on. And on. But learning and applying new food principles that include eating less fat and more fiber puts the brakes on this not-so-merry-go-round.

The second specifically female hormone, progesterone, is a factor in creating the cravings that play nasty tricks on your appetite. Tricks that can make you feel hungry for certain foods, even when your tummy is relatively full. Tricks that can derail a diet and lead to all-out bingeing. But there are food solutions to help you deal with cravings, too, as I pointed out in the previous chapter.

Both estrogen and progesterone are *female* hormones.

They contribute to a special kind of sex discrimination by making it harder for us to get slim and stay slim than it is for men. No wonder men are puzzled—and skeptical—when we moan and groan that the diet that seemed to zap pounds off them doesn't do the same for us. Well, the Bodyrhythm Diet was developed to help counter that discrimination. It works, in part, by moderating some of the profat activities of our female sex hormones.

Insulin, the Unisex Fat Maker

Now we're going to take a look at still another hormone that plays a role in the get-fat, stay-fat syndrome. This one, though, affects both women and men (though in one way, as you will see, it does pose more problems for us). And according to some researchers, it's the most insidious fat-making, fat-storing, fat-trapping hormone in the human body. Anyone, female or male, who wants to lose pounds and keep them off needs to know a few important facts about insulin and how to keep it in balance and under control.

To begin with, the pancreas, a gland located behind the stomach, releases insulin soon after a meal or snack. This hormone's primary job is to drive sugar and fat from the food we eat out of the bloodstream. Insulin escorts blood sugar (glucose) to cells throughout the body, where it becomes available for use as fuel. But insulin packs most of the fat right into the fat cells for storage.

When you eat something that stimulates a sudden gush of insulin, the hormone goes tearing off through your bloodstream, rapidly clearing it of sugar. Blood sugar levels plunge. Your brain, which runs on blood sugar, interprets lowered sugar levels as a need for more food, and flicks the hunger switch to the "on" position.

Haven't you ever felt famished within a few minutes after eating a sugary, high-calorie treat? And haven't you wondered *why* you're so hungry again so soon after you ate? It was probably because the sugar triggered a sudden outpouring of insulin, which then went to work to sweep that sugar out of your blood and deliver it to the cells that make up your body. Your brain sensed the drop in blood sugar and sent out a call for more food. It *commanded* you to eat, especially more sugary stuff, to quickly push blood sugar levels back up, and you probably had to exert all your willpower to resist.

Hunger inspired by a sudden flood of insulin is reason enough to begin eating in ways that modify the effects of this hormone. But it's not the only reason.

Some of the fat in the food you eat is burned immediately as fuel—"fried" might be a better word. But the body is "designed" to run best on blood sugar. It doesn't "like" to burn additional fat stores unless or until its fuel of choice runs low.

If that fat doesn't get burned off as energy, insulin rounds up the fat as it courses through your bloodstream, floats it off to special storage sites—your fat cells—and shoves it inside. Once the fat is safely put away, insulin helps keep it trapped in there. In a sense, insulin is the guardian of your body's fuel supplies, making sure that sugar is available for fuel and fat stays locked away in storage. The more insulin produced, the better it is at these jobs of storing and locking away fat. And with more fat stored and trapped, the less fat you'll burn off as fuel—on a diet or off.

That's not all it does. Insulin also helps convert and store excess sugar as fat. Remember, as the body's fuel of choice, sugar is delivered to the cells and burned. But when there's more sugar in the bloodstream than your body can use for energy or store away, your liver, by a complex process, converts some of its excess stored sugar into fat. The fat is rerouted to the bloodstream. Insulin picks it up and packs it into—you guessed it—those ever-ready-to-expand-and-multiply fat cells! Once again, the more insulin there is on the job, the more efficiently it accomplishes its job of turning excess sugar into fat. And then trapping that fat into fat cells.

Insulin, of course, is vital to your body's normal

functioning. In diabetes—the condition in which the pancreas produces insufficient insulin—too much sugar circulates in the blood. Unless insulin is supplied via external sources, the health consequences can be serious and even fatal. (Interestingly, rapid weight loss is one of the consequences of inadequate insulin). You wouldn't want a drastic decrease in insulin, even if you could arrange it. But as we've seen, high insulin production has some real disadvantages: it makes weight gain easier and weight loss harder.

Insulin Inciters

Many factors influence insulin levels. Some contribute to fat-making, fat-storing, fat-trapping imbalances. Others help moderate the flow, stoke up the fat-burning mechanisms, and ease the weight-loss process along:

Body fat. Fatness, itself, for example, increases insulin output—and that, in turn, promotes a further pileup of body fat. More fat means more insulin, and so on.

Here's how this not-so-merry-go-round works. One of the functions of insulin is to float fat out of the bloodstream and shove it into the fat cells. But when those cells are already bulging and swollen with their greasy contents, the receptors, or "doors" leading into the cells, are thought to become blocked and difficult to locate. (In the same way, the roll of fat that used to hang over the waistband of my jeans made it harder for me to find the zipper!) When moderate amounts of insulin aren't enough to squeeze more fat into the cells, the body responds with an insulin increase. More insulin for rounding up more fat from the bloodstream. More insulin for packing more fat into fat cells and trapping it there. More insulin for converting more sugar into fat and stuffing *it* into cells.

Time of month. During the last half of the menstrual cycle, just when levels of progesterone, the craving hormone, are highest, cells of the body tend to "bind" to insulin. This "residual" insulin, which the cells hang on to, plus "new" insulin released each time you eat, add up to a net insulin increase at this time of month.

More insulin, of course, ultimately means lower blood sugar and intensified hunger and cravings. (Did you know that when blood sugar is low, your sense of smell and taste become keener, making food even more difficult to resist? It's true! Maybe nature planned it that way so we could sniff out food better and eat more at premenstrual times when pregnancy is possible.) But just as day follows night, all-out surrender to cravings—especially at this time of month—is followed by bigger, badder cravings. That's because when you feed those cravings indiscriminately, more insulin is produced, more is held fast by the cells, more is available to push blood sugar levels down further.

Type of food. Even smallish amounts of certain foods can trigger a gush of insulin. These are foods to avoid when the goal is to pare away pounds.

Among the major insulin inciters are carbohydrates. Simple carbohydrates in particular. Simple sugars, to be specific.

There are many different kinds of sugars, some simple, some complex. Chemically speaking, "simple" sugars are made up of relatively few molecules.

Glucose, for example, the simplest sugar of all, has a single molecule. Table sugar (sucrose) is a double sugar, with two molecules (glucose and fructose) strung together. Fruit tastes sweet because it contains simple carbohydrates, or sugars.

Simple sugars, because they are so "simple," are quickly and easily broken down during digestion. The bottom-line, end product of sugar breakdown is glucose. In fact, glucose and blood sugar are one and the same. It is glucose that mobilizes insulin.

Let's say you eat a dish of ice cream. It's as if an alarm went off inside you. Your body quickly changes the sugar in the ice cream into glucose (some calories get burned off, of course). Your blood sugar level might push off into the stratosphere, but a flood of insulin is quickly pumped out to deal with the concentrated load of sugar (as well as the fat) in the ice cream. Insulin races sugar and fat into storage. Within minutes, literally, blood sugar levels take a fall. You may feel hungry even as insulin is still on the job, helping to make excess sugar into fat, and floating it off to your body's favorite storage sites, wherever yours are—hips, thighs, stomach, arms, chin, or anywhere *your* body "likes" to pad on the pounds.

Simple sugars excite an exaggerated insulin response. More hunger-creating, fat-making, fat-storing, fat-trapping insulin is released more quickly when you eat something sweet than with any other type of food. The more insulin coursing through your body, the more fat it can squeeze into your fat cells, and keep there. And the less fat you'll burn off as fuel.

Size and frequency of meals. Sugar is the single worst insulin inciter, but there's a dramatic surge in this profat hormone after every large meal. The longer it has been since the previous meal or snack, the bigger the insulin gush.

This is one reason why meal skipping is such a bad idea... on a diet, or off. Not only will you be hungrier—and less able to exercise appetite control—when it has been hours and hours since the last time you ate, but the rush of insulin acts to extract more sugar and fat from your bloodstream for storage.

We all have to miss a meal occasionally, or put off eating till a more convenient time. But when meal skipping is a habit, the body seems to train itself to become more efficient at grabbing and storing nutrients when they're available... and then burning them more slowly!

Caffeine. Caffeine-containing drinks—coffee, tea, colas, cocoa—stimulate the brain, step up the nervous system, increase your heart rate and trigger a release of stored sugar from the liver. You get a lift—or a jolt—may even feel jittery. Soon after the insulin rise, blood sugar drops. Hunger, even light-headedness and food cravings, can follow. And, of course, fat storing. Beware of caffeine, especially on an empty stomach or between meals, when hunger may be intensified with the coffee, tea, or cola breaks.

Artificial sweeteners. You may *think* you're getting something for nothing (sweetness without calories) when you use sugar substitutes. However, your body might just "read" that sweet taste in your mouth as a signal that the real thing has entered your system, and mobilize the insulin troops to rush out and round up the "sugar." We don't know if it happens with everyone, but it's clearly the case for some.

Of course, you do save calories when you substitute artificially sweetened foods for those high in real sugar. But the imitations might not be such terrific bargains after all if they incite an outpouring of the fat-making, fat-storing, fat-trapping hormone, and slow down your fat-burning mechanisms.

Hyper-responsiveness. Just *looking* at tempting food is enough to start a flow of insulin in some people. That's right. Even before it hits the stomach, even before it passes the lips, the body begins to prepare for it by producing more insulin. For these people, the sight, smell, even (oh, no!) the *thought* of food can do it. Insulin, cruising through the bloodstream, sweeps up available sugar and the hunger switch goes on. All this without ever taking a bite!

By the time the hyper-responder actually does eat, he or she's primed to overeat. With insulin output already high, hunger is increased, less of the snack or meal is burned, and more of it is quickly and efficiently stowed away and trapped as fat.

What's Your IQ?

Based on what you've just read, how would you assess your IQ (insulin quotient)? Are you overweight or overfat? Do you count calories and then spend most of them on sugary treats? Do you often fast and binge, or skip meals and then make up for it by overloading? Do you drink a lot of coffee? Consume lots of artificial sweeteners in beverages, in diet drinks, low-cal salad dressings, jellies, etc.? Do you salivate and get hungry at the sight, smell, thought of food?

A string of yes answers means that your fat-making, fat-storing, fat-trapping hormone needs taming.

You're not alone, of course. In fact, you are typical of overweight women. No other group indulges in as many odd, insulin-inciting food habits, which is part of the reason why no other group meets with such little diet success.

Most weight-loss plans ignore the insulin factor. On many diets the calorie is king (you can eat what you like as long as you don't exceed a certain number). Others emphasize certain food groups to the exclusion of others. You know about them. You probably tried them: the high-protein diet, for example, or one of the high-fat diets that allow few or no carbohydrates. The newer high-carbohydrate, low, low-protein diets. The mostly fruit diets. The egg, grapefruit, and tomato regimes. Hardly any give you what you need to keep blood sugar levels steady and arm yourself against insulin. But the Bodyrhythm Diet is different. You'll see.

Insulin Disarmers

Lucky for us, Bodyrhythm Diet food strategies are synergistic and interactive. They enhance each other, and the eating principles that help subdue one fat-making factor tend to modify the effects of many of the others. That's why some of the insulin disarmers that follow will be familiar. You read about them in previous chapters, but in different contexts.

1. Reduce fats. Fat restriction, as you know, is a must for breaking out of the estrogen-powered female fat cycle. But once you start consuming less fat, your cells seem to become more sensitive to insulin, which means your body won't need to produce as much of this profat hormone.

There's another important reason why, on the Bodyrhythm Diet, you'll be consuming far fewer calories in the form of fat. It has to do with the fact that the fat you eat is very much like the fat you store. Your body doesn't have to do much to convert dietary fat into the greasy stuff that insulin floats out of your bloodstream and into your fat cells. From the lips to the hips . . . it's almost as simple as that. In fact, the body "works off" almost 25 percent of carbohydrate calories in turning them into body fat, but melts down only a tiny 2.5 percent in working to turn ingested fat calories into body fat. That's a net gain of nearly 98 calories for every 100 fat calories you eat!

All diets, including the Women's Bodyrhythm Diet, contain *some* fat. A completely fat-free diet, if possible, would be hazardous to your life, never mind your health. Even a drastic fat cutback can be risky. It might interfere with your body's ability to absorb certain minerals and fat-soluble vitamins, like vitamin A, necessary for maintaining smooth, healthy-looking skin. Worse, your immune system might suffer, increasing your risk of infections or deadly diseases. Since certain fats help build sex hormones, a fat-poor diet might cause a low enough drop in estrogen to rob your skin of youthful moisture, make your menstrual cycle go haywire, even botch up your sex life.

Some fat is not only unavoidable, it's *necessary*. And not just for your health, but also to better your chances for success on a diet. Small amounts at each meal help you feel more satisfied between meals. It makes your food taste better. It also tends to ease cravings—cravings that for women, can be an even bigger block to weight loss than hunger.

Fat is essential. But the human body being what it is, insulin will "want" to convert, store, and lock away ingested fat into fat cells. By reducing your fat intake, you give insulin less to stuff away.

On the Bodyrhythm Diet you'll be getting just enough

fat. Enough for good health and good looks, but not enough to interfere with the weight-loss process. You'll find complete information on how much, what kind, and when to eat it in the diet section, beginning in Chapter 8.

2. *Boost fiber to the max.* Remember what happens when you eat sweets or other foods with sugar as a primary ingredient? A flood of insulin is released to stow away the sugar and convert the excess into fat for more storage. But with a gush of insulin, blood sugar falls, and suddenly you're hungry again. Your hunger may be even more intense during the last half of your menstrual cycle, when "residual" insulin (bound to cells at that time of the month), plus new insulin knocks blood sugar down with a double whammy.

The reason sugar triggers such an exaggerated insulin response has to do with their "simple" chemical makeup.

Think of it this way: sweet-tasting, simple sugars—including table sugar, raw brown sugar, honey, corn syrup, and other sugars—with their relatively few molecules, are like a necklace of just a few beads strung together. So few beads, in fact, that they are easily and quickly snapped apart and broken down by the body into the simplest sugar of all, glucose. Sugar breakdown is so fast that a lot of glucose gets dumped into the bloodstream all at once, and the result is a rapid full-scale mobilization of insulin.

There's also another group of sugars. They're called "complex sugars" (or complex carbohydrates) because they're made up of hundreds and thousands of sugar molecules. Wheat, rice, and other grains, legumes (peas and beans) and starchy vegetables, such as potatoes and corn, and the fiber in fruits and vegetables are all complex carbs.

Like the various sugars, complex carbohydrates are also broken down by the body into glucose. But, to go back to the necklace analogy, because they're made of hundreds of beads, the breakdown process takes longer. Glucose enters the blood more slowly and gradually. And insulin doesn't have to race out in large forces to deal with a sudden sugar intake, but trickles in at a lower and more moderate rate.

Complex carbs with a high-fiber content are better yet. When you eat foods containing whole grains, unprocessed cereals such as "old-fashioned" oatmeal, the skins of starchy vegetables, dried beans, squash, broccoli (to name just a few high-fiber, complex carbohydrates), the roughage further slows down the breakdown into glucose, so insulin is produced at an even slower, more even pace. Less of the profat hormone is available, so fewer calories are converted into fat, and more are burned. And with high-fiber carbohydrates, blood sugar levels tends to remain more even and steady. The result is, the hunger switch stays off for longer periods.

I've become a real fiber fan; it's such a terrifically useful diet tool. As I explained in earlier chapters, it helps to sop up fat from the food you eat, preventing some of it from being absorbed. Fiber itself is fat-free and practically calorie-free, so the more of it there is in your food, the better off you are as a dieter. (But watch out. Though fiber is great, the food it's "wrapped" in may not be such a bargain. Take one of those super-big, dark, and super-moist bran muffins. The bran itself is harmless, but the other ingredients—sugar, flour, shortening, maybe molasses to give it that deep, dark color—can pack a very high-calorie, high-fat, and high-sugar wallop. On second thought, don't take that muffin!)

Fiber also requires lots of chewing, providing more "mouth gratification" than many other kinds of food. And because it's bulky and takes up space in your stomach, it helps you feel full even after a light meal or snack.

But as valuable as high-fiber carbs are, I'm not going to recommend that you eat unlimited amounts, as some diet experts have been doing. Why? Because all carbohydrates, from the simplest sugars to the most complex starches, are broken down into glucose by the body. Yes, it takes longer to snap apart the long chains of molecules that make up the complex-carb "necklace," and longer still if they're high in fiber. And, yes, the insulin outpour is lower with high-fiber, complex carbohydrates than with simple sugars. But no matter how long the breakdown process takes, the end product is always glucose. And a glucose surplus, whether it originally entered your body as candy or as whole-grain bread, is still glucose surplus that will be stored as fat if it can't be used as fuel. The important difference, of course, is that with the candy, more insulin is produced, more calories are stored, and your blood sugar can drop faster and further, while with the high-fiber bread less insulin is produced and blood sugar levels stay more even for longer periods without crashing.

As you will see when you turn to the diet section of this book, on the Bodyrhythm Diet you will be eating generous amounts of high-fiber complex carbohydrates— perhaps more than on any diet you've tried in the past. But you will be eating them in *regulated* amounts. Just enough complex carbs at each and every meal, I find, to supply your body with energy, but not so much that weight loss is slowed. Just enough to ease cravings and keep you comfortably full until the next meal or snack, but not enough to trigger an exaggerated insulin response that will turn up fat storing and turn down your body's fat-burning metabolism.

3. Don't skip meals. Contrary to what you might expect, people who eat frequently tend to weigh less than meal skippers. In fact, in my experience, the stereotype of the fat woman watching the clock, counting down to lunchtime, is all wrong. She's actually more likely to "forget" or to put off eating on purpose—especially when she's trying to lose weight.

It's an old, familiar diet scenario. You have black coffee for breakfast, and more of the same, or perhaps just a green salad for lunch. By midafternoon, you're ravenous. And because you've been so "good" all day, you might feel you deserve a super-snack of gargantuan proportions. Or if you're able to hold out for a few hours more, you may decide to treat yourself to a mammoth dinner—perhaps believing that since this feast will be your only real food, you'll still be ahead of the calorie game at the end of the day.

Sorry, but that's not quite how it works. When you pile food (even "healthy" food) into an empty or almost-empty stomach, you jolt insulin into action. More fat is delivered directly to fat cells—followed soon after by fat "made" by the liver from surplus carbohydrates. Then insulin slams the fat-cell doors shut, keeping the bad stuff locked inside, less easily burned.

Because of what it does to insulin production, loading up on calories all at once can be much more fat making and diet destructive than the same number of calories eaten over a longer period of time. In fact, we now know that the effects of a single pig-out can be long-lasting indeed. It can jack up insulin levels, jam fat in, and keep it there, interfering with weight loss for days, *even if you immediately go back to dieting after your binge*.

And, as I pointed out earlier in this chapter, if the fast-and-gorge pattern is maintained long enough, the body begins to practice its own special kind of fuel conservation: it gets more mileage out of calories by burning them more slowly. That's right. Erratic, irregular eating can actually lower your metabolism. It's exactly the opposite of what you want to happen.

These are fat facts to ponder next time you're tempted to save up calories so that you'll have more to spend on a pig-out later in the day, or on a special dinner two days from now, next week, or whenever.

On the Bodyrhythm Diet, you'll be eating three nutritious fat-fighting meals every day. No skipping allowed. Remember, you won't lose weight faster if you don't eat the recommended amounts at appropriate times. You might not lose at all. You might even gain if you make a habit of banking calories in order to blow them all at once at some future time!

The Bodyrhythm Diet also calls for fruit to be eaten between meals. Fruit snacks will help keep blood sugar levels and insulin in even better balance, keep hunger down and energy up. In fact, fruit, such as oranges, tangerines, peaches, apricots, is the almost perfect snack on this or any diet. Here's why:

Fruit contains fructose, a simple sugar, but one that tends to produce a slower and lower rise in insulin, so blood sugar levels remain on a more even keel. Research also shows that fruit eaten as a snack sends blood sugar up more gradually and lower than high-fiber, complex-carbohydrate snacks, like a slice of whole wheat bread or handful of shredded wheats, or even carrots, the traditional diet nibble.

Fresh, whole fruit (not cooked, frozen, canned, juiced or pureed, dried or overpeeled) is high in fiber, which slows even further the rate at which sugar is absorbed.

Because fructose and fiber contribute to an easy, moderate rise in blood sugar, the insulin response, when you eat fruit, is also slower and more moderate. And that means that more of the sugar is burned as fuel, less is stored.

And of course, fruit's delicious. You can take it with you anywhere in your purse or briefcase. And if you forget, there's almost always a fruit stand or grocery store nearby.

Like three square meals a day, fruit snacks are an integral part of the Bodyrhythm Diet. Don't skip them!

4. Cut back on caffeine. If you're not a heavy coffee drinker, you can skip this one. However, if you ordinarily consume more than two cups a day of regular (not decaffeinated) coffee, I urge you to start drinking less. It could make a difference on a diet.

Remember, caffeine stimulates a release of blood sugar followed by an insulin increase, affecting some people more than others. And, of course, more insulin also means more fat stored, less fat burned, even when the number of calories you consume stays the same.

Some women insist that coffee helps them deal with hunger when they're on a diet, and no wonder. At first the fluid fills up an empty stomach. And blood sugar rises soon after caffeine enters the system. When blood sugar goes up, hunger *is* lessened. At first. For a while. But as insulin rushes out to clear away the blood sugar, hunger returns, often stronger than ever. Unfortunately, the connection between coffee drinking and delayed hunger is blurred by the time lapse between—in other words, you may think coffee "satisfies" a hunger pang because that's how you feel *at first*.

I was a coffee-holic, I'll admit it. I couldn't face the prospect of no more coffee, ever. Still can't. But I did manage to cut back to two cups a day. (Most days, anyway.) And if I was able to do it, I know you can, too.

A few words of warning. Some people who try to quit caffeine cold turkey suffer a range of withdrawal symptoms that include edginess and irritability, fatigue, even headaches. If you're like I am, you are better at everything, including dieting, when you feel good. So instead of cutting out caffeine altogether and all at once, you might have better results if you reduce your intake by a cup or so every few days. Or, if you brew your own coffee, you can gradually substitute decaf for the real thing. Start with mostly regular coffee; over a period of weeks, use more decaf, less caffeinated, until you are down to the two cups daily max, or, better yet, caffeine-free.

As with coffee go-withs, try some of the new blends that are great-tasting black, or add just a splash of low- or non-fat milk. Avoid cream, whole milk, nondairy creamers; they're all too high in fat for us, and the cream substitutes contain corn syrup and other sugars, even though they don't taste especially sweet. Sugar is out, too, as is artificial sweetener, because of their effect on the insulin response.

On the Bodyrhythm Diet, you'll be drinking two cups of coffee per day, tops. (One or none would be better.) If you prefer tea, which is lower in caffeine than coffee, try to limit yourself to three cups. These changes alone won't make you lose weight. But because they'll help keep insulin production more stable and moderate, caffeine cutbacks can aid the cause.

5. *Don't use artificial sweeteners*. I know. They're allowed on most diets. Even some of the better ones. But

this is one more area where the Bodyrhythm Diet is different. Those diets weren't developed to help curb the fat-making, fat-storing, fat-trapping properties of insulin. This one was.

The no-artificial-sweetener rule is important if your body confuses the sweet taste of the fakes with the genuine article and pumps out more insulin to deal with the "sugar." As you know, when that happens, blood sugar levels drop (and hunger mounts), fat storage is enhanced, fat-burning slows. You want the opposite to happen.

There's another good reason to go easy on or give up artificial sweeteners—along with the jams, jellies, sodas, baked goods, puddings, etc. that are doctored up with these products. Often, people who begin to use sugar substitutes regularly to satisfy a sweet tooth, develop an even stronger craving for the real thing. Ironically, instead of extracting the sweet tooth, sham sugar seems to cement it even more securely into place!

Consider this: If artificial sweeteners were effective aids to the dieter, obesity rates would be much lower now that we all have access to those little pink and blue packets, not to mention diet candies, ice cream, pies, cakes, cookies, etc. But that hasn't happened. In fact, one study carried out by the American Cancer Society found that women who use artificial sweeteners were not only more likely to *gain* weight, they gained weight faster, no matter what weight they started at, than women who didn't use the stuff!

Remember, after the sugar—or for some people, even the taste of sweet—comes insulin. After insulin comes hunger. And in the meantime fat storing increases. It's a chain of events we want to avoid, which is why you won't find artificial sweeteners, or foods made with them as an ingredient, on the Bodyrhythm Diet.

6. *Avoid "cue foods.".* This strategy is for hyper-responders whose bodies react with an outflow of insulin and who get hungry at the sight or smell (maybe even the thought) of tempting foods. (If you're not sure whether

you are a hyper-responder, assume you are . . . just to be on the safe side.)

"Cue foods," of course, are the ones that activate your salivary glands the instant you set eyes on them, or your nose gets wind of them, or when images of them pop into your mind. They're not the same for every woman, but they are almost always chockful of sugar, starch, and/or fat. Get them out of your house! Clear them out of your desk at the office! If you can't see them or smell them, you're less likely to think about them. (Out of sight, out of mind.) And less likely to inadvertently turn up your body's hunger-making, profat insulin.

Just as important, when cue foods aren't readily available, you won't be as easily tempted.

Avoiding cue foods is just one of the success strategies that can help you lose more fat more quickly and more surely on the Bodyrhythm Diet. You'll find a whole chapter filled with additional nonfood diet aids, designed to speed the weight-loss process, in Chapter 9.

7. *Get physical.* We don't know for sure if inactivity, all by itself, boosts insulin production. But the opposite does seem to be true. Exercise appears to increase the body's sensitivity to the hormone and the demand goes down. That means, when you begin to use your muscles vigorously and regularly, insulin production will become more balanced and moderate. More fat will be burned, less fat made, stored, and trapped.

I could rattle on for pages about the benefits of exercise—on a diet or off. And in Chapter 10, I'll do just that. For now, the important point is that Bodyrhythm eating and exercise plans can re-form your insulin response as they help reshape your body.

The Good News About Insulin

As we've seen, insulin plays an important role in making you fat and keeping you fat. But you can fight the fat maker and win by following the simple principles built into the Bodyrhythm Diet, including: reducing fat intake, boosting fiber, eating at regular, frequent intervals, taking in less caffeine, and cutting out artificial sweeteners. If you also avoid cue foods and start getting more exercise, you'll be that much ahead in disarming this insidious hormone.

That's the good news. Now, here's more good news. As you lose weight and fat—and you will—the number of insulin receptors, or ''doors,'' on the membranes of your fat cells will increase. With more of these little doors, the cells will become more sensitive to insulin. Smaller amounts of the hormone will be required to clear your bloodstream of sugar and fats, so less will be produced. And with less insulin, there's less fat storing, fat making, and fat trapping. And with less fat trapped, more fuel will be available to be burned off. Not only will you have put the brakes on another fat-making cycle, but you will have reversed it.

Overproduction of insulin is only one of several factors contributing to diet resistance among women. But it's a major one, which is why insulin control is a key element of the Bodyrhythm Diet. The diet plus exercise should coax your body out of the old insulin-powered get fat/stay fat syndrome and into a new cycle of healthier, sexier slimness.

6 | Emotional Eating and How to "Treat" It

Janet was making great progress on a diet she'd clipped from the pages of a popular woman's magazine until her boyfriend told her he needed more "space"—and dumped her. Within a few months she gained back the fifteen pounds she had lost, plus a bonus five.

Elaine had almost reached her target weight of 135 on one of the recently popular mostly protein diets. But as final exams neared, she began to use bags and bags of chocolate candies as "study aids," and by the time she received her test results, her weight had bounced back up to 145 pounds.

Carol simply slumped into the blahs from time to time. Occasionally her blue moods occurred shortly before her period. But just as often, they hit her at other times as well. Sometimes, during her down days, Carol sought out spicy Mexican food or zesty Indian cuisine, perhaps in an unconscious attempt to lift her mood with highly flavored dishes. At other times she cruised in and out of fast-food joints, indiscriminately ordering burgers and fries, because, she said with a shrug, "It's something to do."

Janet, Elaine, and Carol are emotional eaters. They tend to turn to food for comfort, or to ease feelings of stress or tension. Chances are, you're an emotional eater, too. I say this because in all my years of helping women lose weight, I've never met *one* who didn't admit to using food as a feel-good remedy, at least once in a while.

And why not? For most of us, the link between food and emotions was forged soon after birth. As infants, mother's milk or formula actually *did* solve our most serious problem: hunger. And nursing was almost always accompanied by the most delicious warmth and cuddling. In the first days of life, eating became synonymous with love, warmth, security.

Later on, our parents applauded or beamed with pride when we cleaned our plates. Or nagged or threatened if we balked at eating. (Remember this? "Young lady, you just sit right there until you make your meat and vegetables all gone.")

Food may have been associated with excitement, too. At least it was for me. I remember how thrilled and important I felt going out with the grown-ups at night to eat in a restaurant.

Then, too, many of us were rewarded with treats for being good, and deprived of them, as punishment, when we were naughty.

The point, of course, is that we learned in childhood to associate eating with positive feelings—the feeling of being loved, of being good, or being special. And we *still* look to food and eating as a way of recreating those feelings.

Is it any wonder then that Janet overate to compensate for the lover she lost, that Elaine loaded up on chocolates to ease the anxiety she felt about exams, and that Carol combatted blahs and boredom with hot, spicy treats and by whizzing in and out of fast-food restaurants?

For years now we've understood and accepted psychological theories about food and the tendency to eat in order to feel better. But today, we also know that there are real *biological* connections between certain foods and emotional states.

Serotonin, the Calming Chemical

For women, the foods most often used—instinctively, if not consciously—as mood modifiers are those old friends and sometimes demons, the carbohydrates: sugars and starches.

A carbohydrate-dense meal, as you already know, triggers an insulin increase. But in addition to moving carbs and fats out of the bloodstream and into appropriate cells, insulin also moves amino acids (components of protein in the food we eat) to your muscles and tissues.

But one of those amino acids, tryptophan, slips away from insulin's "grasp" and enters the brain. Once there, tryptophan stimulates the manufacture of a chemical called serotonin. Serotonin is special in that it influences moods.

(One point to keep in mind: It's not eating protein that makes serotonin; it's eating carbohydrates that stimulates insulin, which in turn moves other amino acids aside so that the tryptophan can enter the brain to produce serotonin.)

When serotonin levels are low—as can happen if you eat large amounts of protein and/or fats and relatively few carbohydrates—you may begin to feel stressed, crabby, and down in the dumps. You may even have trouble falling asleep. However, a carbohydrate "fix," which boosts serotonin production, often has the opposite effect. A sugar or starch splurge makes you feel more relaxed, even-tempered, and content. You may even be less sensitive to physical pain!

What's so fascinating about the recently documented relationship between what we eat (or don't eat) and how we feel is that our bodies *always* seemed to know which foods would bring us up when we were down and relax us when we felt edgy or grumpy. A kind of inner wisdom— call it instinct—told us to search out sugary or starchy foods. The scientists "simply" figured out, and verified, the biological link between eating carbs and feeling better.

What a relief, if you were ever told (as many women have been) that your urge to eat sweets or starches when you were blue or under stress meant that you were neurotic, or "obsessive-compulsive," or had an "oral personality." Isn't it comforting to know now that researchers have found a solid physiological reason for those carbohydrate urges!

There's another benefit to boosting serotonin production in your brain by eating carbohydrates. When serotonin goes up, your appetite for carbohydrates is turned down. But let serotonin levels fall, and carbohydrate cravings are turned on. When serotonin production is increased again, the craving eases off.

When you want to lose weight, or keep it lost, complex carbohydrates are a boon. By keeping blood sugar levels steady and not setting insulin into hysterical fits of sugar lowering, complex carbs help keep hunger turned off. By getting your brain to keep serotonin relatively even, not surging and falling, they blunt cravings. They help sustain physical energy and emotional equilibrium. In other words, complex carbohydrates are satisfying bodywise and brainwise, hungerwise and cravingwise, energywise and emotionwise.

But don't make the mistake of thinking that if a few extra calories' worth of carbohydrates will make you feel better, loading up on carbs will put you on top of the world. It doesn't work that way. Overeating carbohydrates—sugars *or* starches—may oversedate you and produce an energy drain, causing you to feel tired and sluggish—not to mention bloated, guilty, and *fat*. As so many women have told me, and as I know myself, the response to those bad feelings is often to eat more carbohydrates to "treat" ourselves or to overdose into a carbohydrate-serotonin stupor. And then to feel even worse. Good-bye diet, hello fat!

It's a tricky balancing act. Too few carbohydrates can make you feel tense and mean, or blue, and give you a craving for sugary or starchy food. Too many carbohydrates can make you feel slowed down and sluggish—and prompt you to reach for more, in an attempt to restore your mood.

Balanced, regulated amounts of carbohydrates are what you need. And that is what the Bodyrhythm Diet was developed to do. Just enough, and not too much, of the right kinds of carbohydrates to keep insulin in better balance. I've also suggested the amounts and kinds of carbohydrates for mood enhancement and to help you keep "emotional" eating under control.

Mood Ups and Downs and What to Do About Them

For most women, the mind-body need for carbohydrates isn't steady. It goes up and down. There are times when we crave more carbs, and times when we can do with less.

For example, you probably want more sugars or starches when estrogen and progesterone are on the rise. Remember from reading Chapter 4 how a rise in progesterone close to your period stimulates a physical need for more carbohydrates in order to spare protein. And from reading the previous chapter, you recall that during the last half of the menstrual cycle, cells bind onto insulin, blood sugar levels fall, and hunger and carbohydrate cravings set in and hold tight. And you remember how Stage II eating can help at these hormone-related danger times.

But high levels of estrogen can also affect mood-related cravings. Here's how it is thought to work: Vitamin B-6 is essential for the manufacture of serotonin. But excess estrogen causes the body to utilize vitamin B_6 inefficiently. So when estrogen is high or on the increase, B_6 dwindles, and feel-good serotonin is on the decrease, making you tense, irritable.

And of course, when you feel out of sorts, you crave more carbs so that your brain can make more mood-boosting serotonin. A shorthand way of saying it is that these cravings go hand in hand, up or down, with estrogen production.

There's an estrogen increase beginning midcycle and

rising until a few days before your period. That may be
one reason for preperiod mood nasties, as estrogen inter-
feres with B_6 and mood-moderating serotonin. (Women
who take synthetic estrogens via oral contraceptives may
also be affected.)

But being overweight also seems to intensify cravings
for carbohydrates.

How so? It's another not-so-merry-go-round. Estrogen,
remember, is produced not only by the ovaries, but also
from fatty tissue. If you are overweight and overfat, you
probably produce more estrogen than "normal," which
lowers available B_6, and that, in turn, lowers serotonin
production. When that happens, you can have more mood
fluctuations, more mood-related cravings, and more *intense*
carbohydrate cravings to boost serotonin than men or even
women of normal weight. And each time your already
high estrogen levels climb higher—as happens with each
monthly cycle—those cravings for carbohydrates become
even stronger!

Unfortunately, trying to get through the craving days
without some extra serotonin-boosting, feel-better carbohydrates just adds to the problem.

Diets that are low in carbohydrates to begin with, and
diets suggesting that you, as a woman, should cut back on
carbs during the days before a period, practically set you
up for failure. They create conditions within your body
that can cause you to feel edgy, mean, and more sensitive
to pain (including cramps), while at the same time turning
on cravings full force. Your instinctive response is to reach
for foods that supply the biggest, quickest rise in mood-
modifying serotonin: high-calorie, sugar-dense carbs such
as chocolate, ice cream, cookies, or starchy no-nos, like
chips or rich rolls.

If you wait long enough, and serotonin levels fall low
enough, a massive pig-out is almost guaranteed. Your diet
goes down the tubes, you go up in fat, and the pounds pile
on again until or unless you manage to regain control.

The Bodyrhythm Diet was developed to help you avoid
all that. It calls for foods naturally high in vitamin B_6 at all

times—lean meats, poultry, lots of green leafy vegetables, whole-grain breads. (White-flour products are not only fiber-depleted, but about 75 percent of the vitamin B_6 is removed in the milling process and not replaced, even if the breads or rolls are "enriched.") And the Bodyrhythm Diet is also devised to ease you through the craving days by allowing you to have more mood-modifying carbs at times when *not* to eat them would make you feel miserable and cause big diet trouble.

Now, I'm not in favor of using food to solve problems. After all, getting hooked on food as a source of gratification— as a way of making ourselves feel better—probably helped get us fat in the first place.

But as a realist and diet counselor to overweight women, I also recognize that there are times for every dieter when stress or the blahs make it doubly difficult to adhere to get-slim eating. At those times, *slightly* larger amounts of carbohydrates at meals, and higher-carbohydrate snacks, can save the day and the diet. Stage II of the Bodyrhythm Diet supplies you with those foods.

In Stage II, you'll be eating higher-carbohydrate fruits as snacks and, at meals, more high-fiber, whole-grain breads, naturally rich in vitamin B_6 (the vitamin that enhances serotonin production). During Stage II, you may also choose to eat more of those protein sources higher in B_6 (the "richer" proteins, like lean beef, liver, eggs, salmon). The extra carbohydrate foods, as well as those foods high in B_6, should help you feel better—calmer, less irritable—for longer periods than sugary treats and highly processed starches that can give you a quick lift, followed by an equally quick letdown.

Stage II specifies which and how much of these feel-good extras to eat. But you'll determine when to eat them. You'll do it by tuning in to your moods. Briefly, you'll eat according to Stage I principles (lower carbohydrates, lower-fat protein selections) when you're feeling calm and "normal," and your life seems relatively easy, or at least manageable. Then, if and when your mood slumps (it often happens around the time of a period, but it *could* happen anytime), when you feel tension and anxiety building, and along with them, cravings that you can't wish away, switch to Stage II eating (more carbohydrates, more higher-fat protein choices).

As we've seen, the carbohydrate extras along with the additional sources of vitamin B_6 foods in Stage II seems to help the brain increase serotonin production.

When you're back to normal, go back to lower-carbohydrate, lower-fat protein, Stage I eating. In a sense, Stage I puts you on the diet fast track. Stage II keeps you on track. Together, they help get you where you want to go.

Special to Choco-holics

For some women, chocolate is a real high. It's their first-choice feel-better food. And according to studies carried out by psychiatrist Michael Gitlin of UCLA and Marjorie Schuman, Professor of Psychology at the California School of Professional Psychology, more women than men "self-medicate" with chocolate. These women, they say, tend to be moody, fall in love easily, and are especially devastated by romantic rejection. Many women, I find, turn to chocolate like some other women turn to pills or alcohol to blot out sadness. If they eat enough of it, chocolate seems to bring them up a few notches, and when the "high" wears off, they eat more.

What induces the chocolate high? For one, it could be the super-quick—but super-temporary—energy fix supplied by sugar. And since chocolate also contains caffeine, there's an additional jolt supplied by that chemical. Finally, chocolate is also rich in another chemical upper similar to amphetamines, called phenylethylamine.

There's another nutrient that seems to be linked to chocolate cravings: magnesium. And chocolate has plenty of it. In fact, some researchers suspect that many female choco-holics are actually responding to their bodies' need for more of this mineral, which is in short supply in the standard American diet, and in many reducing diets, too. (An interesting point about magnesium is that it appears to go along with vitamin B_6 in helping reduce the cramping before and during a period, which is why some doctors suggest magnesium and B_6 supplements for women with difficult periods, or a diet that delivers more of these nutrients.)

And then, of course, chocolate is associated with romantic love. Why the connection? Some think the chemical high produced by the naturally stimulating ingredients in chocolate (especially phenylethylamine) create sensations similar to romantic highs, or even a sexual charge. Who knows? But when a man brings chocolate, you know you mean something to him. Maybe we get some of that feeling of being special when we buy it for ourselves. (*I* certainly felt special when I sent Candygrams, gift-wrapped of course, to myself!)

If the women in my diet groups are at all typical of the population at large, choco-holism has foiled the attempts of thousands, maybe *millions* of us to lose weight. But Bodyrhythm Diet eating does seem to help control the habit.

Take the case of Joelle. She fit the choco-holic profile to a tee. A tall, buxom redhead, she was forever trying to get rid of the twenty-five pounds or so that stood between her and a truly spectacular figure. The extra weight was not an initial turnoff to men. She had no trouble attracting them, and, alas, fell head over high heels for each man of the moment.

Why her love affairs were about as sturdy and long lasting as a pair of cheap panty hose is another story. But she always consoled herself with chocolate when "he" walked out.

Joelle joined one of my groups at the beginning of a new relationship. She was radiant, and highly motivated to lose weight. A few weeks later, she walked into the room a different person. Her expression, her posture, even her tone of voice were sad and droopy. "He went back to his ex-wife," she confided when the meeting was over. "But," she added, brightening, "I haven't been drowning myself in a sea of chocolate."

I hesitate to say that it was Stage I and Stage II eating principles that kept Joelle (and others like her) from sinking into chocolate, but I do believe that the Bodyrhythm Diet acted as a kind of life raft. It supplied her with high-fiber carbohydrates at each and every meal and for snacks. So when she was hit with the stress of suddenly having yet another man leave, she wasn't left physically vulnerable because of a carbohydrate deficiency and low levels of mood-steadying serotonin.

Then, immediately after the initial shock, she shifted into Stage II/higher-carbohydrate eating, which encouraged her brain to make more calming serotonin.

Vegetables, high in fiber but very low in calories, such as fresh raw broccoli, cauliflower, and mushrooms, offered her the satisfaction of "chewing out" her frustration, hurt, and anger. Sound farfetched? It isn't. Researchers have found that just the act of chewing—it doesn't matter on what—can reduce anxiety.

Other vegetables, so nonfattening their calorie count is practically negative, also did something else for her. Dark green vegetables, eaten raw or lightly steamed, like romaine lettuce, chard, green beans, and spinach, gave her more magnesium, the nutrient associated with chocolate cravings.

Now, maybe you're thinking, "Broccoli would never do it for *me* when I want chocolate." Possibly not. But if you are an unreformed choco-holic, you're still in the habit of tearing off on a chocolate binge whenever you get the urge, or when you're feeling down, slighted, deprived, or hurt. However, I think you'll discover that once you stop eating chocolate on impulse every time something goes wrong—once you get out of the habit of using it as a crutch—you'll crave it less and less.

That's the way it is about impulses—for chocolate, or spending too much money, or for going for the "wrong" guy. If you give in to these urges, if you try to fool yourself by saying, "Just this one last time," if you indulge them every now and then, those impulses become stronger and your ability to stand up to them dribbles away. But the more you resist, the easier it is to hold out. That's how it worked for Joelle. I'm convinced it can be that way for you, too, once you put your mind to it.

See for yourself. Once you give up chocolate, absolutely swear off it, you'll start to want it less. The Bodyrhythm Diet will help you along by giving you much of what you once got from chocolates. Stage I keeps you fortified with the complex carbohydrates you need for sustained energy, so you won't need to turn to chocolates for fuel. It provides the magnesium you may have been getting in the past from chocolate. And with all the crunchy free foods you're allowed, you can chew away tension and anxiety to your heart's content. When your mood takes a turn for the worse, a switch to Stage II, higher-carbohydrate eating will help your brain make more soothing serotonin. At the same time, the additional whole grains will provide extra magnesium.

Finally, in *staying* with the Bodyrhythm Diet, you'll begin to feel better about yourself. And nothing gives a better high or boosts spirits, self-esteem, and motivation than doing something you know is good for you. Certainly not chocolate.

Feeling Spicy?

You already know from reading Chapter 4 that a desire for spicy foods—like burritos, cheese and crackers, taste-tingling Chinese dishes—can be masked cravings for fats and carbohydrates (sugars and/or starches). Now we're going to take a look at how an urge for highly seasoned dishes is sometimes related to feelings of boredom and the blahs.

How so? Well, think of what it's like when you consume chili, curry, mustard, horseradish, Cajun or Thai cuisines. They literally warm you up. Your metabolism increases and you may even start to perspire (your body's way of cooling itself down). And your tongue burns, your nose runs, your eyes water. Oddly, the pain gives pleasure. It's not masochism. Not exactly, anyway.

It's more like taking a "controlled risk." You know just what you're getting into (or biting into) with these thrill-a-minute foods, and you know you won't really get hurt. All the same, it *feels* like living dangerously. Just like a roller-coaster ride, hot foods give you a jolt that can sharpen your sense of being alive. So, the theory goes, the quest for super-hot is partly a response to the desire to add some spice to your life. Literally.

There is also speculation that the sting of hot foods triggers the release of substances called endorphins. These are the body's natural painkillers and pleasure enhancers. According to this theory, the craving for spicy dishes when you are down or blue may be nature's roundabout way of prompting you to dose up with natural emotional and physical anesthetics when they can do you some good. In other words, reaching for something spicy hot may be an unconscious attempt to relieve an ache—heartache, headache, any ache.

Not everyone loves or wants hotter-than-hot, of course, and you may be one of those who don't. Nevertheless, you probably enjoy variety. The desire for novelty is a basic human trait, and extends even to the food we eat. If you've ever had to exist for more than a few days on a diet of "soft foods" only—or anything only—you know just what I mean. Eat just mushy stuff, and in no time your mouth craves a good, hardy, crunchy chomp. Eat just protein, and soon you'll give most anything for an orange. Eat just fruit, and before long you're dreaming of steak. Eat just bland, and you'll find yourself willing to break all the diet rules for something spicy.

With that in mind, I've provided recipes and spices for lots of taste-appealing dishes that you can use or not as part of the Bodyrhythm Diet—dishes such as chili rellenos, zesty kabobs, pizzazzed pizza, and piquant Oriental chicken. You can incorporate the spices into the diet anytime you want to add some flare to your meals and some spice to your life. They're as suitable for Stage I of the diet as they are for Stage II. However, since Stage II eating was designed specifically to help you through those times when you feel tense, bored, or just plain out of sorts, you may prefer to save the spicy dishes for then. In fact, some taste-zinging foods are specially designed for Stage II eating.

But you never *have* to use these spices or any recipe. Zesty foods are not what make the Bodyrhythm Diet work. You'll have equally good results if you stick with more conventionally seasoned fare. The spiced-up dishes are just in case. I've included them so that you'll have a choice of taste-tingling flavors when and if you want a little more zip in your food and your life—and healthy low-cal alternatives when you are tempted to pig out on greasy, high-cal, spiced-up junk.

When Alcohol Is the Problem

For some women, the problem isn't what they eat, it's what they drink.

Fortunately, of those who drink, most do it moderately and within limits: a cocktail or a glass of wine after a tense day at work, at a party, on a date, or when they want a romantic evening. And they do it for obvious reasons: alcohol *can* be relaxing, and *does* loosen inhibitions.

Too bad that as it relaxes and loosens social inhibitions, it also softens diet resistance. At the same time, many drinks contain some carbohydrates, and "sweet" drinks such as wine, beer, liqueurs, and dessert wines have more sugar. After a drink, the insulin troops are mobilized to clear your blood of sugar. As blood sugar falls, you can be left *ravenous*.

Imagine this: You're at a party. You hesitate, then say yes to a drink. (After all, how many calories can there be in an ounce or three of wine? And anyway, you're intimidate by all those strangers.) You soon feel a little giddy. And a little hungry. You have another drink. You feel a little giddier and a little hungrier. Suddenly you don't care beans anymore about losing weight. You're off and running, eating up every little appetizer that comes your way on a tray, cramming handfuls of party nibbles into your mouth, and later going back to the buffet table for seconds and thirds of everything. Need I add that you hate yourself in the morning?

It's happened to me, and if it hasn't happened to you, it *could*.

And we're not even talking about overdrinking now, but about the feel-good effect of alcohol, and the way it undermines motivation and stimulates hunger. If weight loss is your goal, you *must* skip alcohol until you've lost the pounds you want to lose.

Of course, there are also calorie reasons for avoiding alcohol. Some women who are otherwise quite knowledgeable and sophisticated about nutrition have the idea that alcohol calories don't count.

Sharon, who worked as a buyer for a chain of department stores, was one of them. She followed the diet plan I had given her to the letter. She even xeroxed it several times, she always had a copy with her in her purse, stuck one on her fridge, and taped another to her desk at work.

Yet after six weeks Sharon had lost only three pounds. Now, gradual, steady weight loss is always preferable to crash dieting, which might produce quick and gratifying results in the short run, but practically never works over the long haul. However, a mere three-pound loss after a month and a half of healthy, get-slim eating was going *too* slow. Sharon became discouraged and impatient, and who could blame her?

It finally came out, almost in passing, that Sharon had a drink at lunch that day. Another woman in the group commented that "alcohol isn't on the plan right now." Sharon responded with: "It can't hurt, can it?" And she proceeded to explain to the group that part of her job was entertaining clients at lunch or dinner, sometimes both, and that alcohol was part of the ritual. She seemed genuinely surprised when I explained that the extra calories she was consuming in the form of alcohol no doubt interfered with her attempts to lose weight. It was as if a little light bulb switched on in her brain when she realized how all those weeks had been "wasted" dieting.

Actually, it's a wonder Sharon lost any weight at all, what with white wine (her usual premeal drink) "costing" about 90 calories a glass, and margaritas, her favorite cocktail, running around 400 calories per drink.

Sharon didn't need any more reasons not to mix dieting and drinking. If you do, here they are:

Alcohol is thought to interfere with the liver's ability to get rid of excess estrogen. And high estrogen, as I explained in Chapter 3, makes women more diet-resistant and fat-prone. Excess estrogen, remember, also causes the body to use B_6 inefficiently. And B_6 is necessary for the production of feel-good serotonin. The excess sugar in many alcoholic drinks (and high estrogen) may encourage water retention and the swollen, puffy, undereye bags, tummy, and ankles that go along with it. You don't need *that*! And alcohol is a depressant, making spirits sag. And when mood slumps, you're "stimulated" into wanting sugars or starches to make you feel better.

Sharon, like many social and business drinkers, did stop drinking when she understood how destructive it can be to a diet. It was a relatively simple matter, for her, of substituting a glass of sparkling mineral water with a slice of lemon or lime for the white wine and occasional margarita. Apparently, her clients weren't aware of the change. Or, if they did notice, they didn't mention it. See? It *can* be business as usual without alcohol.

There are no provisions for alcohol on the Bodyrhythm Diet. It's not allowed. Period. Even moderate drinking supplies unnecessary calories and can throw your hormones—insulin and estrogen—out of whack and into fat-storing mode. With increased consumption, it can make you waterlogged, depressed, and hamper production of calming serotonin, your body's natural feel-good chemical. And heavy drinking, of course, is a disease, one that is ultimately more destructive to your looks, your body, and your life, than is obesity.

If you can't control your drinking, no matter how hard you try, recognize you have a problem. A *big* one. Stop trying to lose weight and focus on the serious issue of your drinking. If you can't give it up, get help.

Other Downs and Ups

The get-slim food-and-exercise combination that make up the Bodyrhythm Diet can help you deal better with eating urges brought on by ordinary, everyday blahs, blues, stresses, and anxieties. These downers are often related to disappointment, frustration, or pressure buildups at home, on the job, or in your social life. Sometimes crabbiness or irritability is a result of overwork or lack of sleep.

Occasionally, other factors are at work. Chronic fatigue—blahs to the nth degree—might, if you are overweight, be due to carrying around a load of excess pounds. But don't assume anything. The same symptom could signal low iron.

An insufficiency of iron is most likely to affect women who suffer heavy menstrual bleeding. Unfortunately, when anemia is the cause of that wiped-out feeling, some women reach for sugars or starches to give them an emotional or energy "boost." But when iron deficiency is the problem, you can't eat your way out of it with those foods. And exercise, a great way to boost energy when you are otherwise healthy, can result in even greater fatigue, since running or jogging can lead to a further depletion of iron—a condition known as "runners' anemia."

Fad diets—like an all-fruit diet—can also lead to anemia. The Bodyrhythm Diet provides high-iron foods at all times—plenty of leafy green vegetables, whole grains, lean proteins. And it gives you additional iron-rich foods—more whole grains, as well as dark meat of poultry, eggs, and red-meat choices—during Stage II, which often coincides with those days before or during your period when you need these high-iron foods the most. It's lucky for us that those same foods that help curb cravings are also those foods high in iron.

But if the condition is severe, food isn't enough to remedy it. If you're dragging yourself around and sluggish most of the time, don't tinker with food cures. See a doctor. A heavy-duty prescription of iron supplements or some other remedy may be in order.

Fatigue accompanied by a feeling of never being warm enough—not even in summer, not even when you are bundled up in sweaters—is sometimes indicative of an underactive thyroid gland. Since this gland regulates the rate of calorie burn-off, another result of underfunctioning can be easy, rapid weight gain or extreme difficulty losing pounds if you are on a diet. There is even evidence that women who suffer from symptoms of premenstrual syndrome—weight gain, mood swings, crying jags—may have sluggish thyroids.

Many overweight women would love to assume their problem is due to an underactive thyroid; for a while I even tried this excuse on myself! The truth is, the condition is fairly rare. But it does exist.

By all means, check with your doctor if you are feeling especially tired, cold when everyone else is warm, or have real trouble losing weight on a diet. There are new means of detecting thyroid lows—and a boost in thyroid in pill form can be a simple, medical solution.

There are no food cures for an underfunctioning thyroid gland and the sluggishness that goes along with it. But assuming your thyroid gland is normal, many food researches suggest a simple food tactic you can use to help stimulate thyroid activity, perhaps turn up your metabolism, stimulate your energy, and maybe even lose pounds a little faster: just eat plenty of foods that are naturally high in iodine, since this mineral stimulates the thyroid. Good bets are ocean fish, including halibut, swordfish, tuna, cod, sole, and bluefish. Why not choose an ocean fish as part of your protein portion on the Bodyrhythm Diet?

Another tip: Watch out for cabbage. It's an excellent vegetable for most diets, but anyone concerned about an underactive thyroid should beware. Good as it is, extra large quantities of cabbage, surprisingly, can slow thyroid activity in some vulnerable people.

What If It's All in Your Head?

More and more, researchers are uncovering the links between food and certain moods. We now know that feeling out of sorts or irritable is often related to an insufficiency of serotonin. By eating carbohydrates we can encourage the brain to make more of the calming chemical— and help ourselves feel less stressed. These recent findings help explain the impulse to load up on carbs when we're feeling frustrated or anxious or just plain *nasty*. It's nature's way of bringing us *up*. Stage II of the Women's Bodyrhythm Diet accommodates this impulse by allowing you to dose on the right kinds of extra carbohydrates when your mood slips, but not so much as to interfere with weight loss.

On the Bodyrhythm Diet, you'll also be eating taste-appealing foods to perk and spice up your moods and help prevent boredom eating, foods high in B_6 to aid in making feel-better serotonin, iron-high foods to help prevent fatigue, iodine-rich foods to stimulate the activity-regulating thyroid. In other words, the Bodyrhythm Diet helps give you the food elements vital to good health as well as helping you eat your way out of ordinary, everyday downers while you continue to lose pounds.

But, if you *never* seem to have enough energy, even after a good night's rest—even a restful vacation—or if you suffer chronic emotional distress, don't assume that food is the problem or the answer. "Treat" yourself to a medical and emotional checkup. Go now.

Once any snags are checked up and checked out, you can turn to the Bodyrhythm Diet and feel better than ever.

7 | The Bodyrhythm Diet: How It Works

Now you know more about what you're up against as a dieter in general . . . and especially as a *woman* who wants and needs to lose excess pounds of fat.

You're aware that many diets—even some of the best-known, most-hyped plans—don't deliver on their promises to get rid of fat and keep it off. That's because most of these diets are based on simple calorie counting, or on a "trick" formula that sounds good but fails to take into account many of the biological and psychological causes of overweight.

You've also learned why some of the diets that *do* work for men often don't work as well for us. In fact, no diet that I am aware of addresses the special problems that we, as women, encounter in our efforts to achieve the slimmer, fitter, sexier bodies we want. And that, of course, is why I developed the Women's Bodyrhythm Diet.

The Satisfaction Factor

A diet that gets results for us must work with our female bodies, not against them.

- It must include foods that help us deal with what I believe is the number-one fat-fighting problem for women: not hunger per se, but *cravings*. Especially cravings induced by the ups and downs of our female sex hormones, estrogen and progesterone. They—the hormones and the cravings they trigger—are, I suspect, part of nature's way of fattening us up so that we and our unborn babies (in case we get pregnant) can survive when food is scarce. It's a legacy from the distant past. For most of us now, getting enough to eat isn't a problem, but the cravings remain. And if they aren't pacified, they can build and build. Like water rushing against a dam, they can break down our resistance—and ultimately lead to out-of-control bingeing that undoes weeks of sensible, get-slim eating.

- A diet that works for women should help minimize all the other profat effects of our sex hormones and keep the fat-making, fat-storing, fat-trapping unisex hormone, insulin, in better balance.

- A diet that works for women should enable us to say no to the high-cal, sugary, and/or grease-laden feel-good foods we yearn for in times of emotional stress and strain, and should offer healthy, slimming alternatives that boost production of the body's natural tranquilizer, serotonin.

- A diet that works for women must supply liberal amounts of all the nutrients we need to stay healthy and look terrific—among them, bone-protecting calcium, blood-enriching iron, collagen-forming and cell-rejuvenating protein, and the full range of vitamins and minerals, including mood-enhancing vitamin B_6.

- A diet that works for women must give us enough food in the right proportions to prevent intense hunger, help protect against muscle loss and flab, and keep our bodies energized and purring along at peak efficiency.

- A diet that works for women should satisfy our need for variety and be composed of foods that are good tasting and easy to prepare or order (if we're eating away from home) so that we're not led into temptation by boredom or inconvenience.

In short, a diet that really works for women has to satisfy us hormonewise, moodwise, nutritionwise, and tastewise. Otherwise, we won't stay with it long enough to see it through to success.

The beauty of the Women's Bodyrhythm Diet is that it *does* meet all our special requirements. It has made a major difference in my life, and in the lives of other women who have tried it. Your turn.

The Diet: An Overview

Remember, the Bodyrhythm Diet is a two-part program consisting of Stage I, for maximum safe weight loss, and Stage II with built-in binge insurance and pig-out protection, to get you through difficult craving days while you continue to lose pounds of fat.

Before we go on to the details of the diet, let's take a look at how Stage I and Stage II are alike, and how they're different:

MEALS. You will be eating protein, starch (high-fiber is best), and a small amount of fat at breakfast, lunch, and dinner in *both* stages. All Bodyrhythm Diet meals are complete and well balanced.

PROTEIN. Your daily protein allowance in each stage of the diet supplies you with ample amounts of the amino acids your body needs for cell building and repair. The six ounces of protein you'll be eating each day on the Bodyrhythm Diet is, in fact, about what is recommended by the American Dietetic Association (which recommends five to seven ounces.) As a diet counselor, I've found that women tend to feel more deprived, hungrier, and seem to experience more frequent and intense cravings when protein intake is low—or even at the low end of the ADA recommendations. That recommendation was made in part to get people to consume less fat (untrimmed red meats, sandwich meats, high-fat cheeses, and other popular protein foods are quite high in fat). However, the small amount of fat supplied by the extra ounce or so of protein on the Bodyrhythm Diet is a must for craving control. And since the rest of the diet is low in fat, your intake of this nutrient never rises above healthy, moderate levels.

Note: Many popular diets overload you with protein— some allow unlimited protein, many give you six ounces of chicken, meat, or fish per *meal,* others allow as much as nine ounces a day. Protein may curb hunger, but too much protein may cut down on the making of serotonin— that brain chemical that serves to blunt cravings. And out-of-control cravings, as you know, lead to diet doom, binge eating, and fat.

Stage I proteins are all low in fat and include fish, such as halibut, red snapper, or orange roughy, lean poultry, and low-fat dairy products.

Stage II proteins are somewhat higher in fat, the better to help you resist the urge to splurge when cravings mount. In Stage II, you can select from slightly fattier fish, such as salmon or fresh tuna, dark meat poultry choices, certain red meats, cheeses (low-fat, part-skim if possible) or eggs.

HIGH-FIBER STARCHES are prime ingredients of each and every Bodyrhythm Diet Meal. As we saw in earlier chapters, fiber helps your body deal with excesses of the profat hormone estrogen. And, because high-fiber starches are broken apart *slowly* during digestion, they'll keep you feeling full longer, maintain steadier blood sugar levels, and encourage more balanced insulin production, so fewer calories are stored and more are burned. Starches also nudge the brain to make more serotonin; with serotonin up, you should feel less stressed and better able to control emotional eating. Bodyrhythm Diet starch choices are best if they are *whole-grain choices*—high in fiber as well as vitamin B_6, which seems to be especially helpful in easing women's mood swings.

You will be eating the same *kinds* of starches in both stages of the diet. Hot or cold cereal at breakfast. Bread or rolls at lunch and dinner. (Remember, if you have the

choice—at the supermarket, at the restaurant, at home—
always choose high-fiber, whole-grain cereals, as well as
whole-grain bread or rolls.)

In Stage I, however, all starch servings are limited to
one ounce.

In Stage II, when craving control is important, lunch
and dinner starches are doubled to two ounces.

You'll find a list of high-fiber cereals suitable for both
Bodyrhythm Diet stages on page 104.

FAT is another feature of all Bodyrhythm Diet meals,
much to the surprise of some dieters. This nutrient is
included for some very important reasons. Fat is digested
slowly and contributes to feelings of fullness long after a
meal has ended. (In that sense, small amounts of fat can
actually help keep you on a diet!) Fat enables your body
to utilize certain vitamins—especially vitamin A—essential
to good health and good looks. It also helps keep cravings turned down by allowing your body to spare protein,
instead of wasting it. (As we saw back in the progesterone chapter, protein waste is at the root of many cravings.) And fats also make your food taste tastier, so
you'll feel more satisfied, less likely to scour around for
something "good" (meaning "fattening") to "top off"
a meal.

Stage I and Stage II fat choices and amounts are
essentially the same. They're listed on page 114.

FREE FOODS. Low-cal vegetables, such as broccoli,
bell peppers, and cabbage, are good sources of additional
fiber, vitamins, and minerals. They'll also keep your
mouth busy with chewing and swallowing, providing you
with some of the oral gratification so many dieters seem to
miss on other weight-loss plans.

In Stage I and Stage II, you can have free foods in
unlimited amounts. Enjoy them crunchy and raw, or *very
lightly* steamed, between meals and/or with lunches and
dinners.

Bodyrhythm Diet free foods are listed on pages 115-116.

SNACKS. Certain fruits, because they are high in fiber

and contain fructose, a sugar that causes a slow rise in blood sugar—and thus has a moderating effect on insulin—are *required* snack choices.

You will be eating two servings of fruit in Stage I and in Stage II.

In both stages, one fruit will be a high vitamin C variety, such as a medium orange, two small tangerines, a cup of strawberries.

In Stage I, your second fruit choice will be one with a relatively low sugar content.

In Stage II, your second fruit choice will be somewhat more "sugar dense": the additional carbohydrate is an important part of binge insurance and should help ease cravings.

See page 120 for listings of fruits suitable for Stage I and Stage II eating.

NOTE: You'll probably find that fruit snacks do the best job of keeping blood sugar above the hunger threshold if you eat one midmorning and the other between lunch and dinner. And some women like to save the fruits until after dinner. Go ahead. If you'd rather splurge and have both fruits at once, do so.

CALCIUM REQUIREMENTS. To meet your daily needs for calcium, the mineral so vital to maintaining strong bones and teeth throughout life, you will be consuming two cups of milk in both stages of the Bodyrhythm Diet. Important: Use one, eight-ounce cup of *low-fat* milk with your cereal for breakfast.

On this diet, low-fat is better than skim at breakfast, even though it delivers an extra forty calories in the form of fat. The reason: Those few calories of fat help satisfy hunger and keep cravings reined in and under control. In fact, the fat in your morning cup of milk actually counts as the fat component of your breakfast!

You can pour your morning milk over cereal. If one cup swamps the bowl, use less and drink the rest as is, or in coffee, decaf, or tea.

The second eight-ounce cup of milk is either low-fat,

nonfat, or buttermilk—the choice is yours. Drink it with your meals if you like, or have it with your fruit snack, add it to coffee or tea, or sip it warm at bedtime. Just don't skip it.

The Diet: Stage I

In Stage I, you'll be eating lower-fat proteins and smaller amounts of high-fiber starches than in Stage II, and one of your fruit snacks will have a slightly lower sugar content than your second Stage II fruit. Stage I puts you into high fat-fighting gear.

How do you know when to eat according to Stage I principles? Easy! Follow this part of the diet when you are feeling relatively craving-free. You'll know simply by tuning in to your body.

For many women, cravings—if any—are low level and manageable during the fourteen days or so following the start of a period. That's because at this time of the month the body produces relatively small amounts of the craving hormone, progesterone. Chances are, this time of the month will be relatively food manageable for you, too. EAT ACCORDING TO STAGE I.

You may find when you tune in to your body that hunger and cravings are nonexistent, or turned down low, when you are in an up frame of mind, regardless of the time of month. FOLLOW STAGE I PRINCIPLES.

And, as your body accepts a lower weight, gives up its stores of fat, and becomes less resistant to further weight loss, SOS's for food, in the form of nagging cravings, may be fewer and farther between. (To simplify, when you are fat, your body is programmed to hold on to that fat by urging you to eat more; as you become slimmer, and your body adjusts to a lower weight, the program is interrupted.) STAY IN STAGE I.

The *absence* of cravings is the tip-off that your body and mind are primed for Stage I eating and heavy-duty fat-fighting.

BEGIN THE BODYRHYTHM DIET WITH STAGE I AND CONTINUE IN STAGE I UNTIL CRAVINGS BEGIN TO MAKE DEMANDS AND YOU FEEL THE NEED FOR STAGE II BINGE INSURANCE.

THE STAGE I REDUCED CRAVING FOOD PLAN

Later on, in Chapter 8, you'll find a week of Stage I breakfast, lunch, and dinner suggestions, plus recipes. However, the basic Stage I food plan is always the same. Here it is:

BREAKFAST

1, 8-ounce cup low-fat milk
(Note: low-fat milk supplies some carbohydrate, as well as breakfast-protein, *and* fat-portion requirements)
1-ounce (measured dry) cereal (high-fiber is best)

LUNCH OR DINNER

3 ounces Stage I low-fat proteins
    or, ½ cup cottage cheese (low-fat is best)
    or, ½ cup hoop, pot, or farmer cheese or, 6 egg whites
1, 1-ounce slice bread or roll (whole-grain is best)
1 portion fat
Free foods, as much as you like

CALCIUM REQUIREMENT

1 8-ounce cup nonfat milk, low-fat milk, or buttermilk (in addition to the 1 cup low-fat milk with breakfast)

SNACKS

1 serving vitamin C–rich fruit, anytime between meals
1 serving low-sugar fruit, anytime between meals
Free Foods, anytime you like

IMPORTANT

Don't omit any of the foods included in Stage I menu plans.

All Bodyrhythm Diet meals are balanced. Each element has been included for a *reason*. By skipping one or more elements, you deprive yourself of vital nutrients, set yourself up for intense hunger or cravings, and throw the whole plan out of kilter. Don't do it.

Unfortunately, some women look at Stage I menu plans, see the fat required at lunch and dinner or the low-fat milk at breakfast, and decide not to eat the fat or to use fat-free milk at breakfast in the hope that they'll lose weight even faster without the fat calories. They're using diet oldthink, in which only calories count. It's true, of course, that gram for gram, fat delivers more calories than any other nutrient. It's also true that regardless of how you measure it—grams or gobs—fat is a more fattening calorie since it's so easy to make into body fat. But these facts are more than offset by others: small amounts of fat make the dieter feel more satisfied far longer after meals, help prevent cravings that can lead to real diet trouble, aid in the absorption of other vital nutrients. All in all, the fat you'll be consuming in Stage I is not only essential, it's a bargain.

Don't tinker with amounts, or substitute Stage II foods for the foods called for in Stage I.

Stage I proteins, for instance—including low-fat fish, broiled poultry, and low-fat dairy products—are lower in fat than Stage II proteins, so they're appropriate for full-speed-ahead weight loss. As we've seen, *some* fat is essential to diet success and good health. But when you are in Stage I, and relatively craving-free, you won't need the additional fat supplied by Stage II higher-fat proteins.

The same with Stage I and Stage II fruits. Both will help you feel satisfied between meals by keeping blood sugar at moderate levels and insulin production even and balanced. But the second servings of fruit for Stage I (like blueberries or apricots) are lower in sugar than those you will be eating during Stage II (like apples or bananas), when you need more carbs to boost your mood and for binge insurance to help you deal safely with cravings.

Don't eat it if it's not specifically listed as part of the diet.

Some foods will be conspicuous by their absence. Artificially sweetened diet drinks, diet salad dressings, diet desserts, fruit juices, and, of course, all the standard diet no-nos such as ice cream, cake, fried foods, etc. and etc. Just as every food included as part of the Bodyrhythm Diet is there for a reason, there are equally good reasons for excluding all the others—hormone reasons, mood reasons, calorie reasons. I'd have to write twenty books to cover the why-not's of the many foods that have no place in the Bodyrhythm Diet. Instead, I'll be brief. If you are in doubt about a particular food, check the lists of Stage I and Stage II choices. If it's not on either list, don't eat it.

Follow the guidelines exactly. Your body and the food will do all the rest.

The Diet: Stage II

Stage I is for when you are relatively craving-free. Switch to Stage II eating principles when nagging food urges and mood changes threaten your efforts to lose pounds of fat.

Dangerous days occur, for many women, in the week or so *before* a period, when the hormone progesterone is on the rise, when insulin binds to cells, and cravings often become a problem. It's especially important to stay in touch with your body at this time. If cravings begin to come on strong and you need extra help to deal with them, CHANGE TO STAGE II OF THE DIET.

Blues, blahs, stressed-out feelings, frequently coincide with the rise in progesterone before a period. But just as often, mood swings are a result of disappointments and frustrations in your life and have nothing to do with hormones. When down emotions are accompanied by cravings—regardless of the time of month—you need to eat in ways that will lift your mood and ease the urge to go on a food rampage. TRY STAGE II EATING.

Sometimes sudden fat loss, even the threat of an impending fat loss, triggers cravings. Nature, remember, wants to keep you padded with a reserve supply of fuel, and, I suspect, when that supply dwindles, she does her best to make you replenish it. You may be able to tough out these cravings, but if you feel yourself on the verge of giving in, REINFORCE YOUR WILL WITH STAGE II.

Your body will tell you when you are vulnerable to diet-destroying cravings. Stay tuned in. When you get the signal, make your move from Stage I to Stage II of the Bodyrhythm Diet.

REMAIN IN STAGE II FOR AS LONG AS YOU MUST, BUT *NO LONGER*. A SINGLE STAGE II SNACK OR MEAL MAY BE ENOUGH TO BLUNT CRAVINGS. OR IT MAY TAKE A DAY, OR TWO, OR MORE OF STAGE II EATING BEFORE CRAVINGS EASE OFF. AS SOON AS THEY DO, GO BACK TO STAGE I PRINCIPLES.

THE STAGE II INCREASED CRAVINGS FOOD PLAN

Here's a breakdown of Stage II breakfast, lunch, and dinner menus. Follow these guidelines for as long as your body is in a craving mode. A week's worth of Stage II meal suggestions, plus recipes, begins on page 123.

BREAKFAST (Note: It's the same as Stage I, Reduced Cravings.)

1 8-ounce cup low-fat milk
(low-fat milk supplies carbohydrate, as well as *both* protein and fat requirements for breakfast)
1 ounce (measured dry) cereal (high-fiber is best)

LUNCH OR DINNER

3 ounces Stage II higher-fat proteins
    or, 2 ounces hard cheese (part-skim or low-fat is best)
    or, 2 eggs (or 1 egg and 3 egg whites)
2 1-ounce slices bread or 2-ounce roll (whole-grain is best)
1 portion fat
Free foods, as much as you like

CALCIUM REQUIREMENT

1 8-ounce cup nonfat milk, low-fat milk, or buttermilk (in
    addition to the 1 cup low-fat milk with breakfast)

SNACKS

1 serving vitamin C rich fruit, anytime between meals
1 serving higher-sugar fruit, anytime between meals
Free Foods, anytime you like

IMPORTANT

Don't omit any of the foods included in Stage II menu plans.

All meals are balanced and designed to help you face up to cravings without giving in to that urge to splurge. If you skip a meal, or part of one, you won't be getting the full benefit of Stage II binge insurance. Remember, if you are feeling vulnerable enough to change over into Stage II eating, you *need* the higher-fat proteins, increased amounts of starch, and the higher-sugar fruit stipulated in this part of the diet. And you need them in the amounts indicated.

Don't tinker with quantities or substitute Stage I foods while you are in Stage II of the diet.

Portions in Stage II are balanced. They're planned to be large enough to help blunt cravings, but not large enough to reverse weight loss.

Though it's not always possible to weigh and measure portions, you can *always* use good judgment and, by "eyeballing" your food, arrive at a close approximation of the proper amount. Do your best.

Don't eat it if it's not specifically listed as part of the diet.

For obvious reasons, ice cream, doughnuts, french fries, and other sugary and/or grease-laden foods are taboo on the Bodyrhythm Diet. But keep in mind that a few foods, even some that play an important role in other diets, are also off limits on this one. Some of those foods (like diet drinks, unlimited coffee or tea, fruit juices) are out of bounds because of what they may do to insulin production. Others may be low in calories (like pickles, sauerkraut, unlimited sodium-rich seasonings, or frozen diet dinners), but are just too high in salt, encourage water retention, may increase absorption of starch calories, and may adversely affect moods as the retained water presses in on emotional centers of the brain. Other foods (like cream cheese, sandwich meats, rich rolls, or granola) are so high-cal and/or offer so little in terms of fat-fighting, mood modifying, or craving control, they don't merit inclusion. When you're not sure whether a particular food is okay on the Bodyrhythm Diet, check the lists at the back of this book. It it's not there, don't put it in your mouth!

What About Stage II Slowdown?

In Stage II, you'll be consuming more calories. They're programmed in in the form of larger amounts of high-fiber starches, higher-fat proteins, "sweeter" fruits. These extra calories are not just any old calories that you choose for yourself at random. They're *planned* calories, supplied by foods that should help ease cravings and prevent the binges that would take weeks of strict eating to undo.

But, you may be wondering, will the extra calories in Stage II result in weight-loss slowdown? I'm afraid that's a hard one to answer. Some women do lose less in Stage II. Others continue to lose just as rapidly as they did in Stage I. However, virtually *all* women hit a plateau from time to time, whether in Stage I *or* Stage II, or, in fact, on any diet.

Remember, weight loss hardly ever proceeds indefinitely at a steady uninterrupted quick clip. Even if you ate exactly the same low-calorie food every day, day after day, month after month, it's extremely unlikely that the scale would register a loss of, say, a pound or two a week, no more and no less, every week you were on a diet. In fact, it's practically impossible, because your female body tends to retain water at certain times of the month. You may even be more prone to water retention when you are under greater-than-usual stress. There's also the fact that your body wants to hold on to fat precisely when it gets the message that its fat reserves are threatened and in danger of being depleted. Take heart. If you don't allow impatience and discouragement to throw you off the diet, your body will, finally, let go of water, fat—*pounds*.

Accept weight-loss slowdown in Stage II, if it does indeed occur, as you would accept those other interruptions in the fight against fat: as frustrating but temporary and minor delays. Your body *will* adapt. Cravings *will* ease up. And when they do, you should quickly shift back into Stage I eating and faster fat reduction.

It's only natural to want to lose as many pounds as possible as quickly as possible. But, as you may have discovered from personal experience, super-speedy weight loss is almost always followed by equally rapid gainback, at least for women. That's partly because we're so vulnerable to hormonal and emotional food cravings. All those dozens of diets that promise almost-instant results tend to be disappointing precisely because they *don't* address the craving question. The Bodyrhythm Diet, with built-in craving control and binge insurance, is different. Follow it exactly and it will help you go all the way to the slimmer, fitter body you want. Isn't that better than initial quick success that fizzles into failure and more fat?

How to Listen to Your Body

I've encouraged you to "tune in to your body" several times in this chapter. Listening to what your body has to say about hunger and cravings is the best way to determine when to follow Stage I principles and when to make the switch to Stage II. In fact, it's the only reliable way.

But I've known some women who have trouble with the concept. They are often women who have been overweight most of their lives. (It may even be that they are overweight *because* they've never tried to listen to their bodies.) I tell them what I'm going to tell you now. But before I begin, I want to reassure you that it isn't difficult to tune in to your body and gauge when to use Stage I and Stage II. It boils down to learning how to distinguish between ordinary hunger pangs and gnawing cravings.

It's unrealistic, when you go on a diet, to expect that you won't ever experience some hunger. It's not the fault of this, or any well-balanced diet. It's simply that your body becomes accustomed to a certain number of calories, a certain amount of body fat, and certain eating habits. Hunger is a consequence of change.

To simplify, hunger is the feeling you experience when your stomach is empty and wants to be filled. It's almost always the result of missing a meal, or delaying a meal, or eating a meal that doesn't supply enough of the foods that keep you feeling comfortably full until the next meal or snack.

If you follow Bodyrhythm Diet guidelines, which include *not* skipping meals, *not* omitting any of the foods included on breakfast, lunch, and dinner menus—and if you eat at *regular* intervals—*real* intense hunger shouldn't be a major problem.

Nevertheless, if you do feel hungry, think back: Was your last meal a complete one? Did you skip or skimp on one of the foods? Has it been more than four or five hours since you ate a meal or snack? If the answers to any of these questions are yes, you probably *are* hungry.

This hunger, the kind we're talking about now, is relatively easy to deal with: your next meal should fix it. Or, if it's going to be a while until lunch or dinner, fill up on "free foods" or have a fruit snack. The vegetables will help fill up an empty stomach. The sugar in fruit should help turn off the hunger switch by gently lifting blood sugar levels back up toward normal. (Because fructose—combined with fiber—doesn't cause an insulin gush, a fruit snack actually pacifies hunger better than "real" sugar, enabling you to hold out until you can sit down to your next meal!)

Stay in Stage I if you feel this slight hunger. (It could mean your body is getting ready to give up fat.) But if a Stage I meal doesn't satisfy your hunger and that gnawing in your stomach intensifies, go to Stage II for your next meal or snack.

Cravings, however, are far more mysterious and exert a much more powerful influence over your eating behavior than "simple" hunger. For one thing, cravings can occur independently of hunger. They can nag at you even after a meal. In fact, meals made up of certain combinations of food (like those that eliminate starches, those that skim off all fat, or those that skimp on protein) seem to "stoke" cravings, making them flare up the way a fire roars higher after you pour oil on it. That's because cravings, as I've explained elsewhere in this book, are related to hormone changes and mood swings.

If a Stage I snack or meal doesn't pacify your urge to eat, that urge is probably a craving. A craving is hunger of a specific nature. That is, you experience a desire for *specific* foods, usually rich sugary sweets (like chocolate, ice cream, or cookies) or greasy foods (such as french fries, cheese toast, chips), or spicy cuisines (Mexican or Chinese dishes). If you find yourself thinking of certain nibbles, treats, or dishes, experiencing that intense "want" for specific foods—hungry or full—not just for a fleeting

moment, but *most* of the time, you are certainly dealing
with a craving.

Go to a Stage II meal or a Stage II higher-sugar fruit
snack if you're dueling with cravings.

To reiterate, tuning in to your body, as I've been using
the phrase here, is really the process of distinguishing
between hunger and cravings.

Unfortunately, cravings are worse than obsessions. That's
because cravings are not *just* psychological—they're not
just "in your head"—but more importantly for women,
cravings are more likely to be biological—they're *also in
your body*. When you try to ignore cravings altogether,
they become more urgent. And chances are, if you don't
give your body *some* of what it emotionally wants and,
more important, physically *needs,* the craving will intensify, eventually overwhelm all your good intentions, and sap
your will to resist. When you finally give in, you're out of
control and it's pig-out time.

Thin women, when cravings hit them, tend to do what
comes naturally: they respond by eating moderate amounts
of what their bodies demand. The Bodyrhythm Diet helps
you learn how to deal with cravings as the skinnies do, by
allowing you to eat small amounts of the foods your body
cries out for.

But before you go from Stage I to Stage II, tune in to
your body and try to figure out what you are really dealing
with: "simple" hunger, or a craving.

And don't jump the gun. Don't leap into Stage II every
time the sight or smell of food activates your salivary
glands. Don't use Stage II eating to help you deal with
every minor frustration or disappointment, or to pull you
up out of every passing down mood. Don't grab for Stage
II choices when hunger seems manageable. In other words,
don't look for excuses to switch.

Wait. Tune in to your body. Was that urge to eat easily
satisfied with a snack? If so, stay in Stage I. If it continues
through a snack or meal and just won't leave you alone,

however, recognize that you are up against something more.

In that case, don't try to tough it out. Don't pit your willpower against your body's insistent demands. (Unless you're Wonder Woman, your body will win!) Do as thin women do. Respond to the craving with increased amounts of the foods that will help pacify it, and in the process nip binges in the making. You can do it with Stage II eating.

Depending on the factors contributing to a craving, it could last just a few hours. Or your body might remain in a craving mode for days and days. Stay in tune. Monitor the craving. Try to be just as aware of its going as you were with its coming. When a craving passes—and it will—don't linger in Stage II. Switch back to Stage I.

Before You Begin the Diet

With the advice of dietitians, I developed the Bodyrhythm Diet to supply all the nutrients you need to maintain your health, your looks, your energy, in amounts calculated to help you win the war against fat. Though I have no way of knowing your present foods habits, I'd be willing to bet you'll be eating a lot better on the Bodyrhythm Diet than you are right now. If your diet is anything like the standard American diet, for example, you'll be consuming better-balanced meals composed of less fat, more fiber, more calcium-rich foods, enough protein to supply all your body needs for this important nutrient, and fewer calories. It's just what all the doctors are ordering these days.

Nevertheless, don't go on this or any diet before checking with a physician. Explain your weight goals and show her or him the menu plans for both stages.

Once you get the go-ahead, go for it. A slimmer, thinner, healthier, better body is practically yours for the eating.

8 | The Bodyrhythm Diet Details

You've reached the heart of this book. All the information you need to lose weight is in this section. Here you'll find the details of what and how much to eat, as well as menu planning suggestions and recipes for Stage I and Stage II of the Women's Bodyrhythm Diet.

The program is based on information I gathered in my years of helping overweight women slim down, and was developed with the help of nutritionists, psychologists, and researchers in the field of obesity. The result, I believe, is the best fat-fighting plan for women yet.

Of course, you must play by the rules. That means adhering to the food choices and amounts "prescribed" for each stage of the diet. It means eating according to Stage I principles when you are relatively craving-free. And it means switching to Stage II eating *only* when your body shifts into a craving mode. Follow the guidelines exactly, and the Bodyrhythm Diet will work with your distinctly female physiology to pare off pounds of fat and help get you to a slimmer, trimmer shape.

Stage I and Stage II Breakfasts

Breakfast in both stages of the Bodyrhythm Diet consists of a one-ounce serving of dry or cooked cereal and eight ounces of low-fat milk. It's as simple as that!

To select a cereal, read labels carefully.

Dry Cereals

Do NOT choose sugar- or honey-coated dry cereals, or cereals containing dried fruits (such as raisins or dates) or those with nuts or seeds. Of course, don't eat cereals with marshmallows or other candy bits.

Good—low-sugar and high-fiber—dry-cereal choices include:

All-Bran (There's a new "Extra Fiber All-Bran")
Bran Flakes
Bran Chex
Corn Bran (A personal favorite)
Fiber One
Kelloggs' Nutri-Grain
Shredded Wheat (An oldie but goodie—either spoon-sized or bowl-sized.)
Shredded Wheat 'N Bran (A newer model)
Uncle Sam Cereal

Many other dry cereals—puffed, flaked, squared, or budded—are acceptable. The words "whole grain" as the first ingredient indicate more fiber. And the more fiber, the less sugar, salt, and fat, the better. (Note: The word "natural" can be misleading. For example, "granolas" have the word "natural" blazoned on their boxes from top to bottom. But many are full of sugars—brown sugar, honey, dried fruits—as well as fats—oils or nuts. Might as well eat crumbled oatmeal cookies for breakfast.)

A one-ounce serving of an appropriate cereal yields about 100 calories. But an ounce of some cereals gives you only a scant quarter cup, while others puff up to much more than a cup, so it's important to measure. To measure a one-ounce serving, spoon cereal into a container and weigh on a postage scale. (Weigh the container first and subtract that amount.) Or use the equivalent cup measurement on the package.

Cooked Cereals

Avoid cooked cereals made with added sugar, salt, and dried fruits.

Among the best cooked cereal choices are:

"Old-fashioned" oatmeal (better than "instant" or "quick-cooking" in terms of fiber.)

Oat bran (I still like it, even if it may not be the wonder-breakfast food.)

Whole-wheat cereals (such as Wheatena)

Mixed grain cereals (There's a chewy "7-grain Natural Cereal"; also a "4-grain" variety.)

Other cooked cereals are acceptable provided they are not made with added sugar or salt. (Read labels.) "Whole-grain" cereals are best since they're fiber-maxed. To measure a one-ounce serving, spoon dry uncooked cereal into a bowl and weigh on a food scale. (Subtract the weight of the bowl.) Or, use the equivalent measurement on the package.

Low-fat Milk

An eight-ounce cup of low-fat milk—not nonfat—is an essential part of every Bodyrhythm Diet breakfast. It supplies the protein and fat components of the meal.

Pour milk over your cereal. Drink the rest, or use it to lighten breakfast coffee, decaf, or tea.

STAGE I AND STAGE II BREAKFAST GUIDELINES

• Skip fruit at breakfast time. Fruit plus cereal boosts the carbohydrate content of the morning meal. The combination could result in an initial feeling of being full, but may be followed by hunger as insulin kicks in and drags blood sugar levels down.

- For variety, and to take advantage of the benefits of various types of fiber (oatmeal, for example, may help reduce cholesterol; wheat bran can aid in preventing constipation), have several cereals on hand and alternate them. You might choose hot oatmeal one morning, bran flakes the next, a mixed grain cereal the following day, etc.

- Watch out for sugar in disguise—brown sugar, honey, molasses, dried fruits, dextrose, corn syrup. These all come down to the same thing: sugar. The more of these sweeteners listed on a label, the more sugar dense the cereal. And surplus sugar in the morning, can set you up for hunger and sugar cravings all day long.

- Make it easier on yourself and don't buy overly appealing cereals. Many women find the large boxes of dry cereal too tempting to have around. The open box calls out for nibbles. And it's hard to stop at one flake or even one handful—like eating chips or nuts. You might want to limit your purchases to those individual, premeasured, boxes of dry cereal, or to cereals that must be cooked.

WHY YOU MUST EAT BREAKFAST

I know. Many women gag at the thought of breakfast. You may be one of them. Or, perhaps, mornings at your house are so frantic you never thought you had time to make and eat breakfast.

Sorry, but you are going to have to change your ways if you are serious about wanting to lose pounds of fat. Breakfast is a must on the Bodyrhythm Diet. It actually helps rev up the body's calorie-burning mechanism. And without the starch, protein, and fat supplied by this meal, you will be much more vulnerable to midmorning urges for something sugary and high-cal.

No time? Get serious! How long does it take to pour cereal and milk into a bowl?

Some women tell me they don't like breakfast because it makes them feel sluggish or seems to trigger increased hunger a few hours later—or both. But sluggishness is almost always the result of eating too much fat (eggs and bacon; three-egg omelets, etc.). And delayed hunger can be the result of eating a no-fat breakfast (such as cereal with *skim* milk, or just dry toast). Postbreakfast hunger and that zonked-out feeling may also be caused by too much or the wrong kinds of carbohydrates (cereal, *plus* toast, *plus* orange juice, for example, not to mention breakfasts like pancakes with syrup).

You shouldn't experience hunger and/or sluggishness after a Bodyrhythm Diet breakfast. It supplies carbohydrates, protein, and fat in planned amounts that can keep you going full-tilt, but not enough to make you feel stuffed and groggy. And with moderate carbohydrates, you don't get a gush of fat-storing, fat-making, fat-trapping insulin.

Maybe you don't fancy the thought of breakfast now, but start eating it anyway. You may learn to love it.

Here's the "Breakfast Master Plan."

BREAKFAST MASTER PLAN
(For *both* Stage I and Stage II)

1 ounce cereal
(high-fiber, low-sugar, and low-salt cereals are best)
8 ounces low-fat milk

Stage I and Stage II Lunches and Dinners

Breakfast in both stages of the plan is the same. But there are crucial differences between Stage I and Stage II lunches and dinners.

To simplify, in Stage I, when you are relatively craving-free, you'll consume lower-fat proteins and a single serving of starch. In Stage II, when your body and mind shift into a craving mode, you'll eat proteins with a slightly higher fat content and double servings of starch.

Basic menu plans for Stage I and Stage II lunches and dinner look like this:

LUNCH AND DINNER MASTER PLANS

STAGE I LUNCH AND DINNER	STAGE II LUNCH AND DINNER
Reduced Cravings	Increased Cravings

Protein

3 ounces Stage I low-fat proteins (cooked weight)	3 ounces Stage II higher-fat proteins (cooked weight)
or, 6 egg whites	or, 2 whole eggs (or 1 whole egg, 3 whites)
or, ½ cup softcheese	or, 2 ounces hard cheese (part-skim or low-fat are best)

Starch

1 slice bread (1 ounce)	2 slices bread (2 ounces)
or, ½ roll (1 ounce)	or, 1 roll (2 ounces)

Fat

1 teaspoon margarine, oil, or mayonnaise	1 teaspoon margarine, oil, or mayonnaise
or, 2 teaspoons salad dressing	or, 2 teaspoons salad dressing

Free Foods

unlimited	unlimited

STARCHES FOR LUNCHES AND DINNERS

The only difference between the starches for Stage I and Stage II is *quantity*. In Stage I, when your body and mind aren't hassled by cravings, one portion is enough. But when and if you feel threatened by mysterious and insistent food urges, you move into Stage II and double the starch portions.

Theoretically, there are dozens of high-fiber starches that would fulfill the special Bodyrhythm Diet requirements. But in the interest of keeping things simple, unconfused, and less tempting, I want you to limit your selections to the following.

Bread—select high-fiber, whole-grain, if possible. A standard slice comes to about one ounce. You can have *one* slice with Stage I lunches and dinners, and *two* slices during Stage II.

Rolls—select high-fiber, whole-grain, if possible. Half an average-size roll weighs in at about one ounce, which is just right for Stage I lunches and dinners. Take one whole (two-ounce) roll for Stage II lunches and dinners.

STARCH GUIDELINES

- It goes without saying (but I'll say it anyway) that you shouldn't *slather* your bread or roll with gobs of jelly, cream cheese (even "diet" cream cheese), butter, or margarine.
- Important: When you buy bread or rolls, don't select the biggest, fattest, heaviest slices or buns you can find. You *know* what an "average" roll looks like. That's the kind to get. (When in doubt, weigh your selections.)
- Use bread or rolls that don't call out to you. Those with seeds, nuts, dried fruits, or those that are overly sweet with extra honey or sugar are most tempting. And the sugar and fat could throw the diet off balance. Stick to "ordinary," plain, whole-wheat bread and rolls.
- Freeze the loaf of bread or the bag of rolls to help prevent impulse nibbling.
- Look for the words, "whole" and "100-percent" as the first ingredients—such as "100-percent whole wheat." "Whole" means more fat-fighting fiber.

PROTEINS FOR LUNCHES AND DINNERS

Stage I and Stage II proteins differ in their relative fat content.

When cravings aren't a problem and your body is primed for maximum safe weight loss, you will be eating the lower-fat proteins called for in Stage I. These include fish with a minimal fat content, low-fat poultry, low-fat soft cheeses, and egg whites.

Stage II proteins are higher in fat. They'll help you stay in control and on track when food urges mount. Among your choices are fish with slightly higher-fat content, dark meat of poultry, most cuts of lean beef, pork and lamb, low-fat hard cheeses and eggs.

No matter which stage, at lunch and dinner eat three ounces (cooked weight) of the appropriate protein.

Here are complete listings of protein suitable for Stage I and Stage II of the Bodyrhythm Diet.

STAGE I PROTEINS	STAGE II PROTEINS
("Light" choices both in terms of color and calories.)	("Dark" choices; darker proteins are higher in fat.)
Fish (3 ounces cooked) "Light" fish	Fish (3 ounces cooked) "Dark" fish

(Note: Like meat and chicken, light-colored fish generally has less fat, while the darker fish are higher in fat content.)

Favorite light choices:	Favorite dark choices:
cod	bluefish
flounder	salmon
haddock	shad
halibut	swordfish
orange roughy	trout
perch	tuna, fresh
sea bass	
sole	
snapper (a reddish fish, but still low-fat)	
"seafood"—oysters, clams, mussels, crab, shrimp, lobster, etc.	
tuna, canned white meat (no oil)	

Poultry (3 ounces cooked)
"Light" meat
including:
white-meat chicken
white-meat turkey
Cornish game hens
(Note: Game hens are
mostly "light" meat.)

Poultry (3 ounces cooked)
"Dark" meat
including:
dark-meat chicken
dark-meat turkey

White Meats (3 ounces
cooked)
veal

Red Meats (3 ounces cooked)

beef
lamb
pork

Eggs
6 eggs whites

Eggs
2 whole eggs
1 egg, 3 whites

Cheeses
"light" cheeses
are soft cheeses
(except cream cheese,
of course)
Such as:
cottage cheese (low-fat
is best)
farmer cheese
hoop cheese
pot cheese

Cheeses
"richer" cheeses
are hard cheeses
(preferably low-fat,
part-slim cheeses)
Such as:
part-skim mozzarella
feta
jack
Muenster
Swiss

PROTEINS TO AVOID

Remember, play by the rules. If it's not listed, don't eat it. Sounds easy enough, but I know from working with the women in my weight-loss groups that questions concerning certain protein foods always arise.

For example, many dieters wonder why "nonanimal"

proteins are excluded. It's true that beans, peas, grains, nuts, and seeds are protein sources and that they deliver protein without the cholesterol that accompanies proteins of animal origin.

But women lose pounds better and faster by limiting their protein intake to fish, chicken, and certain meats. Why so? Perhaps it's because plants always supply carbohydrates along with protein. Maybe it's because some of the popular, tasty vegetarian proteins—such as nuts, seeds, peanut butter—are high in fat. Whatever the reason, plant proteins just don't seem to work as well.

Dairy proteins (soft and hard cheeses) are included only as concessions to non-meat-eaters and because sometimes the lowest-fat choice on a menu is cottage cheese. (Also, a couple of ounces of low-fat hard cheese in an otherwise fat-controlled meal could save you from succumbing to a craving for a billion-calorie burrito pig-out or a grease-out with a whole pizza.) *But*, because cheeses contain sodium and carbohydrates, and hard cheeses can be high in fat, many women lose more slowly if they eat cheeses regularly. So, when possible, always have fish, chicken, or meat instead of *any* type of cheese.

Processed meats are off limits on this diet. By processed meats, I mean items such as cold cuts (bologna, salami, pastrami, etc.), smoked fish (lox, finnan haddie, smoked cod, etc.), hot dogs, sausages, bacon, packaged turkey and chicken slices, and so on.

Many processed meats are too fatty. Fat alone would disqualify them. But, in addition, most of these meats are prepared with large amounts of salt, which can slow your progress by causing your body to retain more water. And according to some recent research, sodium increases starch absorption, so that more calories are sucked in per gram of carbohydrate.

You won't find the new "imitation" shellfish on the Bodyrhythm Diet either. Though fake crab (sometimes called "Krab" or "snow crab"), imitation shrimp, and other make-believe shellfish are low-cal, their high sodium content could work against you.

Finally, certain cuts of meats and poultry are out-of-bounds because they're so fatty, and the fat is so difficult to remove. Among these are beef or pork ribs and the backs and wings of chicken and other fowl. (The fat is deposited in small "pockets" in the backs of poultry. As for wings, they're mostly skin, bones, and fat.)

Remember, if it's not specifically listed here as suitable for use in Stage I or Stage II, it's not part of the Bodyrhythm Diet.

PROTEIN GUIDELINES

• Canned proteins such as tuna, salmon, and chicken are fine, but get the kind packed in water. (Even in Stage II, you don't need all that excess oil.) Keep in mind that canned food is packed with added salt unless the label clearly states that the product has no added salt or sodium. Remove the salt by rinsing canned fish or chicken under running water. (Best way: Place contents of can in a sieve and hold it under the tap.)

• Because ready-to-eat seafood (crab, shrimp, lobster, etc.) is generally cooked in salted water or preserved in salt before being sold, rinse these, too. And rinse shellfish (oysters, clams, etc.), all naturally high in sodium. When eating out, instead of shellfish or clawed seafoods, order "finny" fish; it's less risky in terms of sodium.

• Remove the skin from chicken, turkey, or other poultry *before* cooking. Otherwise, fat just under the skin will be liquefied by the heat and soak back into the bird. If you are eating away from home, order your poultry broiled and remove the skin as discreetly and with as little fuss as possible. Of course, when roasting a turkey or chicken, you'll leave the skin on during cooking. (Did you ever try to roast a skinned turkey? Don't.) But *remove* the skin before eating the meat. (And don't eat the skin after it's removed.)

• Red meat should be lean to begin with and trimmed of all visible fat *before* cooking.

• Broiling, steaming, and microwaving are the best ways to

cook fish, meat, or poultry because in all three methods fat is liquefied and easily poured off. Sautéing is okay, but don't add fats. Use a nonstick pan or a nonstick spray and drain off any juice or fat.

- In restaurants, always order fish, chicken, or meat "*dry*-broiled," which means with no added fat. If you simply ask to have your protein "broiled," the chef might feel free to use butter or pour on a sauce. Of course, don't order (or accept) anything sauced (even "lightly") or creamed—you'll be taking a chance with gobs of grease on your food first and on your body next.
- Do not cook Stage II, higher-fat proteins in liquid or in their own juices. This means no stewing, no casseroles, no soups made with beef, lamb, pork, or dark-meat poultry. The reason: When higher-fat proteins are cooked in liquid, any fat in the juice will be reabsorbed—and you don't need that much extra fat, even in Stage II.
- As for cooking Stage I, lower-fat proteins (white-meat poultry, game hens, fish) in soups, casseroles, or stews—go ahead. But remove the skin and loose fat before cooking. If you have the time, chill or freeze the cooked poultry or fish dish; skim, sieve, or chisel off all grease before reheating.
- Allow for shrinkage when you buy, prepare, and cook. Boneless, skinless poultry, fish fillets, and trimmed meat will shrink by about one ounce during cooking. In other words, to get a three-ounce cooked portion, start with about four ounces of boneless, skinless, fat-trimmed raw protein.
- Allow about *three ounces* extra for unboned, unskinned, untrimmed protein. For example, a six-ounce raw chicken breast, with bone in and skin still on, yields about three ounces when skinned, boned, and cooked (one ounce for skin, one for bone, one for shrinkage). Similarly, a six-ounce piece of untrimmed meat, with the bone in, (lamb or pork chop, T-bone steak) gives you about three ounces after cooking. (Count one ounce for the fat you trim off before cooking, one ounce for the bone, and one ounce for shrinkage during cooking.)

- A three-ounce cooked portion of protein looks like a deck of playing cards—about half of what restaurants serve. Cut off your portion *before* you start to eat.

FATS FOR LUNCHES AND DINNERS

Each and every Stage I and Stage II meal, remember, must include a small amount of fat. Fats are slowly digested, so you feel fuller longer. They enhance the availability of certain vitamins, enabling your body to make better use of them. And they make food taste better, satisfying hunger and helping prevent diet boredom.

At breakfast, the fat is supplied by the forty calories of fat in the low-fat milk.

At lunches and dinners, in both stages, you will be adding a portion of fat.

The fat choices are:

Fats
(One choice at lunch and dinner both stages)

1 teaspoon margarine (2 teaspoons if you use "diet margarine")
1 teaspoon oil—corn, safflower, soy, sunflower, olive, peanut, or sesame (great taste) oils are all appropriate
1 teaspoon mayonnaise (double that for "diet mayo")
2 teaspoons bottled salad dressing, such as Italian, French, herb (don't use "diet" dressings—you need the fat in "real" dressings)

FAT GUIDELINES

- Naturally, I don't expect you to eat a teaspoon of margarine plain, or to swallow down two teaspoons of salad dressing. Instead, use margarine as a spread on your lunch or dinner bread or roll. Or use the fat requirement to stir-fry vegetables.
- Salad dressing can be poured over free vegetables or as a "dip" to dunk veggies.

- Don't use "diet" or "low-cal" dressings—you need the fat in the "real" dressings. In addition, diet dressings are often high in sodium.
- Margarine, oils, or dressings can also be used in cooking. (I'll provide recipes later in this chapter.)
- Be fat smart. Especially at first, don't guess at amounts. Measure your allotment with a measuring spoon.

FREE FOODS

Bodyrhythm Diet "free foods" are all low-carbohydrate vegetables. They're "free" because you can have them in unlimited amounts anytime you want.

Use them to add vitamins, minerals, as well as color, texture, and flavor—not to mention bulk, fiber, and chewing satisfaction—to lunches and dinners. You can also fill up on free vegetables between meals.

Don't make assumptions about which vegetables are "free" on the Bodyrhythm Diet. Some veggies, even a few that are okay in unlimited amounts on other diets, don't qualify as free foods on this one.

Carrots and beets, for example, though low-cal, are too high in sugar to be considered Bodyrhythm free vegetables.

The old dieters' standby, celery, doesn't meet Bodyrhythm Diet free-food standards either, because of its naturally high sodium content.

Canned vegetables are out as *unlimited* freebies. Unless labels say otherwise, canned vegetables are salt-loaded. Also, a certain amount of cooking is part of the canning process, which breaks down plant cell walls, decreasing fat-fighting fiber and freeing sugar. Canning also takes the crunch out of vegetables, and for many women the crunch, chomp, and chew helps work off frustrations. No crunch, no anti-anxiety value.

As for frozen vegetables, they can be used only as a second choice to fresh. Frozen vegetables are often peeled, resulting in less fat-fighting fiber. And the freezing process somewhat "cooks' the vegetables. Result: The fiber is broken down, making the calories more absorbable. It's better always to use fresh vegetables at meals and for free foods. But for convenience sake or "emergencies," frozen vegetables are acceptable, provided they don't contain added trinkets—nuts, pasta, cheese, butter, sauces, salt, or seasonings. (Read labels carefully.) Be sure to buy only frozen vegetables listed on the "free-food list" and steam them only very briefly.

Only the vegetables on the list below are "free," and they are free only if you eat them *fresh* and *raw* or *very* lightly steamed. When in doubt about a vegetable, check the list. If it's not on the list, it's not a Bodyrhythm Diet free food.

Free Vegetable List

Go for Green:

All green vegetables are free, except peas and lima beans—they're actually members of the peanut family. (Don't peas and limas look a little like peanuts?)

Good green choices include:

asparagus, bell peppers (even "mature" red or yellow bell peppers), broccoli, Chinese pea pods (also called snow peas), "greens" (such as beet greens, collard greens, mustard greens), cilantro, parsley, leafy vegetables (such as spinach and Swiss chard), chili peppers (including green, red, yellow, or white), watercress, and, of course, all lettuce.

Go for White:

White or pale vegetables are free, too, *except* "root" vegetables—potatoes, onions, turnips, etc.—and celery.

Good white choices are:

bean sprouts, cabbage (even red cabbage), cauliflower, cucumbers, iceberg lettuce, mushrooms, summer squash (such as, crookneck, patty pan, or zucchini squash).

FREE FOOD GUIDELINES

- As you've seen, most "greens" and "whites" are "free." Go for greens and whites. Other hints: Stop at "orange." Orange vegetables—such as carrots, winter squash (acorn, pumpkin, banana) yams—are higher in sugar and are not "free." In addition, stop at the "roots." Root vegetables— potatoes, onions, jicama, rutabagas, beets, celery, etc. —are all higher in starch and sometimes salt, making "root" vegetables unqualified as free foods.
- Always eat vegetables whole if possible, with no—or only minimal—peeling or paring. The peel is fiber-high.
- Free foods *must* be eaten either raw or very lightly steamed. Remember that cooking, including steaming to the point of softness, boiling, microwaving, canning, and baking, breaks down the fiber and frees up sugar.
- Since canned vegetables are all soft-cooked, don't eat those. Frozen vegetables are okay at meals, but don't use as freebies. At meals, steam frozen veggies only briefly. And use frozen vegetables without almonds, cheese, salt, "flavorings," soy sauce, or other sauces, onions, corn, or carrots. In other words, stick to frozen green veggies— other than peas and limas—unseasoned, ungarnished, unsauced.

SEASONINGS

The zippy spices and herbs, flavorful sauces and vinegars, and aromatic vegetables below can be used to jazz up Bodyrhythm Diet Stage I and Stage II lunches and dinners. Experiment. Make up your own salt-free seasonings or fat-free sauces. Try unusual combinations such as fresh ginger, sliced red onions, and lemon juice, or chili, cumin, and curry powders to give fish, poultry, meat, and vegetables new taste appeal without adding salt, which can cause water retention or rich sauces, which will cause fat accumulation.

Note that only a few of these seasonings can be used in unlimited amounts. The rest are subject to restrictions.

Unlimited Seasonings:

Use as desired:

Fresh lemon or lime juice—terrific "salt substitutes"

Dry (powdered) mustard—sprinkle on fish or chicken, before cooking for a tasty "crust" (Hint: Look for dry "Oriental" mustard for a spicy treat.)

Pepper—fresh ground tastes best

Any seasoning blends containing no added salt or sodium; labels will tell you which these are.

Spices, herbs (fresh or dried), extracts and flavorings if they contain no added salt or sodium: such as, chili powder, ginger, nutmeg, anise, basil, dill, garlic, thyme, vanilla extract, peppermint extract, rum flavoring, etc.

Vinegars—not just white or cider, but raspberry, champagne, balsamic, and rice vinegars.

Limited Seasonings:

Because of sodium, use limited amounts of the following—

Canned sauces—like tomato, chili, or spaghetti sauces (Hint: Spread over fish before broiling.)

Bottled sauces—such as horseradish, hot sauce, prepared mustard, salsa, steak sauce, soy sauce, Worcestershire sauce

Flavor-enhancing vegetables:

Because of natural sodium/and or natural sugars, limit the following—*1 per meal*

Celery—1 stalk, cooked or raw. Note: A stalk is one long stick.

Tomato—medium, cooked or raw.

Onions—medium sized, white, yellow, or green; also leeks and scallions—cooked or raw.

Carrots—1 long carrot, cooked or raw.

A note about artificial sweeteners: Artificial sugars are missing entirely from the list of flavorings above. If you read Chapter 5, you know why. To recap briefly, artificial sweeteners seem to fake out the brain, which interprets the sweet taste as the real thing, and ups insulin production for some people.

I've also found that for many women, sham sugar, rather than pacifying the urge for sweets, actually appears to intensify cravings for sugars, candies, baked goods. The more they eat of the artificial kind, sooner or later, the more they want of the real thing! Some women will eat more of any food that's artificially sweetened—that goes for gum, sweetened drinks, "diet" cocoa, or "diet" candies. One woman *drank* a whole jar of diet jelly. Many women have binged on "diet" desserts—and even sugar-reduced cakes mount up calories when eaten out of control.

Artificial sweeteners have no useful role to play on the Bodyrhythm Diet. Don't use them on cereal, or in coffee or teas. Don't drink "diet" sodas and other artificially sweetened beverages. As for diet candies, jams and jellies, and desserts sweetened with imitation sugar. NO!

FRUITS

Fruit helps ease hunger and cravings that could lead you astray in the hours between or after meals. All fruits contain simple sugars in the form of fructose and glucose, but selections in Stage I are less "sugar dense" than those recommended for Stage II. That's because when you need help in craving control, the additional sugar in Stage II fruits can block a binge in the making and continue the fight against fat.

Each day on the Bodyrhythm Diet, you will be eating *two* fruit portions. Every day, pick one high-C fruit, whether you are in Stage I or Stage II. If you are in a reduced-craving state, choose your second fruit from the lower-sugar fruit list. If cravings mount, and you move to Stage II, your second fruit should come from the higher-sugar fruit list.

High-C Fruits
(One each day, either stage)

Cantaloupe, ¼ medium (6 inches in diameter)
Grapefruit, ½ small
Orange, 1 small
Papaya, 1/3 medium
Strawberries, 1 cup
Tangerine, 1 large or 2 small

Stage I Fruits (Lower-Sugar Fruits)	Stage II Fruits (Higher-Sugar Fruits)
Choose One On Reduced-Craving Days:	Choose One On Increased-Craving Days:
Apricots, 2 medium	Apple 1, 2-inch diameter
Berries, ½ cup	Banana, 1 small (8-inches)
Kiwi, 2 medium	Cherries, 20 large
Melons, 2x7-inch wedge	Grapes, 1 cup
Nectarine, 1 small	Guava, 1 medium
Peach, 1 medium	Mango, 1 small
Plums, 2 (about 2-inch diameter)	Pears, 1 small
Any high-C fruit	Pineapple, 1 cup
	Watermelon, 4x8-inch wedge

SNACK GUIDELINES

- Save fruits for after meals. Bodyrhythm meals are designed to provide enough carbohydrates in the form of high-fiber starches to pacify hunger and supply you with long-lasting energy. Too many carbohydrates (even fruit) can overload your body with excess carbs and trigger the release of excess insulin. And you know what increased insulin can mean—more calories stored and more intense hunger soon after a meal.
- Fruit juice doesn't count as fruit. Juice has little or no fiber and is too quickly absorbed and digested. In fact,

drinking fruit juice is almost like drinking sweetened, vitamin-rich water. You get the calories and vitamins, but not the fat-fighting, hunger-easing properties of whole, high-fiber fruit.

- Don't choose canned fruits. Canned fruit often comes with added sugars. Canned fruits are also peeled and cooked, reducing fiber and freeing sugar. Of course, you don't get the same chewing and chomping satisfaction from canned fruits that you get from fresh. (Can you really munch on a canned peach or sink your teeth into crisp applesauce?)
- When choosing frozen varieties, select only fruits prepared without added sugar.
- Do eat fruit unpeeled (except for oranges, bananas, kiwi, and other fruits that need to be peeled, of course). The peel is fiber-high.
- Tip: Why not really be good to yourself and buy the freshest, most beautiful, unblemished—though not necessarily the largest—specimens you can find? Luscious, perfect fruit is a treat for eye and palate that can make you feel as if you're feasting like royalty!
- Many dieters get more "mileage" from their fruit snacks when they have one midmorning (a sweet and satisfying substitute for coffee-break sweet rolls or doughnuts) and enjoy the other a few hours after lunch, when it picks them up out of the afternoon slump. I encourage you to do the same. However, there may be times when having both fruits at once can reinforce your will to say no to the greasy and/or sugary junk food. When the going gets rough, a fruit mini-splurge (two fruits only, of course) could help.

CALCIUM REQUIREMENTS

Two cups of milk, in conjunction with exercise and normal levels of estrogen, can reduce your risk of developing osteoporosis later in life.

An eight-ounce serving of low-fat milk is an important

part of every Stage I and Stage II breakfast. Not only does it supply the protein and fat components of the meal, but it makes up half your day's quota of calcium.

Make your second choice from the "milk choice" list.

Milk Choices

(In addition to the eight ounces of low-fat milk at breakfast, choose one of the following anytime during the day.)

8 ounces nonfat (or skim) milk
1/3 cup nonfat dry powdered milk
4 ounces evaporated skim (Beware: Don't make the mistake of drinking "regular," or worse, sweetened condensed milk.)
8 ounces 1-percent milk (You can mix your own 1-percent milk—use half skim milk, half low-fat milk.)
8 ounces low-fat (Also called 2-percent milk. Read the label: use low-fat milk that's 120 calorie per 8-ounce cup.)
8 ounces buttermilk (Check the label—use the brand that contains no more than 120 calories per 8-ounce cup.)

After your eight ounces of low-fat milk at breakfast, the second choice is up to you.

You can have your second eight-ounce cup of milk anytime during the day, on its own, as an accompaniment to a meal or snack, or as a lightener for coffee, decaf, or tea. Use it as you like.

As for me, I've always been a bedtime binger. Daytime dieting was never that hard. But evening was another story. I'm still most tempted to eat something (or anything and everything) I shouldn't at evening time. If you're like I am, you might want to save that second cup of milk and one fruit before bedtime. You might even want to make a special blender shake, as I sometimes do. Recipes are in the menu section at the end of this chapter.

Stage I/Stage II Menu Specifics

Now that you know about the components of Stage I and Stage II, I'll show you how to put them all together to make nutritious, good-tasting, fat-fighting meals.

The menu suggestions and recipes that follow are all designed to serve one. Adapting them for two or more is a simple matter of doubling (or tripling, or whatever) the ingredients.

Nondieters may want larger portions or seconds. Keep that in mind and cook extra for family or guests. They might also appreciate an additional starch—a baked potato, some rice, or pasta.

The important thing, however, since you are the cook, and you are also the dieter, is to do whatever is simplest—and least likely to cause *you* problems. Example: If you've never been able to resist pizza or chocolate cake, don't make it or buy it for others, no matter how much you want to please them. Instead, serve Bodyrhythm Diet foods everyone can enjoy—broiled chicken, fresh green beans, and a bowl of luscious raspberries.

Don't let more than seven hours elapse without eating. If you must wait longer before you can sit down to a real meal, quiet your hunger with free foods, a glass of milk, or a fruit snack. Preplan snacks into your day to prevent hunger.

Do NOT eat anything that is not part of the Bodyrhythm Diet Plan. You don't want to invite hunger, activate cravings, or inhibit weight loss.

SAMPLE STAGE I AND STAGE II MEALS

I've worked out seven sample Stage I and seven Stage II menus.

Use Stage I for those days when cravings are manageable and your body and mind are primed for weight loss. Stage I of the diet, remember, puts you into high, fat-fighting gear. Stay alert, listen to your body, and remain in Stage I for as long as cravings are under control.

If and when you feel you need extra help resisting the urge to junk out, of course, switch over to Stage II eating. *Caution: Most women NEVER need to stay in Stage II for an entire week. One day, two meals, or even just one higher-sugar fruit snack is all that's needed to pacify their cravings.*

Note: Where there is an asterisk next to a food selection, the recipe follows later in this chapter.

SAMPLE ONE

Stage I Days	Stage II Days
(Reduced Cravings)	(Increased Cravings)

BREAKFAST

1 ounce 100-percent Bran Flakes
8 ounces low-fat milk

SNACK	SNACK
1 small orange	1 small orange

LUNCH	LUNCH
Turkey Sandwich	Turkey Sandwich
1 slice whole-wheat bread	2 slices whole-wheat bread
3 ounces turkey breast	3 ounces turkey dark meat
1 teaspoon mayonnaise	1 teaspoon mayonnaise
½ thinly sliced tomato	½ thinly sliced tomato
1 slice of red onion	1 slice of red onion
romaine lettuce	romaine lettuce
(Use lettuce as a "lid" over your open-faced sandwich.)	
Free Foods:	Free foods:
raw cauliflower	raw cauliflower
snow peas, mushrooms	snow peas, mushrooms

(Hint: Dip vegetables into exotic vinegar, such as tarragon, raspberry, or balsamic.)

SNACK

SNACK

Free foods

Free foods

(Hint: Prepare extra vegetables when making "free foods" for lunch. Season with "Mrs. Dash" or other no-sodium seasoning.)

DINNER

DINNER

1-ounce whole-wheat roll
3 ounces broiled halibut
Salsa*
Gingered Vegetables*

2-ounce whole-wheat roll
3 ounces broiled salmon
Salsa*
Gingered Vegetables*

SNACK

SNACK

8 ounce buttermilk
1 peach

8 ounce buttermilk
1 small banana

SAMPLE TWO

BREAKFAST

1 ounce "old fashioned" oatmeal (measured dry)
8 ounces low-fat milk

SNACK

SNACK

½ grapefruit

½ grapefruit

LUNCH

LUNCH

Chicken Pita Pocket
Chopped "free" vegetables
3 ounces chicken breast
2 teaspoons salad dressing
1 ounce whole-wheat pita

Chicken Pita Pocket
Chopped "free" vegetables
3 ounces dark-meat chicken
2 teaspoons salad dressing
2 ounces whole-wheat pita

SNACK

SNACK

1 cup low-fat milk

1 cup low-fat milk

(Hint: Buy a two-cup thermos; pour in heated milk, and add a cup of coffee or decaf with a dusting of cinnamon. Your "café au lait" stays hot and comforting all afternoon.)

DINNER

3 ounces Foiled Fish*
  (using "white" fleshed
  fish)
Steamed bell peppers,
  mushrooms, broccoli
1 teaspoon margarine
1 slice whole-wheat bread

SNACK

½ cup fresh raspberries

DINNER

3 ounces Foiled Fish*
  (using "red" fleshed
  fish)
Steamed bell peppers,
  mushrooms, broccoli
1 teaspoon margarine
2 slices whole-wheat bread

SNACK

Baked Apple*

SAMPLE THREE

BREAKFAST

1 ounce Shredded Wheat 'N Bran
8 ounces low-fat milk

SNACK

1 large tangerine

SNACK

1 large tangerine

LUNCH

Chicken Surprise*
1-ounce whole-wheat roll

LUNCH

Egg Salad*
2 1-ounce whole-wheat rolls

SNACK

¼ cantaloupe

SNACK

20 cherries (Count them.)

DINNER

3 ounces Oven "Fried"
Fish*
  (using white-fleshed fish
  and 1 slice bread)
Steamed snow peas
  and mushrooms

DINNER

3 ounces Oven "Fried"
Fish*
  (using red-fleshed fish
  and 2 slices bread)
Steamed snow peas
  and mushrooms

SNACK	SNACK
¾ cup low-fat milk heated with instant decaf and vanilla extract	¾ cup low-fat milk heated with instant decaf and vanilla extract

(Note: Part of your milk used in "frying" fish—see recipe below.)

SAMPLE FOUR

BREAKFAST

1 ounce 7-grain hot cereal
8 ounces low-fat milk

SNACK	SNACK
1/3 papaya (Hint: Squirt with lemon juice)	1/3 papaya

LUNCH	LUNCH
Chicken Toast-ada*	Toasted Taco Salad*

SNACK	SNACK
2 apricots	1 apple

DINNER	DINNER
3 ounces roast turkey breast Steamed green beans and red bell peppers Topped with: Herbed Croutons* made with 1 slice bread	3 ounces Vacation Beef* Steamed green beans and red bell peppers Topped with: Herbed Croutons* made with 2 slices bread

SNACK	SNACK
Egg-Less Nog*	Egg-Less Nog*

SAMPLE FIVE

BREAKFAST

1 ounce oat bran (measured dry, before cooking)
8 ounces low-fat milk

SNACK	SNACK
2 medium plums	1 cup grapes

LUNCH

LUNCH   **LUNCH**

Turkey Surprise*
   with 3 ounces
   light-meat turkey

Turkey Surprise*
   with 3 ounces
   dark-meat turkey

(Hint: Bake a whole turkey. Slice and freeze in 3-ounce portions to have on hand for sandwiches, salads, or dinners. But be careful: If I cook a whole turkey, I want to eat the whole turkey.)

½ whole-wheat
   English muffin

1 whole-wheat
   English muffin

SNACK

SNACK   **SNACK**

8 ounces low-fat milk
   heated with maple
   flavoring

8 ounces low-fat milk
   heated with maple
   flavoring

DINNER

DINNER   **DINNER**

Chicken Chili*
   (with 3 ounces white
   meat)
1-ounce whole-wheat roll

Chicken Chili*
   (with 3 ounces dark
   meat)
2-ounce whole-wheat roll

SNACK

SNACK   **SNACK**

½ grapefruit

½ grapefruit

SAMPLE SIX

BREAKFAST

1 ounce Bran Chex
8 ounces low-fat milk

SNACK	SNACK
1 cup strawberries	1 cup strawberries

LUNCH

Hen's Hen*
1 slice whole-wheat toast
2 teaspoons diet margarine
Steamed vegetables

LUNCH

Oriental-Oriented Kebobs*
2 slices whole-wheat toast
2 teaspoons diet margarine
Steamed vegetables

SNACK

Free Foods
(Hint: Dip veggies into "dressing" of rice vinegar and Dijon mustard.)

SNACK

Free Foods

DINNER

3 ounces orange roughy
    broiled with 1 table
    spoon Dijon mustard
Steamed crookneck squash
    green and red bell
    peppers with onion
    flakes
1-ounce whole-wheat roll
1 teaspoon margarine

DINNER

3 ounces fresh tuna
    broiled with 1
    tablespoon Dijon
    mustard
Steamed crookneck squash
    green and red bell
    peppers with onion
    flakes
2-ounce whole-wheat roll
1 teaspoon margarine

SNACK

Berry Blended*

SNACK

Banana Cream*

SAMPLE SEVEN

BREAKFAST

1 ounce Fiber One Cereal
8 ounces low-fat milk

SNACK

2x7-inch wedge of honey-
dew melon

SNACK

1 cup grapes (Hint:
    Eat grapes frozen.
    They're like mini-
    Popsicles. ™)

LUNCH

Pita Fold-Ups:
Free Vegetables
½ tomato
½ cup low-fat cottage cheese
2 teaspoons salad dressing
1 ounce whole-wheat pita
(Stuff everything into pita pocket. Bake at 350° for 10
minutes)

LUNCH

Pita Fold-Ups:
Free Vegetables
½ tomato
2 ounces low-fat hard cheese
2 teaspoons salad dressing
2 ounces whole-wheat pita

SNACK

1/3 cup nonfat
    powdered milk
    added to hot coffee
    or decaf

SNACK

1/3 cup nonfat
    powdered milk
    added to hot coffee
    or decaf

(Hint: Be sure to pour the coffee in the cup *before* adding the
powdered milk—or you'll have a wad of milk-glue at the
bottom of your cup.)

DINNER

3 ounces red snapper
    broiled with lemon juice
Stir-fried Vegetables*
1 slice whole-wheat bread

DINNER

3 ounces trout
    broiled with lemon juice
Stir-fried Vegetables*
2 slices whole-wheat bread

¼ cantaloupe

<u>SNACK</u>

¼ cantaloupe

Getting Started

There's nothing to stop you now. If you don't already have an okay from your doctor, get it. Then stock up. Treat yourself. Look for the freshest, most colorful vegetables, the most perfect, juicy fruit. Sample fish you never tried before. Splurge on fresh herbs and spices from the seasonings list. Experiment with some of the new vinegars, such as balsamic, raspberry, and rice vinegar. There's plenty of room for creativity on this diet. In fact, I think you will be delighted and surprised at how well you can eat, how satisfied you'll feel, how much energy you'll have as the pounds depart.

And with your first meal, you'll be on your way to the slimmer, shapelier body you want.

Bodyrhythm Diet Recipes

As you'll note, many of these recipes can be changed to use in either stage. It's a simple matter of substituting proteins and/or changing the amount of starch in the recipe.

MAIN-COURSE RECIPES

FISH DISHES

Because fish is low in fat and high in iodine, which may help stimulate a sluggish thyroid and boost calorie-burning metabolism, make fish your first choice among proteins. If you use canned fish, select water-packed and rinse to remove salt. Rinse shellfish and seafood as well. To be on the safe side, sodium-wise, select fresh "finny" fish as your primary choice.

Fish-Veg-Out

4 ounces fresh fish. (Use salmon for Stage II; halibut or red
   snapper for Stage I)
½ leek, washed, trimmed, and cut into small strips
½ cup mushrooms, sliced
½ carrot, cut into small strips
fresh parsley
1 bay leaf
a few slices of lemon, cut thin
squeeze of fresh lemon juice
freshly ground pepper

Tear off a sheet of aluminum foil large enough to cover
fish and vegetables. Place fish on foil. Pile vegetables and
the rest on top. Fold foil over fish. Fold edges to make a
packet. (Squeeze foil tightly or your oven will be a fishy
mess.) Pop in hot oven (500°) for 8 to 9 minutes or until
the fish flakes when tested with a fork. Take out the bay
leaf before serving.

Foiled Fish

The trick to making fish is to avoid drying it out; foil does
the magic. For Stage I, use any low-fat fish—sea bass,
halibut, red snapper, or orange roughy are favorites. For
Stage II, use a higher-fat fish. Salmon or fresh tuna are
popular choices.

4 ounces firm, thick fish fillet
1 tablespoon fresh ginger root, sliced
2 teaspoons chives or green onions, finely chopped
½ teaspoon lemon peel, grated
pinch freshly ground pepper
chopped fresh spinach, zucchini, parsley (any amounts)
juice of 1 lemon (or lime)

Place fish in center of foil. Top with everything else. Fold
up foil. Place foil packet in casserole dish at 400° for 10 to
12 minutes. (Hint: Remove the ginger slices before serving; they're hard on the teeth. Hint #2: Make extra

packets and freeze in foil. Heat up later for your own, "Frozen Diet Dinners.")

Oven "Fried" Fish

4 ounces fish (Use halibut, snapper, cod, or any *firm*, low-fat fish for Stage I; use salmon, fresh tuna, or other higher-fat fish for Stage II.)

1 slice whole-wheat bread, toasted and made into crumbs (For Stage II, use an additional slice of bread.)

¼ cup low-fat milk (Note: This is part of your daily milk requirement. Drink the other ¾ cup milk at meal or snack time.)

1 teaspoon margarine

1 green onion, minced

Dip the fish into milk. Dab or roll in bread crumbs. Place fish in small baking pan that has been sprayed with nonstick coating. Top with any remaining bread crumbs and milk. Smear the margarine on top. Sprinkle with minced green onions. Bake for 10 minutes at 450° or until fish flakes. (Hint: For microwaving, follow recipe, but microwave uncovered at full power for 6 minutes, or until fish flakes easily with fork. Cover and let stand for 5 minutes to complete cooking without drying out the fish. Note: Too long in the microwave oven results in fish leather, so "nuke" the fish for no more than the 6 minutes. It'll cook the rest of the way while "standing.")

POULTRY DISHES

Be sure to remove the skin and loose fat *before* cooking.

Chicken Chili

¼ onion, minced

1 glove garlic, minced

1 tomato, chopped

1–2 tablespoons green chili, seeded and diced

¼ teaspoon chili powder
¼ teaspoon ground cumin
1 tablespoon salsa
1 tablespoon tomato sauce
2 teaspoons garlic or herbed salad dressing
3 ounces cooked, cubed skinless chicken

(Note: Use light meat for Stage I; dark meat for Stage II.)
¼ cup water or ''vegetable water'' (water left over from
   steaming vegetables). (Hint: Freeze ''vegetable water''
   in ice-cube tray; pop out when needed.)

Put everything in a pan. Stir it around. Cover and simmer
for about 10 to 15 minutes. Add more water, if needed.
Serve in a bowl. Dab up sauce with a whole-wheat
roll—1-ounce roll for Stage I; 2 1-ounce rolls in Stage II.

Chicken Surprise

Didn't you used to hate those recipes with ''surprise''
tacked on? The ''surprise'' usually meant recycled leftovers. Here, the ''surprise'' is a chicken salad without gobs
of fatty mayonnaise.

3 ounces cooked chicken (Light meat for Stage I, dark
   meat for Stage II.)
2 teaspoons diet mayonnaise
1 tablespoon lemon juice
1 teaspoon mustard
pinch curry powder
1 teaspoon dried dill
½ stalk celery, finely chopped
½ green onion, finely chopped
1 tomato, cored and seeded
paprika

Mix everything together except tomato and paprika. Stuff
or smash all into the tomato shell. Sprinkle with paprika.
(Hint: If you want a hot lunch, stick the stuffed tomato in
the toaster oven and broil for a few minutes.)

Chicken Toast-ada

A calorie saver: Instead of a fried taco shell, you'll have a toasted pita for this "toast-ada."

   1 ounce whole-wheat pita (Use 2-ounce pita for Stage II.)
   Free vegetables: lettuce, cilantro, or parsley, red cabbage, green and red bell peppers (any amounts desired)
   ½ tomato, diced
   1 tablespoon onion, diced
   3 ounces cooked chicken breast
   (Note: For Stage II, use dark-meat chicken.)
   2 teaspoons garlic-flavored salad dressing
   1 tablespoon salsa
   1 tablespoon tomato sauce

Toast pita until very crisp. Chop up "free" vegetables. Add everything else. Mix well. (Hint: Use your hands— less to wash later.) Pile on top or inside toasted pita.

Hen's Hen

My favorite "party" recipe. My *only* party lunch recipe. You can roast a batch of these hens, freeze them, and take out one to reheat or zap in the microwave on days you don't want any fuss. That makes your own "takeout" lunch. And a no-fuss lunch *is* a party—even if you are your only guest.)

   ½ smallest Cornish game hen you can find.
      (Use 4 ounces skinless, dark-meat turkey for Stage II.)
   ¼ teaspoon ground cumin
   1 tablespoon lemon juice
   1 glove garlic, crushed
   pepper
   paprika
   ½ red onion, sliced

Skin the game hen. (Not difficult: It's like pulling off a snug T-shirt.) Remove loose fat. Mix cumin, lemon juice, garlic, pepper, and paprika. Massage into the hen. Broil hen for about 20 to 30 minutes. Baste with juices. Top with slices of red onion and broil a few minutes longer or until the meat is no longer pink inside. (Hint #1: Do the same for turkey thigh, but check to be sure it doesn't overcook. Hint #2: Broil on foil—keeps the oven cleaner. Don't you just hate having to scour the broiler after a party? Or anytime? Hint #3: Quarter hens before serving, so guests don't have to do battle with the hens.

RED MEAT DISHES

Although "red meats" are designed for use in Stage II when you increase fat to help pacify cravings, use these same basic recipes for Stage I, but substitute a low-fat protein—such as chicken breast, halibut, sea bass, or shellfish.

Oriental-Oriented Kabobs

4 ounces trimmed, skinless dark-meat turkey, lean beef, or pork for Stage II. (For Stage I, use 4 ounces any firm fish, boneless, skinless chicken breast, or shrimp.)
2 teaspoons soy sauce
1 tablespoon lemon juice
¼ teaspoon dry Oriental mustard (Check the "ethnic" section of any supermarket, or use equal parts mustard powder and tumeric.)
½ red bell pepper, cut into slices
½ green bell pepper, cut into slices
½ red onion
5 cherry tomatoes

Cut meat into cubes. Mix soy sauce, lemon juice, and mustard. Dab meat in sauce. Thread meat onto skewers, alternating with peppers, onion, and tomatoes. (Hint: Instead of skewers, I used metal knitting needles. They're reusable, sturdier, and I can hang on to them when yanking off the meat.) Broil, basting with sauce.

Toasted Taco Salad

4 ounces lean hamburger or ground turkey
(Note: For Stage I, substitute 4 ounces turkey breast or chicken breast.)

¼ cup red onions, chopped
⅛ teaspoon garlic powder
lettuce and red cabbage, chopped
½ tomato, finely chopped
2 teaspoons garlic-flavored salad dressing
1 tablespoon prepared salsa
2-ounce pita (Use 1 ounce for Stage I.)

Toast pita and break into chips. Put meat in a nonstick pan. "Fry" until the meat is no longer pink, drain off the fat. (How? I dump the meat in a sieve, shake it over the trash can. Don't pour the grease in the disposal; it clogs the disposal's arteries. Plop the meat back into the pan.) Add red onion, garlic powder, and stir to heat. Toss the lettuce, cabbage, tomato in salad dish. Add the meat mixture, the dressing and salsa. Mix the whole business with your hands. Serve with pita "chips."

Vacation Beef

The vacation? This recipe tastes like it comes from a faraway tropical island. Better yet, it requires little fuss in the kitchen—and that's a vacation, island or no island.

    juice of 1 lime
    ¼ medium red onion, sliced
    a bunch of cilantro (some prefer parsley)
    1–2 cloves garlic, minced
    ½ teaspoon ground cumin
    4 ounces well-trimmed lean chuck steak or other lean red
        meat or turkey thigh meat. (For Stage I, you could use 4
        ounces skinless, boneless chicken breast, for Vacation
        "Chicken.")

Combine the lime juice, onion, cilantro, garlic, and cumin in a pan. Add meat. Blot all sides of the meat in marinade. Cover and let stand for 2 hours. Remove the meat. Grill on barbecue or under broiler to desired doneness. Dab with marinade. (Hint: The longer meat cooks, the more fat drips off. Just be careful you don't cook it too long and end up with Vacation Beef Jerky.)

DAIRY DISHES

Because cheeses contain sodium as well as carbohydrates, and because the hard cheeses are high in fat, many women lose weight more slowly when they make a cheese choice. However, if cheese pacifies a craving, it's better to make the choice to lose slowly than to pig out and gain quickly.

Chili Rellenos (For Stage II, only)

2 large green chilis, cut in half, seeds and veins removed. (Hint: The more seeds, membrane, and "ribs" you leave in, the hotter this gets—some like it sinus-opening hot; others don't. Use gloves when preparing chilis; the oils can burn your skin. Don't rub your eyes!)
2 slices whole-wheat bread
1 ounce low-fat Jack cheese, finely grated
dried onion flakes
1 green onion, minced
1 egg (or use 1 white and a touch of the yolk)
2 teaspoons diet margarine

Prepare chilis. Steam them until soft. Dry by blotting with a paper towel. Toast bread and make into crumbs. Mix onions with grated cheese. Dab cheese-onion mix in center of each chili. Beat egg. Dip chilis into egg mixture to coat. Roll chilis around in the crumbs; back to eggs. Repeat. Melt the margarine in a nonstick pan. Place the chilis in the pan. Pour over them any remaining egg mixture and crumbs. "Fry" a minute or so to melt cheese inside. Turn once.

Egg Salad

1 hard-boiled egg and 3 hard-boiled egg whites. (For Stage I, use 6 egg whites—with the seasonings, it tastes like egg salad. As for the yolks; give them to your dog, the birds, the garbage can.)
1 teaspoon mayonnaise (or 2 teaspoons diet mayo)
2 teaspoons salsa
1 teaspoon dried dill
¼ teaspoon curry powder

1 green onion, minced

Mash eggs. Mix in the rest. (Hint: If you use this recipe to make a sandwich—2 slices for Stage II; 1 slice for Stage I—and have to pack it for later, don't use "diet" mayo. It's made with added water. By lunchtime, your bread will be soggy.)

SAUCES

You'll find these recipes add zest, without water-retaining salt and/or pound-creating fat.

Salsa

You can use this recipe as a sauce or a vegetable dip.

3 cups diced tomatoes
2 green onions, sliced
½ serrano or jalapeño chili, minced
2 gloves garlic, minced
1 tablespoon lime (or lemon) juice
1 teaspoon dried oregano
¼ cup red onion, chopped
¼ cup fresh cilantro, chopped

Combine all ingredients. (Actually, I can't be bothered chopping, seeding, mincing, or measuring. I just plop everything, whole, in the blender and whirl away.) Let stand for a couple of hours for the flavors to blend.

Tangy Dressing

You can make this one at any restaurant. Just ask for the ingredients, plus a cup for mixing.

½ teaspoon mustard—Dijon, if available
2 tablespoons vinegar—ask for wine vinegar or balsamic
2 teaspoons Italian dressing
chives
fresh pepper

With your fork, mix everything together.

STARCHES

For Stage II, when you eat double portions of starch, just add one more slice of bread to these recipes.

Herbed Croutons

2 teaspoons garlic salad dressing
¼ teaspoon Dijon mustard
1 green onion, finely chopped
1 slice whole-wheat bread, cut into cubes
    (Use two slices for Stage II.)

Use a nonstick pan or spray a small frying pan with a nonstick coating. Dump everything into the pan. Sauté gently. Stir so it doesn't stick. Sprinkle over salad or vegetables.

Herbed Stuffing

1 slice whole-wheat bread (or 2 slices for Stage II)
1 teaspoon margarine
¼ teaspoon "poultry seasoning"
1 stalk celery, finely chopped
½ onion, minced
paprika

Toast bread. Tear into crumbs with your fingers. Blend in margarine and poultry seasoning—also with fingers. Add celery and onion. Place in a "custard cup." Sprinkle with paprika. Bake in hot oven until browned. (Hint: Don't cook this stuffing inside or under chicken. The chicken grease that melts off will be absorbed right into the stuffing, and then into you.)

VEGETABLES

I've suggested vegetable combos and spices I enjoy. Change the recipe to suit your taste. Watch sodium-containing spices. And use only "free vegetables" in these recipes.

Gingered Vegetables

For either stage, but may be appreciated in Stage II, a time of cravings for zesty foods. This one will "spice up" any meal.

2 teaspoons diet margarine
water
1 tablespoon fresh ginger, chopped
1 clove garlic, minced
red bell pepper, cut into strips
snow peas
broccoli, cut into chunks
freshly ground pepper
1 green onion, finely chopped.

Put everything in a nonstick pan. Sauté vegetables until crisp. (Add water or lemon juice if needed.) Serve at once. (Well, if not at once, as soon as you get everyone to the table.)

Stir-fried Vegetables

Free vegetables: snow peas, broccoli, bean sprouts, green and red bell peppers, and/or mushrooms are colorful and crunchy choices
2 teaspoons Italian, herbed, or garlic dressing
water or "vegetable water" (water left over from steaming other vegetables)

Cut vegetables into small chunks. Spray small frying pan with nonstick spray or use a nonstick pan. Place vegetables in pan with salad dressing. Heat gently, adding water as needed. Cover briefly to steam. (Hint: If you like, you can use 1 teaspoon olive or sesame oil in place of dressing.)

SNACKS

Some of these recipes can be used *only* in Stage II.

Banana Cream (For Stage II, only)

Almost like ice cream . . . almost.

¾ cup ice water
2 teaspoons pure vanilla extract
1/3 cup nonfat skim-milk powder
1 banana, frozen, cut into cubes

Place water and vanilla in blender. Add powdered milk, a spoonful at a time. Blend. Slowly add banana cubes. Add more water if needed, but add only a tablespoon at a time.

Baked Apple (For Stage II, only)

> 1 medium apple
> ½ teaspoon "apple-pie spice"
> a few drops brandy flavoring

Core the apple. Sprinkle insides with ½ teaspoon apple-pie spice. Cover with foil. Bake in a custard cup at 375° for 20 to 30 minutes. (Less cooking means more sugar stays trapped inside the fiber walls.) Or cover the apple with microwave plastic wrap. Zap on "high" for 5 to 6 minutes, or until the apple is steaming hot, but not mushy. (Hint: If you save part of your milk, you can pour cold milk over the hot apple. Yum!)

Berry Blended

> 2/3 cup ice water
> 1–2 teaspoons *pure* vanilla extract
> 1/3 cup nonfat dry powdered milk
> 1 cup frozen strawberries

Place ice water and vanilla in blender. Add powdered milk, a spoonful at a time while blending slowly. Drop strawberries in, one at a time. Leave some strawberries chunky. Add more water if your blender jams.

Egg-less Nog

> 8 ounces well-chilled low-fat milk
> 1 teaspoon *pure* vanilla extract
> 1 teaspoon brandy or rum flavoring
> dash cinnamon
> dash nutmeg

Mix extracts into milk. (Some use a "regular" blender. Others use one of those small hand-held blenders. I use a glass and a fork.) Pour milk into iced glass. Top with cinnamon and nutmeg. (Hint: Try this heated and poured into a mug. Use a cinnamon stick to stir and flavor.)

9 | Success Strategies

The Bodyrhythm Diet addresses your special *female* diet needs by helping you overcome your body's built-in resistance to weight loss. It's the first and only diet that does. I think you, like so many of my clients, will discover that Bodyrhythm Diet guidelines give you the ammunition you need to fight fat better than ever before.

The Stage I/Stage II format provides the mix of foods you need to stay on track while coaxing your body to give up its stores of fat. Just as important, it helps you stand up to food cravings and *win*. All this, and it can help keep you on a more even emotional keel, too. Just follow the menu plans, starting with Stage I and continuing in Stage I for as long as you are relatively craving-free. Then, if you sense an urge to splurge on fatty, sugary, or starchy foods, switch to Stage II and stay there until you feel more in control.

Obviously, what you eat, and don't eat, is crucial to your success on the Bodyrhythm Diet. However, there are certain techniques which, when used in conjunction with the diet, will help you get even better results.

These success strategies can help you lose more surely and more steadily, from day one of your diet, to the final day, when you reach your target weight. And beyond, since many of these same tricks are invaluable aids in maintaining ideal weight as well. Some are Spencer "originals" that I developed in my work with overweight women. Other strategies you may have run across elsewhere. All can make a difference, but only if you *use* them.

Setting Goals: The Ten-Percent Solution

A target weight gives you something to aim for and a handy yardstick for measuring your progress. Setting individual weight goals, in fact, is one of the first things I work on with the women in my diet groups. But as it turns out, my definition of what's a reasonable, achievable, and maintainable goal is often different from theirs.

Some women come to the first class with their minds already made up about how many pounds they *should* lose. Often, these are women who were slim, or slimmer, in their teens and early twenties. What they usually hope to do is diet back down to the weight at which they looked and felt their best when they were younger.

Katherine, for example, weighed about 125 pounds from her sixteenth birthday until she became pregnant for the first time at the age of twenty-eight. Three babies and ten years later, she joined one of my diet groups, tipping the scales at 187. When Katherine and I discussed her weight goals, she said it would be "heavenly" to get down to 125 again, "but I'll shoot for 130." Suddenly, the eager expression on her face was replaced by one of uncertainty. "Oh, no . . . that means I have to lose *62 pounds*. That's an awful lot. . . ."

Maybe you're like Katherine. You were slender years ago, but a high-fat diet, a sedentary life, a couple of pregnancies, or all of the above resulted in a pileup of pounds. What you want now is to have your "old" sleeker body back again. That's fine. Your former weight may indeed be a good one for you. (You might even achieve a slimmer, fitter body than before!) But it's not a realistic goal for the short run—unless you only need to lose fifteen or so pounds to achieve it.

Or maybe you were never trim. Maybe you are one of the many, many women who have been burdened with excess fat for so many years—since childhood, or even infancy—that you can't even imagine how you might feel or look at various weights. I've worked with hundreds of women like you. Lacking any prior personal experience with slimness, you might refer to the Metropolitan Life Insurance Company's height/weight charts for guidance. (Or try to match your weight to your thin neighbor's, or your favorite TV star's, if she's about the same height you are.)

Lucinda was like that. At the age of five, she weighed almost 70 pounds; at twelve, 150. When I first met her, she was thirty and weighed 200 pounds. Consulting the 1983 Metropolitan Life chart, Lucinda noted that a woman her size—5 feet, 4 inches tall, with a medium frame—should weigh between 124 and 138 pounds. She was inclined to shoot for the midpoint of that range, and set a goal of 131 pounds. Then, after a quick mental calculation, it hit her. "Sixty-nine pounds! I'll never make it."

I have no quarrel with the aim of regaining former slimness (I'm all for it), or with using Metropolitan Life Insurance Company charts, or even your sister-in-law's body, to determine a range of desirable weight for you.

But I do have a problem with setting an initial goal based on the final results you want to achieve, because it's impossible to predict whether the goal is right for your body. Just as important, I've seen how demoralizing it can be when a woman suddenly realizes she has to lose fifty, sixty, seventy, or more pounds to reach her target weight. As one woman put it, "I feel defeated just *thinking* about all the weight I have to lose."

Exactly! Any major undertaking is daunting when you view it as a gigantic whole, and see success only in terms of final results.

But when you think about a big, long-term project as

something that can be accomplished in smaller steps, your perspective changes. It all seems more doable.

That's why I try to discourage women from starting with a long-term ultimate goal and suggest instead that they plan *as a first step* to lose 10 percent of their body weight.

I'm going to urge you to do the same.

If, say, you weigh 200 pounds now, your first goal should be to lose 10 percent of that, or 20 pounds. Don't even *think* about how many more pounds you want to get rid of. Make 20 your magic number and aim for that 20-pound loss. If you weigh 170, your immediate goal should be to lose 17 pounds (10 percent of 170 is 17). Concentrate your efforts on making those 17 pounds disappear.

Almost everyone who ever accomplished anything worthwhile somehow discovers a variation on the theme of breaking up a big, seemingly overwhelming project into smaller parts. It's what one efficiency expert calls "Swiss cheesing," because you keep nibbling holes in the job until bit by bit there's nothing left of it, and it's completed!

I call it ten-percenting. Time and again I've seen the positive psychological difference it can make to the dieter.

Meeting an immediate goal of losing 10 percent of your body weight represents a quick mini-success. It will keep your motivation way up there and do marvelous things for your morale. For example, when Lucinda lost her first 10 percent she was thrilled. It had been a long time since she weighed less than 200. Buoyed by the initial loss, she felt eager and confident about losing the next 10 percent. Now, at 146, Lucinda is still a bit overweight and plans to lose more. But she's ecstatic about her progress so far. Long and hard as she had tried to diet in the past, she had never lost that much before.

Lucinda attributes her victory mainly to the Bodyrhythm Diet with its built-in provisions for craving control, but also to the fact that for the first time ever, her goals were truly achievable.

Time Out?

After you lose the first 10 percent of your body weight on the Bodyrhythm Diet, what next?

If you're feeling flush with success, full of confidence and enthusiasm, eager to keep going, then forge on and lose the next 10 percent. Of course, continue alternating Stage I and Stage II eating, as explained in Chapter 7.

Some women, however, find it helpful to take time off from dieting after their first 10-percent loss. Maintaining their weight at the new lower level gives them an opportunity to settle in and get comfortable with the changes that have taken place in their bodies, their lives, and their eating habits.

All change is stressful, including change for the *better*. The physical, mental, and emotional changes—as well as the changes you should make in your environment (more about them later on in this chapter)—that occur when you commit yourself to fat-fighting may throw you off balance for a while. A brief vacation from dieting (while still maintaining your weight), allowing you time to adjust to your different, healthier way of life, can relieve some of the stress associated with those changes. And it can put you in an even stronger position physically and mentally to lose more when you go back to serious fat-fighting.

How do you know if you should take a break from dieting? It's your decision, and you should base it on how you feel and whether you think you'll benefit from a break. Some women seem to be able to forge ahead and lose all the pounds they want to lose in one uninterrupted stretch. Others seem to do better when they concentrate on stabilizing their weight after every 10-percent loss.

There are other circumstances when a break can be beneficial:

1. Consider a break *any* time you need to play catch-up—to give your body and mind an opportunity to adjust

to new ways of eating and living. Moving from the diet proper to Stage III, the maintenance part of the Bodyrhythm Diet (see Chapter 12) can help you deal with those changes without the unwanted consequences of weight gainback.

2. Many women find their weight loss stalls for one, sometimes two weeks out of the month. It's only natural. Not your fault, or the diet's. The hormonal changes that occur shortly before your period dam up water in your body. In fact, I warn women that there are really only two "good" weeks during the month when your body easily gives up weight.

But, if your weight loss stops for more than three weeks, your body could be telling you it's time for time off. Remember, we are genetically "programmed" to hang on to fat. When fat stores—really reserve fuel supplies— are threatened, as during dieting, the female body can become more resistant to weight loss.

This may never be a problem for you, but if it is, see what happens when you make a change to Stage III. Regulated, controlled Stage III eating should keep you comfortably at your current weight. You might even discover that the increase in calories actually jogs the weight-loss process along, and you begin to lose pounds again! (Yes, it's a paradox, but it sometimes happens that when calorie consumption goes up a notch or two, there's a corresponding rev-up in fat burning. It's almost as if the body needs assurance that more food is on the way, and there's no need to horde fuel, before it will give up more fat.)

One thing you definitely should *not* do when weight loss slows to a standstill is put yourself on a deprivation diet that severely restricts your intake of carbohydrates, protein, and fat. Oh, sure, semistarvation will reward you with the loss of a few pounds. But as a special "bonus" you will end up with less muscle tissue, as your body literally cannibalizes itself for nourishment. Believe me, I've seen what drastic deprivation dieting can do, and it's not pretty: hanging skin draped across the stomach, loose, flapping underarm flesh, thighs that roll and wobble with every step. Ugh!

That's not all. Off-balance dieting forces your body to turn its fat-burning functions way down in a last-ditch effort to conserve fuel. Then, when normal eating is resumed, your slower metabolism can result in an alarmingly rapid weight gainback—or worse, gainback *plus*.

To reiterate, consider taking time off from dieting if your progress is nil for three plus weeks. At that point, use Stage III maintenance eating guidelines to help keep your weight steady. A week or so should do it. Do *not* attempt a drastic cutback in calories. The possible consequences just aren't worth it.

3. You might need a diet break over the holidays, when you are on vacation, or during other super-busy or high-stress periods. These can be dangerous days because you are probably focused on matters that have nothing to do with the state of your shape. Your determination to lose weight is more easily undermined by lurking food temptations, major breaks with routine, and the strain of having so many things to do and so little time to do them. These are also times when you might be more susceptible to either/or thinking: either diet, or forget about weight control. I've seen it happen with the women in my groups. Good intentions are put aside, good eating habits are thrown out, and by the time their lives are back to normal, they've gained five, seven, ten or more pounds. In fact, I often tell them that just keeping their weight stable when the going gets rough is almost as good as dropping a few pounds!

Obviously, when the long-range goal is to lose pounds of fat, taking a diet break doesn't mean giving yourself permission to eat everything and anything in unlimited amounts. The technique of time off is the opposite of going out of control: it's a way of retaining control. Stage III of the Bodyrhythm Diet can help you do it.

Don't Play the Weighing Game

Haven't you noticed? When you are trying to lose weight, scales suddenly become irresistible. Even women who once ran from weigh-ins often hop on a scale every chance they get when they begin a diet.

The problem, of course, is that the bathroom scale doesn't always reveal what we want to see: quick progress.

Most of us know rationally that pounds hardly ever disappear at a smooth even rate, and that a diet progress chart rarely looks like this:

but more often—especially with our tendency to retain water at certain times—it looks like this:

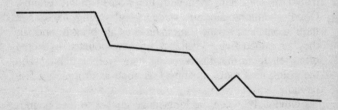

But no matter how knowledgeable we are, no matter how well we understand the slow progress by which fat is released from the cells, metabolized, and eliminated, we're still not ready to accept the fact that even when we've been "good," or "perfect," there are times when fat-fighting isn't reflected on the scale.

It's always discouraging when the needle gets stuck at

a certain weight for more than a couple of days—as it inevitably does on *any* diet. And when it happens, you may begin to wonder if it's worth it to continue denying yourself the foods that made you fat. Morale goes down; so does motivation.

I think daily weigh-ins are counterproductive because they can lead to disappointment and frustration. So I discourage women from checking their weight each morning. Once a week is better. A weekly weigh-in will give you a more accurate indication of what's *really* happening within your body. You are much more likely to see progress if you allow several days to elapse between each rendezvous with the scale. (Plateaus may come and go without you ever being aware of them!) Just as important, you will be less likely to be demoralized by what *appears* to be a lack of success.

For the best, most accurate assessment of how you're doing on your diet, follow these guidelines:

1. Have a scale that is in good working order. If yours is an old clunker that's been rusting away in your bathroom lo these many years, invest in a new one. It's worth it. I suggest a real "doctor's" scale—a balanced scale. With one of these, you avoid the major drawback of conventional spring-type scales, which give a fluctuating reading when you get on and off. The worst choice, as far as I'm concerned, are the digital scales. A friend of mine bought one and thought she was losing pounds at a rapid clip—even though she'd been sneaking ice cream—when actually, the battery was wearing down. When she stepped on a balanced scale in her doctor's office, she learned the awful truth!

Tip: You should be able to get a good deal on a balanced scale at a discount store or at a doctor's supply house. Doctors frequently trade in their scales for newer models, even though the old ones are still in good working condition. These scales, in fact, are terrific bargains; they're practically indestructible, always accurate, and give you immediate feedback on how you're doing.

· 2. Weigh yourself soon after awakening on your first

day of the Bodyrhythm Diet. (Get undressed and go to the bathroom first.)

3. In a notebook reserved for this purpose, jot down your weight and the date.

4. Do not weigh yourself again until seven days later... same time, same scale.

5. Jot down your new weight and the date.

6. Repeat seven days later, and so on.

How to Keep Your Weight Moving Along

If your weight hovers at or very near the same number on the scale for more than three weeks (and you don't want to take "time out" into Stage III maintenance eating), it's time to do some mental stock taking.

The first and most important question to ask yourself is whether you have been adhering faithfully to Bodyrhythm Diet food guidelines. An honest answer may make all the difference between having the body you want and being stuck with the body you have.

Think carefully. Have you been eating or drinking any "extras"? A glass of wine in the evening, even "lite" beer, can cause weight loss to grind to a halt. One woman thought the nondairy creamer she added to the several cups of coffee she drank each day was harmless. (It's not. Weight loss resumed when she used some skim milk from her "milk requirement" to lighten her coffee.) Another woman didn't understand the free-food concept, and thought it was okay to eat any vegetable, cooked in any way, in any amount—including carrots (they're a "starchy" vegetable) and celery (too salty). Still another woman was under the impression that dietetic candies are calorie-free. (They're not; some are nearly as calorific as regular candy. Once she stopped popping mints, she lost weight and experienced fewer sugar cravings!)

The foods, free and otherwise, that you *can* have on the Bodyrhythm Diet are listed according to type at the end of the preceding chapter. When in doubt, check. If the food in question is not included, it's not suitable for Stage I or Stage II eating.

Another common stumbling block to weight-loss success is a too liberal interpretation of serving sizes called for in the food plans. Lyn, for example, always chose the very largest fruit specimens she could find. As a result, instead of two fruit snacks a day, she was eating the equivalent of three or four!

Another woman, Joanne, gave herself oversized protein portions. Her reasoning: On some of the other diets she tried, she could have practically unlimited amounts of steak, chicken, and cottage cheese, so it followed that plenty of protein must be okay on the Bodyrhythm Diet, too. Of course, she was wrong. It's important to get enough protein, but not too much, since it's almost always accompanied by fat—and fat calories are the most fattening of all. But don't think large amounts of low-fat proteins are slimming. The body does not store excess protein and draw on it when protein is needed for cell repair. Instead, the extra protein can be stored as fat. You need a steady, even intake of protein throughout the day for cell building and body maintenance—not all at once and not large quantities. And besides, protein in excess has been shown to affect serotonin production, intensifying cravings for sugars and starches.

The latest health "revolution" sings the praises of complex carbohydrates. And they *are* great. In moderation, starches keep your energy up and spirits sailing. But excess starches, even high-fiber, nutritious, whole-grain ones, can let you slip into a post-eating slump. And the reaction to that slump is often to crave sugary foods for a "pickup"—only to go on a roller-coaster ride of ups and downs, to say nothing of weight gainback. You need enough complex carbohydrates (starches) for energy and to prevent mood slumps, but not so much that you find yourself nodding off after meals.

For simplicity and ease in measuring (it's easy to get carried away with portion sizes when you're eating pasta, rice, or other starches) whole-grain breads are the bread choice recommenced for Stage I and II of the Bodyrhythm Diet.

To be absolutely sure you're not overfeeding yourself, choose medium-size fruits instead of those gargantuan freaks of nature. When the menu plan or recipe specifies a certain number of ounces of food, weigh it out on a kitchen scale. Do the same with measuring cup or spoons when you need to determine amounts of food or "limited" seasonings.

If you're certain you are following my food guidelines to the letter, yet you're still not losing, don't give up. *Any* woman can make a better body for herself if she wants to badly enough. You are no exception. To drag more fat out of your fat cells, however, you may need to take stronger measures.

EXERCISE

From a health standpoint, and also because of greater effectiveness, getting more exercise is preferable to eating less as a way to speed weight loss. Increased physical activity not only results in more rapid calorie burn-off, it also fights fat in other ways. In fact, I recommend it to *every* woman losing weight, and not just to those who are marooned on a vast diet plateau. For more about the why's and how's of exercise, see Chapters 10 and 11.

DIET MODIFICATION

Some women just don't have enough time to increase their exercise. And a few can't because of physical limitations. When upping activity levels is not possible or practical, a further revision of eating patterns could rev up weight loss.

1. *Eat enough*. Usually, it's "cheating" or eating more, that slows progress. But sometimes cutting out or

cutting back on certain foods can have the same effect. As I mentioned earlier in this chapter, too few calories can cause metabolic slowdown. When that happens, the body conserves fuel, burns less, and makes better use of every little scintilla of nourishment from every tiny calorie, and weight loss grinds to a halt. If you have not been eating all the foods specified in the Bodyrhythm Diet guidelines—or if you've been eating less than I've recommended—see what happens when you begin to follow the diet *exactly* as written. You might be surprised to discover that adding back what you've subtracted from the diet is enough to reregulate your fat-burning mechanism and reignite the weight-loss process.

2. *Watch out for lurking sodium.* You already know that salty and high-sodium foods tend to cause water retention, and that when you are waterlogged, fat loss may be masked by water weight.

Now, new evidence indicates that when meals are high in sodium, more of the starch in those meals is absorbed by the body. That means each gram of starch delivers a bigger calorie punch when the starch is salted or eaten with foods that are salt- or sodium-rich! And if starch absorption is increased, there is reason to suspect that there is a corresponding increase in production of the fat-storing, fat-making, fat-trapping hormone, insulin.

The message is clear: Avoid salt and sodium. It may not be enough to refrain from using the saltshaker. You should also be aware of those ''hidden'' sources of salt:

- Canned fish, including canned tuna—even the kind packed in water—has lots of sodium. Dump it in a sieve and rinse it before you eat it. Tip: Dietetic water-pack tuna is almost salt-free.
- Shellfish—clams, oysters, lobster, shrimp—are all fairly high in sodium. ''Imitation'' shrimp and crab are loaded with the stuff. If you suspect that too much sodium is slowing your progress, omit all these foods from your diet for a few weeks. It might make a difference.
- Other animal proteins. Some butchers, packers, and dis-

tributors make a practice of dipping protein foods such as beef, chicken, fresh fish, and shellfish in a brine or salt bath to keep it looking fresh. For this reason, it's a good idea to rinse all animal proteins before cooking.

• Processed foods. Unless a label says the product is sodium-free, you can assume that canned and processed frozen foods have been prepared with fairly large amounts of sodium. (Frozen vegetables without added salt are okay to use, but generally have less fat-fighting fiber than fresh, raw, or lightly steamed.) Why not just use fresh foods instead?

• Condiments and flavor enhancers. Watch out for catsup, steak sauce, soy sauce (even low-sodium soy sauce), barbecue and cocktail sauces, salsa, and canned tomato sauce. These are allowed in both Stage I and II eating, but since they contain some sodium, you use them in measured amounts. (See "Seasoning List" in the appendix for amounts.) Herbs and seasonings without salt or sodium are allowed in unlimited amounts. The "Seasoning List" will give you all the added zest and flavor you desire, without adding excess salt to your food.

When in doubt, read labels. Even a product advertised as having "no salt added" could contain sodium—which is almost the same thing. Keep in mind that sodium comes in many guises and is often listed on labels as bisodium, disodium, monosodium, etc. Use only in the limited amounts as indicated in the "Seasoning List."

In addition to reducing sodium in your diet, you can encourage your body to release more water by drinking more water! Sounds crazy, but lots of water—eight glasses a day—actually helps flush sodium out of your system. (Water also helps fill you up, cutting down on eating.) As water and sodium are eliminated, the difference should show up on the scale.

It might also help to try one or more natural diuretics. Asparagus, watercress, and camomile tea act to ease water retention. And because vitamin B_6 can aid in a release of water, be sure to eat foods high in this antiwaterlogging vitamin—whole grain breads (not refined white bread), fresh, green leafy vegetables, as well as liver and fish.

3. *Have fish more often.* If any protein food seems to speed weight loss along, it's fish, partly because it's so low in calories. Simply substituting fish for beef, pork, lamb, and even chicken is one way to reduce calorie intake without unbalancing your diet.

There are other reasons why fish might help you lose faster. One has to do with the fact that fish are free of growth stimulants still given to some cattle and chickens—stimulants that are used to make these animals fatter and market ready at an earlier age. When you eat beef and chicken, you may be ingesting small amounts of these profat hormones. And though we don't know for sure, it is certainly possible that they have the same effect on us as they do on the animals.

Finally, ocean fish is high in iodine and iodine acts to perk up a sluggish thyroid, the gland that regulates metabolism.

With all the good things fish has going for it, it's worth taste testing until you find the ones you love.

4. *Spice things up.* Not only do spicy foods add zest to your meals, perking food without fats and helping prevent "cheating" or even pig-outs due to diet boredom, but researchers at Oxford Polytechnic have found that spicy foods give a jolt to your metabolic rate. Of course, eating jalapeño peppers won't burn off a binge and a heavy sprinkling of Oriental mustard or sinus-opening curry won't get you skinny, but hot seasonings and spicy vegetables might just be the "kick" your metabolism needs to get into higher gear. If nothing else, a spicy meal makes you reach for water, and the more water you drink the fuller you feel and the more waterlogging salt will be lost.

Arranging a Fat-Fighting Environment

I haven't said much about willpower so far. That's because on the Bodyrhythm Diet, with its mix of foods that minimize hormone- and mood-related cravings, you shouldn't need a will of steel in order to lose weight.

Still, there's no point in courting temptation. The more you do to arrange an environment that helps rather than hinders your efforts, the easier it will be to keep the fat moving out of your fat cells, and the needle on the bathroom scale moving down, down, down.

Here's how to manage your environment, at home and away:

Don't keep impulse foods in the house. Day one of the diet is what I call the "black-bag day." Go through your refrigerator and kitchen cabinets and toss into one of those big plastic garbage bags all the diet no-nos that sing out your name as you pass by. Out of sight, out of mind—and off your hips, thighs, and stomach.

My suggestion to rid the house of taboo baddies is always met by a chorus of "but's." "But I *can't* throw out the ice cream; my husband loves it." "But the children *expect* cookies when they come home for school." And so on. I've heard dozen of reasons why fat-proofing the house is impractical, and almost all of them have to do with other people.

Well, you are a person, too. What you want is at least as important as what your husband, roommates, and children want. Keep that fact firmly in mind and urge the people you live with to indulge their taste for fattening foods when they are away from home.

Most reasonable adults have few objections to this arrangement, especially if they care about the well-being of the dieter. As for kids, they're usually delighted to be given money and sent to the store to buy their own treats. (Just remind them not to bring the goodies home.)

If your children are too young to go to the store on their own, they're still young enough for you to have a positive influence on what they eat. At snacktime, give the little ones the same healthy foods that you eat between meals. And for heaven's sake, don't feel guilty about it. Your kids won't be deprived if you don't give them sugary soft drinks, cookies, and cake between meals. On the contrary. You are promoting healthier eating habits. And who knows? You may also be helping your children avoid the struggle you're currently having.

You don't have to go so far as bare cupboards or an empty fridge. Besides having a brimming fruit bowl and plastic containers filled with crisp veggies for everyone to enjoy, I have on hand certain foods that don't call to me. For example, I can't stand ginger snaps, but I stock them for family and guests. Ditto with sherbet. Creative compromises *can* be made.

Eat "in" as often as possible. There's no place like home for maintaining control over your meals. Nondieting family members or roommates can enjoy Bodyrhythm meals along with you, though the skinnies in your life will probably want and need to augment diet fare with extras, or take larger portions.

Important: Plan and shop ahead so that you'll never be caught short of the food you can eat and won't be tempted to substitute with high-fat, high-calorie foods you shouldn't eat. Think out your meals in the morning—including what, where, and when you'll eat later in the day. The planning process helps you keep firmly in mind the idea that you are on a diet, and aim to lose weight.

Develop restaurant savvy. For me, eating at home is definitely best. But many women seem to do better when they eat out. In a restaurant, they don't have to deal with the temptations they meet with when they cook, serve, and clean up in their own kitchens. And, most of us wouldn't dare overeat (to say nothing of pigging out) when others are around to watch.

Regardless of your own preference, however, chances are you'll be eating away from home several times a week. No problem if you pack your own lunch (Bodyrhythm Diet lunches are designed to be portable) and eat at your desk, the company cafeteria, or park bench when the weather is fine.

But what if brown bagging is impossible because of business obligations? Again, no problem if you choose an appropriate restaurant and order wisely.

In general, the best restaurants for the dieter are those that serve "American" (as opposed to ethnic) food. These can be counted on to include on their menus plain grilled or broiled fish, chicken, veal, and beef. Be sure to ask the waiter to serve your order "dry-broiled." I say this because I've sometimes asked for food with no butter and no sauce and been shocked to find my fish or chicken placed in front of me swimming in oil. "Dry-broiled" signals that you want no butter, no sauce, no oil, no fat of any kind.

Vegetables, of course, should be steamed, boiled, or raw—never sautéd, buttered, oiled, fried, or sauced.

If you order chicken or turkey, remove the skin and the underlying fat before you eat it.

In Stage II of the diet, when roast beef or steak are acceptable protein choices, be sure to trim away all visible fat. (Hint: Well-done meat has less fat.)

Ethnic restaurants are iffy at best. Avoid them if possible. Unless you are knowledgeable about these cuisines, you might get stuck with something highly calorific, salt-loaded, richly sauced, and dripping with fat. If you must eat in one of these restaurants, ask the waiter to suggest the simplest grilled, broiled, or steamed protein entrée served plain, no salt, no sauce, no butter, nothing. (Ask for fresh lemon for a squeeze of flavor if you like. Or use any of the "unlimited seasonings"—like fresh chives, ground pepper, exotic vinegars—or "measured additions" —such as mustard, horseradish, soy sauce—from the "Seasonings List" page 118.)

For Stage I, your starch portion at lunch and dinner is one slice of bread. For Stage II, it's two slices at both lunch and dinner. To prevent the temptation to nibble on surplus carbs, ask your waiter for extra vegetables (from your "free food" list) in exchange for the starch that comes with your entrée. (Later on in Stage III, when you are maintaining your weight, you'll have a wider choice of starch selections—rice, pasta, potato, etc.—but bread is the fat-fighting and craving-control plan for Stages I and II.)

If possible, choose high-fiber, whole-grain bread. (Some

super-motivated women take along a slice or two of whole-wheat bread in a plastic bag tucked in their purse! All the better to assure they get fiber plus essential vitamin B_6.) But watch out for that premeal basket of bread. In my opinion, the best way to deal with the temptation posed by bread or rolls that arrive at the table soon after you are seated is to take your serving and then to ask your dining companion if he or she would mind having the rest removed. Not as good, but better than having the bread just sit there practically daring you to eat it, is to cover it with a napkin. If you don't see it, it's easier to ignore, and may trigger less of the pro-fat insulin that can get juiced up just by the sight of tempting foods.

When your entrée is placed before you, look it over. If you ordered your meal cooked without fat or sauce and it comes to the table drenched with either, tell the waiter please to ask the chef to prepare your food again—this time as you ordered it. Make it a command, not a question.

As you survey your plate, check to see if there's too much of anything. Ask for a doggie bag (this is still at the *beginning* of your meal) and place inside it the excess protein, high-starch vegetables, plus any other food that's not part of the Bodyrhythm Diet. Then give the bag to your dining partner! If you can't carry off the doggie-bag maneuver, you can always oversalt the portions you shouldn't eat. That should erase any temptation.

Use "fake eating" tactics at dinner parties. At a restaurant you at least have a range of selections from which to order. As a dinner-party guest, you don't. What to do?

One woman, who had an unusually busy social life, accepted invitations with the understanding that she would arrive after the hors d'oeuvres and cocktails but before dinner. It's a good tactic for anyone who needs special help resisting zillion-calorie canapes.

As for the meal itself, in my experience there is almost always, on every dinner-party menu, at least one or two dishes that don't violate Bodyrhythm Diet get-slim principles. Stick to these, and if necessary whisper to your host or hostess that you would like to have your entrée, vegetables, and salad without sauce or dressing. If that's not possible, discreetly scrape away the sauce, and simply eat around the high-fat portions of the meal.

Remember, no matter what Mom used to say, you don't have to clean your plate. And you shouldn't if the food will set you back on your goal of a better body.

Now, here's a little trick to try: If you talk with enough animation while simple "toying" with your food on your plate—cutting it into bite-sized pieces and moving them around with a fork—it's possible to get away with eating very little without offending host or hostess. In fact, without anyone even noticing. The important thing is to rearrange the food so that it *looks* different from the way it did when presented. Try it. It works. And the reason it does is that the others at your table will be so focused on their food, they won't be aware, much less care, what you eat.

People Problems

Some of the people in your life, even close friends and relatives, can make dieting more difficult than it needs to be. Usually, they don't intend to interfere with your fat-fighting efforts, at least not on a conscious level. Yet they make trouble, by word or deed or both.

Parents can be notorious diet saboteurs. Patricia, a woman in her early twenties, who ultimately lost 100 pounds, put it as succinctly as anyone: "My mother and dad always criticized me for being overweight. Yet, when I go to visit, Mom usually bakes a huge cake—my favorite chocolate layer cake! Then she acts hurt when I don't eat it."

There are also the people I call "food friends." You know who they are. They're the ones who suggest going out for something to eat whenever you get together with them.

One of my close friends was like that. Marla is and

always was reed slim. Whenever she came to town for a visit, she would inevitably steer us to a little café for "coffee." Only, "coffee" for her meant coffee plus a sweet roll, cake, or pie. Marla never gained an ounce, no matter what she ate. I, however, was fat, always on a diet, and forever famished.

Every time we went out, I promised myself to have just coffee. But watching her eat the sweets I craved was too much for me, and I always walked out with a hot fudge sundae under my belt making its way inexorably to my hips and thighs. (Or I would be "good" in front of her, but once alone, I gobbled anything I could lay my hands on.)

That was years before I developed the Bodyrhythm Diet, with its built-in binge insurance and craving control. But even now I try to avoid sharing meals with Marla or other food friends. They're big eaters, and just looking at what they order is a turn-on for *my* insulin and *my* hunger. As a FFP (formerly fat person), I have to work hard on not letting anything interfere with my efforts to stay slim!

I believe that the best way to deal with relatives and friends who unknowingly make dieting more difficult is simply not to get into food situations with them. It won't be easy, especially if you want to maintain close ties. Just keep in mind that nowhere is it written that time spent with important people in your life has to be planned around eating. There *are* other things to do. Instead of meeting for lunch or dinner, you could go to a movie or museum, browse in the stores, hike, bike, or simply settle down on the sofa for a good, long talk.

If they insist on sharing fattening food, be honest. Tell them how important it is for you to lose weight and that you would appreciate not being coaxed to eat things that will keep you fat. And if they still won't go along with your wishes, tell them you'll have to stay in touch by phone. Harsh, perhaps, but better for you in the long run.

Men can pose special problems. When the woman he loves goes on a diet, a man often views it as the first step in leaving him. Your man may need to be reassured that you are losing weight because you want to look better and feel better—not because you're getting ready to go out shopping for a new guy.

Strangely enough, fat friends can exercise the most negative yet subtle influence of all. Misery *does* love company, and there is often an unspoken agreement between two heavyweights that they're in it together. When one begins to change her body and her life, it's as if a pact has been broken. The friend who stays fat feels abandoned, even betrayed, and yes, jealous.

I've had women tell me that when they started to slim down, their fat friends suddenly began to make remarks that seemed calculated to slow diet progress and drain away morale. Remarks such as: "You used to be so pretty, but now your face is all caved in"... and "men like women with more meat on them"... and "you've changed; I liked the old you much better." Often they were hurt as their fat friends became morose, distant, or even turned away entirely.

Fat friends can put you in a bind: lose weight and lose a friend. Or keep your fat *and* your friend. The best way out of the dilemma is to persist in your efforts to lose pounds, and at the same time try to inspire your friend to do the same. With a little encouragement, support, and understanding, it just might work, and you'll both be rewarded with better bodies. In any event, stick with your diet. Loyalty is a virtue, but when it prevents you from changing and improving yourself, loyalty can turn self-destructive.

What to Do If You Fall Off the Diet?

The Bodyrhythm Diet is a different kind of diet. Because it helps defuse cravings caused by hormone swings and mood shifts, it requires less from you in the way of willpower. It's easier to stay on. Nevertheless, it's not foolproof. No diet ever is. Some women slip up and fall off. What if that happens to you?

Shrug your shoulders, tell yourself you're going to do better in the future, and see what you can learn from your mistake. For example, if you pigged out on potato chips, the lesson is clear: You must never again imagine that you can have one or two chips and leave it at that. You have to stay as far away from chips as you can. If you lost all control at the buffet table, you know that for the sake of your diet, you might ask a friend to make the right choices for you—and that's what you'll do, next time. If unsatisfied cravings resulted in a binge, you've learned to stay tuned in to your body and to move directly into Stage II eating the moment you feel a craving in the making.

For heaven's sake, don't beat up on yourself when you go astray. I know how it is, because I've been there. Falling off a diet used to make me feel so worthless and down on myself, I'd think, "What's the use? I'll never get thinner, so I may as well just keep on gorging." There's nothing more debilitating than that line of reasoning. Don't get caught up in it.

Almost as bad is to try to make up for your mistakes by skipping or skimping on the next few meals. This only sets you up for repeat bingeing as hunger—*intense* hunger—combines with cravings and you finally give in all over again and stuff yourself with more of the wrong foods.

There is a way to break out of the binge/fast/binge cycle and that is to give your body *small* amounts of carbs and fats after a bout of overindulging. *To go directly from a binge into Stage II of the Bodyrhythm Diet,* in other words. Stage II foods will help ease the cravings and help put you back in control of your eating. You'll be on the safe, solid middle ground between overeating and fasting. And in a good position to withstand further food urges.

Many women resist the idea of eating more starches after a binge. As one put it, "It doesn't make sense." Maybe it doesn't make sense to you either. Think of it this way. Overeating tends to stimulate cravings for more food, particularly carbohydrates. "Starving" your body of the very foods it wants—especially after an eating spree when you ate an excess of those foods—just aggravates and accentuates the cravings. You'll have to exert every ounce of your willpower to hold out against your body's hormonal and mood-related urges for more. And unfortunately, in any match between willpower and nature, willpower usually loses. But when you give your body what it wants, through controlled Stage II eating, you'll be working with it, not against it. Stage II carbs will help you get back on track, more easily and with diminished cravings and hunger.

Continue in Stage II for three days. Then, assuming cravings have subsided, switch to Stage I for maximum, safe weight loss. Lose no time moving back into Stage II, however, if cravings begin to reassert themselves.

Isn't it nice to know that with the Bodyrhythm Diet not only do you have binge insurance, but a valuable tool for terminating the binge/fast/binge cycle?

Special to the Super-Diet-Resistant Woman

As I explained earlier in this book, almost all women are diet-resistant, at least when compared with men. But some of us are such slow losers, we make other women look like weight-loss speed demons. We're the ones who tend to be pear-shaped, or bottom heavy (with more numerous fat cells). Our faces, chins, necks, arms, even our waistlines may be relatively slender (with normal numbers of fat cells), but watch out below. From the waist down, it's saddlebag hips, rhino rears, thunder thighs.

Does this sound like you? If it does, and if you ever managed to lose a few pounds on an ordinary diet, you may have been appalled to see your face shrivel, your breasts shrink, and your arms turn into toothpicks (as those fat cells shrank down)—while your bottom half continued to be almost as large and lumpy as ever (as the numbers of fat cells remained). You might have become *so* upset and frustrated that you threw in the towel—and threw out the scale—and decided to live with your pearish contours.

Will the Women's Bodyrhythm Diet help *you*? I believe it can. But you've got to stay with it. Persistence is the key.

Of course, broad hips are often a matter of bone structure, and no amount of dieting will change the shape of your skeleton. And (other than surgery) there may be nothing you can do to remove the *numbers* of existing fat cells. But the *amount of fat* in the fat cells of your hips, rear, and thighs is also estrogen-related. Estrogen, remember, stimulates fat cells in those areas to produce greater amounts of the enzyme lipoprotein lipase. LPL in turn pulls *more* fat out of your bloodstream and coaxes it into those very same fat cells. Or worse, a whole new generation of fat cells can be created in your fat-prone areas anytime you gain weight rapidly—such as pregnancy, or when unsatisfied cravings lead to binges that not only restuff existing fat cells, but may even make more of them. The results: even bigger thighs, a broader rear, and more bulging hips.

The low-fat, high-fiber foods you'll be eating in all stages of the Bodyrhythm Diet put a brake on excess estrogen. Less LPL is stimulated. As a result, less fat is attracted to problem areas. At the same time, reduced calorie intake and increased exercise helps deplete and shrink the fat cells already padding out your hips, rear, and thighs. In addition, Stage II helps defuse cravings, preventing the massive overeating that stuffs up fat cells, bulging them out and, perhaps, even creating a whole new generation.

I can't promise that the Bodyrhythm Diet will make you as skinny from the waist down as a fashion model. Some women are programmed to be pear-shaped, no matter what. But if you are *persistent,* chances are good that you'll be a better-proportioned, less exaggerated, peared-down pear. Better yet, by combating cravings, you'll fight off binges, weight gain, and the formation of even more numerous fat cells.

Even some of the most diet-resistant women lose pounds and inches from hips, rear, and thighs when they stay with get-slim eating. And because the Bodyrhythm Diet helps keep the profat hormones in better balance, less fat is stored, more fat burned—but without the toneless, saggy-baggy skin and brittle hair that are the ugly side effects of many diets.

Maybe you'll never have a boyish rear and streamlined hips and thighs. I know I won't. But I'm thinner in those areas than ever before, and so are the women who stayed with Bodyrhythm eating long enough. With persistence, why should it be any different for you?

10 | Fat-Fighting with Exercise

I almost dread beginning this section by telling you what you've already heard umpteen million times before: Exercise is *good* for you. Because if you're like I am, whenever you're told over and over again how *good* something is for you, you become a little suspicious. (It's probably because we learned as children that so many of the things *they* kept telling us were "good for you" we did didn't like one bit. Going to bed early, for example. Or creamed spinach.)

Nevertheless, it's true. Exercise is not just good, it's fantastic! Few things do so much for you. As a human being, as a woman, and especially as a dieter who wants to lose pounds of fat and look and feel her absolute best.

You're already familiar with many of the benefits of exercise. You know that it promotes stamina and endurance, reduces the chances of having a stroke and developing heart disease, and even protects against bone-thinning osteoporosis. You're certainly aware that physical activity helps burn off extra calories, thus speeding the weight-loss process.

But there's more. So *much* more to get from exercise, that I've made it an integral part of the Women's Bodyrhythm Diet.

Of course you can lose pounds simply by adhering to Stage I and Stage II eating principles. Others have done it. You can, too. But why cheat yourself of all the special diet-enhancing effects of increased activity? Why just sit there when you can look better, feel better, lose weight more quickly, and achieve a trimmer, toned up, and more attractive body just by getting a move on?

Even a little extra activity can make a difference. Hard to believe? Believe it!

The Active/Passive Vacation Syndrome

When I say that even a mini-increase in physical activity can have a positive influence on how much and how fast you lose—and also on how well you maintain your weight loss—I really mean it.

Some of the most striking examples of the relationship between exercise and weight control arise out of women's vacation experiences, of all things. Let me explain.

Many women enroll in my diet groups for the express purpose of shaping up before going away on vacation. Once they lose the weight, however, they start to worry that they'll gain it all back, and then some, while they're away.

Now, many return and are astonished to find they haven't gained even a pound—and a few even lose weight—despite the fact that they had relaxed their diet vigilance for a couple of weeks. Others of course literally shriek with horror the first time they step on a scale back home.

In almost every instance, those who didn't gain were *doers*. They spent their vacations wandering around museums, exploring ruins, inspecting historical sites, poking around in boutiques and department stores, biking down country lanes, or dancing till all hours of the night.

By contrast, the weight gainers were sitters. They planted themselves on a blanket at the beach, or sprawled in a deck chair on shipboard. They lolled by a pool, or spent days and evenings curled up at fireside at a resort.

They also tended to sleep late and take naps during the day.

It wasn't that the doers put themselves on an exercise program while they were away. But they were up and around, moving their bodies much of the time. The sitters vegetated. And the difference was enough to show up on the scale.

The lesson is clear: Even small extra amounts of physical activity count.

If you're still in doubt about the potential benefits of being just *slightly* more active, consider the results of a recent study on "fidgeters," conducted by the National Institute of Health. In this experiment, groups of fidgeters— people who habitually shift around in their chairs, drum their fingers, wring their hands, tap their feet, chew on pencils, etc., burned anywhere from 200 to 850 calories per day. No, I'm not advocating fidgeting for calorie burn-off. Fidgeters, I suspect, are born not made—and they also tend to drive the people around them to distraction! I mention the study merely to underscore the point that where calorie expenditure is concerned, *any and all movement* can make a difference.

Think of it! If fidgeting can cost 200-plus calories a day, imagine how many more extra calories you could burn by walking, climbing stairs, gardening, housework. The list could go on and on. In fact, the options for additional calorie burn-off are limited only by your imagination. I'll tell you about how to use more calories by being just *slightly* more active—without engaging in strenuous Exercise with a capital E—in the next chapter.

For now, let's take a closer look at some of the lesser known but extremely important benefits of capital E Exercise. Once you're aware of them, I think you'll want to get up and out of that chair and start moving via a program of aerobic activity that suits your needs and your life-style. And you'll want to do it *now*.

Exercise and the Pro-Fat Hormones

A particularly valuable advantage of exercise for us, as women, is its moderating effect on the female sex hormones, estrogen and progesterone, and the fat maker, insulin.

Estrogen

This female hormone is so profat that for years ranchers added the powerful synthetic estrogen, DES, to cattle feed because animals on a DES-supplemented diet got fatter faster and more cheaply (with less feed) than animals who ate plain cattle chow. The practice of putting synthetic estrogen into livestock food was later banned out of fear that traces of the chemical in meat were being ingested by humans. But it's interesting, isn't it, that cattlemen were aware of—and acted on—a principle that diet experts too often ignore or deny: Estrogen encourages fast fat storage, with comparatively little feed.

Physiologically, we are not so very different from those cattle. Estrogen produced by our bodies, as well as hormone supplements taken for medical reasons, can make us fatter, too. The higher our estrogen levels, the more fat we tend to store. More estrogen, in turn, is "manufactured" in body fat. And on and on. It's the female fat cycle, remember?

As we've seen, one way to break the cycle is to switch to low-fat, high-fiber Bodyrhythm Diet eating, which reduces estrogen levels. As estrogen levels begin to taper off, fat is less likely to be stored in those cells. Exercise hastens the process, helping to pull even more fat out of storage. With less body fat, less fat-storing estrogen is made and released from that body fat. In fact, when amounts of estrogen are measured in athletic and nonathletic women, the exercisers tend to have lower levels of the hormone. And compared to nonactive women, those who have made exercise part of their life-style have significantly lower rates of cancers of the breast and uterus, no doubt due to their lower amounts of the hormone.

In terms of women, estrogen helps make you fat and keep you fat. I developed the Bodyrhythm Diet to aid in subduing the profat properties of this hormone. The low-fat, high-fiber diet alone should do it. But I think you'll see, as have so many of the women I've helped, that when exercise plays a role in your estrogen-moderating strategy, fat just doesn't stand a chance.

Progesterone

Physical activity also appears to counter some of the effects of progesterone, the "craving" hormone. It is progesterone, remember, that stimulates the urge to junk out on high-cal, high-fat, high-sugar stuff, and/or super-rich starchy foods.

As with estrogen, so with progesterone; women who are physically active tend to produce less progesterone than nonexercising females. In view of this, it would be reasonable to expect that active women would experience less intense cravings. And that seems to be the case! In some of the women I see—the ones who adhere to Bodyrhythm Diet food principles and who *also* exercise regularly—hormone-induced cravings are practically zapped out of existence.

Stage II of the diet, with its built-in binge insurance, can help you hold out against progesterone-related cravings and block potential pig-outs before they begin. But with diet *plus* exercise, you'll be in an even better position to resist.

Case in point: It was Stage II eating, along with increased physical activity, that finally enabled Nancy, a twenty-five-year-old social worker, and one of my "star" clients, to lose sixty pounds.

Like many overweight women, Nancy lost quickly when she first began to diet. "The fat is just melting off," she said with delight.

But by the time she had shed twenty pounds, her body had adapted to her new way of eating and went into a holding pattern. Food cravings, which hadn't bothered her in the early months of her diet, once again began to taunt and tease.

On her own, without talking it over with me, Nancy decided to stay with Stage I eating, instead of taking advantage of craving control. She worried that the additional carbohydrates and the higher-fat protein foods called for in Stage II would cause weight gain. Poor Nancy. Without Stage II binge insurance to help her deal with cravings, she set herself up for a massive eating orgy: three days of nonstop gorging on cheese pizzas, washed down with gallons of Coke Floats.

Several days later and ten pounds fatter, she turned up at my office, tears streaming down her face. "I don't know what happened. I totally lost control. I'm so disgusted with myself," she wailed.

Once again, I explained the connection between progesterone and cravings, and reemphasized the role Stage II eating can play in helping to defuse those cravings. Then I took a harder line.

"Nancy, I want you to get right back on the program. Now. And I want you to start with Stage II. When and if cravings become intense, walk away from them as fast as you can."

She looked puzzled. "Walk away from them?"

"Exactly," I said. "Better yet, don't wait for the cravings. Just start walking. Every day for fifteen minutes. You'll start burning extra calories and begin to lose weight again. And because brisk walking could bring progesterone down a bit, it may prevent another eating orgy."

She began to protest. "I'm too fat to exercise, and besides, I hate it."

"Nonsense!" was my response. I reminded her that she was young and healthy. Further, despite her recent ten-pound gain, she was still thinner than when she started to diet. And then the clincher: "Tell me, Nancy, which do you hate more? Being fat or being active? It's your choice, you know."

She grumbled, but in the end she made the decision I knew she'd make: slender and active was better than fat and sedentary.

Soon after starting her walking program, Nancy's weight

began to drop again. And she found she was able to manage her food cravings simply by shifting into Stage II eating when she felt tempted.

The difference between Nancy then and Nancy today is incredible. Now she's a slender five-foot, six-inch beauty with a body that practically stops traffic. And guess what? Not only is she still a walker, she joined a health club and works out several evenings a week with weights and Nautilus equipment. Last time I saw her, she told me she had so much energy, she doesn't know what to do with it all.

And energy, as you know, is another exercise bonus. Physical activity seems to generate more energy, both physical and mental. The why's of this phenomenon are not completely understood. But for women, especially in the days just prior to menstruation, the effect of exercise on progesterone production might be a contributing factor.

The craving hormone, you see, is also the culprit responsible for the slowed-down, drained, dragged-out feelings many of us experience in the preperiod phase of the menstrual cycle. When increased physical activity rebalances progesterone production, we may then begin to feel less sluggish, more up, and *alive* . . . and even more inclined to exercise. (Now, that's what I call a terrific two-for-one bargain: Fewer, less intense food cravings, *plus* more energy, all for the price of a few minutes of vigorous exercise each day!)

Insulin

A boost in physical activity also often helps disarm the third pro-fat hormone, insulin. For why this is so, consider the fact that many diabetics are urged by their doctors to get plenty of exercise. In part that's because physical activity helps the diabetic make more efficient use of the small amounts of insulin produced by his or her pancreas. To put it another way, exercise makes the diabetic more *sensitive* to the hormone. In fact, those same studies of athletic women referred to above also found that the exercisers had lower rates of diabetes.

It's the same insulin facts for the dieter. With exercise,

your body becomes more sensitive to insulin, meaning that it begins to make better use of smaller amounts of the hormone. When that happens, your pancreas no longer needs to pump out floods of insulin because less is needed to clear sugar and fat from your blood. When the demand decreases, so does the supply. And with less insulin circulating in your blood, less fat is stored, more fat is burned.

And as exercise makes your body more sensitive to insulin and less is produced, blood sugar levels don't fluctuate as wildly. There are fewer of those steep drops that trigger your brain to send out hunger and craving signals. With less hunger and fewer cravings, staying on a diet becomes that much easier!

Isn't it ironic that the best appetite suppressant of all doesn't come in a bottle or little foil-wrapped packets, doesn't have any dangerous side effects, and doesn't cost a penny? I'm talking about exercise, of course.

Yellow Fat, Brown Fat...and Exercise

Frankly, when I begin to explain the distinction between yellow fat and brown fat, and how exercise affects both, some women groan out loud.

"Oh, nooo . . . you mean there are *two* kinds of fat, and we have to worry about both?" is a typical reaction.

Yes and no, I say. There's only one that you have to "worry" about. And then I go into my spiel.

First, there's ordinary "yellow" fat, the greasy gunk that is packed away in your fat cells. When we talk about body fat, we are referring to yellow fat. It's lazy, gloppy stuff that just piles up, distorting your shape and making you feel miserable. It's main function is to act as a reserve fuel supply to be drawn on for energy and heat when food is scarce.

Yellow fat is the bad fat you want to get rid of. The one to "worry" about.

"Brown" fat, on the other hand, is much darker in

color because it is richly supplied with blood vessels. Whereas yellow fat is rather evenly distributed throughout your body, with somewhat more padding hips, breasts, thighs, and rear, brown fat is confined to certain areas, primarily those immediately surrounding vital organs, including the large veins and arteries leading to and from the heart. Indeed, one function of brown fat seems to be to warm those organs, especially when temperatures drop.

Brown fat is good fat. The more you have of it, the better.

Unlike ordinary, lazy, yellow fat, brown fat burns calories, producing heat. It's metabolically *active*. Inside every brown fat cell, minuscule globs of ordinary fat are "fried." Heat from this combustion is carried off and used to warm vital organs. Brown fat cells, in fact, have been compared to tiny metabolic furnaces, burning off calories.

Researchers believe that skinnies not only have *more* brown fat than fat-prone people, but that the brown fat furnaces of thin people are actually switched on *more of the time*. In several studies, thin volunteers actually gobbled up 5000 to 7000 *more* calories a day than usual, and still did not gain an ounce. How come? The extra food seemed to stoke up their brown fat. And, like the little furnaces they're compared to, it is thought that these brown fat cells automatically increased their activity enough to "fry" off the excess calories. This process is known as "adaptive thermogenesis"; the body adjusts, "adaptively," to overeating by turning up its thermostat, making more heat and burning more calories. The extra food is not stored and does not result in obesity.

Adaptive thermogenesis could be one of the answers to the great mystery that has confounded doctors and dieters ever since obesity was first perceived to be a problem. The mystery of why some people can eat everything and anything from morning till night and still stay slim. Or, to turn it around, the mystery of why some of us are fat even though we *know* we eat less than our thinner friends.

Can we make adaptive thermogenesis work for us? Can we get more of this brown fat? And can we get the brown fat we already have to switch on its heating mechanisms and stay turned up higher for a longer period of time to vaporize more of our calories?

Yes. Yes. Yes. And yes, say the brown fat experts. And you probably guessed how. Exercise. Vigorous physical activity on a regular basis is not only thought to increase the total *amount* of fat-burning, brown fat, but exercise also appears to "fire up" the brown fat we already have so that more calories are just sizzled away.

But the mechanism that stimulates brown fat functioning seems to kick into play only when you eat regularly, as you will when you start to follow Bodyrhythm Diet principles. Crash dieting or skipping meals only turns down *total* calorie burning. With too few calories, yellow fat, the kind that acts as reserve supply, is horded within the fat cells. And the calorie-burning functions of brown fat are also turned down.

If you've ever tried a drastic diet, you probably remember feeling chilled and wanting to turn up the heat while others were peeling off their sweaters. This was partly because your metabolism, the rate your body burns fat, was turned down in an attempt to save fuel. Eating, on the other hand, warms you. Your body says, "Okay, there's food here, so I'll burn off some of this fatty yellow grease for warmth. And while I'm at it, I'll go ahead and turn on calorie-frying brown fat."

Score one more for safe, sane, moderate eating plus exercise. Together, they'll help keep metabolic rate up, turn on your brown fat, and help fry off the yellow fat.

Hips, Hips, Away

If you're still not completely sold on the idea of combining Bodyrhythm Diet eating with an increase in exercise, this should clinch the deal: Exercise just might whittle away at those very parts of your anatomy that are least affected by diet—hips, thighs, and rear.

No, I'm not talking about "spot-reducing" exercises.

Sad but true, when exercises focusing on specific parts of the body work at all, they don't actually get rid of fat in the problem areas. Instead, they improve muscle tone, resulting in greater firmness. (The fat's there; it just doesn't jiggle around as much, in other words. . . .)

Rather, I'm referring to almost any vigorous activity and its potential for changing the ratio of "receptors" on fat-cell surfaces.

I'll explain. There are two kinds of fat-cell receptors. There are the "alpha" receptors that attract fat like magnets, lock it into the fat cells, and then figuratively throw away the keys. Then there are the "beta" receptors, which encourage fat breakdown and release.

As a woman, even if you are relatively thin, you probably have more fat-holding alpha receptors on the fat cells of your hips, thighs, and rear. Diet, especially a balanced eating plan such as the Bodyrhythm Diet, which results in steady weight loss, will drag some of the fat out of cells equipped with alpha receptors. But to really reshape your shape, you need more of the fat-releasing betas in those areas that tend to bulge.

But guess what? Researchers tell us that there's at least a "hint" that vigorous activity—not spot-reducing exercises—shift the receptor ratio away from fat-holding alphas toward fat-releasing betas. As women, we need to pay attention to hints like this.

Exercise may also help to deactivate LPL. This is the enzyme, remember, which, in the presence of estrogen, tends to draw fat to the "female" parts of our bodies, padding our breasts and making some of us bottom heavy. We already know that vigorous exercise affects rat LPL. In lab tests, when groups of rodents were deliberately overfed and fattened up on a diet high in fat and sugar and then put on a running program (don't ask me how researchers accomplished that!), LPL activity was diminished, and the rats lost weight and fat. However, when the rats quit their exercise routines, their fat-storing LPL shot right back up again.

Now rats aren't human, and everyday life is different

from a controlled lab situation. But I think it would be unwise to dismiss these test results as meaningless.

We don't know yet whether vigorous activity for women does indeed decrease LPL production enough to allow significant fat reduction in the stubborn problem areas below the waist. But since exercise does help modify estrogen levels, there's every reason to believe that regular workouts will also subdue LPL. This is because of the close relationship between estrogen and LPL—if more exercise equals less estrogen (and it does), it should also mean less LPL.

But exercise, at least, *seems* to work in areas where diet doesn't.

When I was fat, I longed for sleek hips, a trim little behind, and bulge-free thighs, and was convinced these attributes would be mine if I just cut calories and got down to normal weight. What a disappointment. No matter how many pounds I lost, my bottom half always seemed out of proportion to my top. It was only after I began to follow Bodyrhythm Diet food principles and started to exercise regularly that I lost the look of an hourglass with all the sand sunk to the bottom.

No, I still don't have the streamlined hips and thighs of a fashion model. But there is a noticeable improvement in my proportions. I can put on a bathing suit, peek in a mirror, and say to myself in all honesty, "Well, Spencer, the old bod isn't perfect, but compared to before, it's not bad . . . not bad at all."

I know women who've had similar experiences. Weight loss slimmed them all over, but didn't alter their proportions.

Exercise did.

Was it because regular vigorous physical activity changes alpha/beta receptor ratios? Or deactivated LPL? Or was there some other physiological mechanism at work. Who knows?

The important thing is that diet plus exercise seems to accomplish what diet alone can't. Give women better-proportioned, more attractive, toned-up bodies.

Staying "Up" with Exercise

Here's another one for the exercise bonus file: Many doctors and mental health professionals now view brisk physical activity as an inexpensive, versatile, and potent "wonder drug," with the potential to ease nervous tension, alleviate stress symptoms, lift sagging spirits, help insomniacs sleep sounder and longer—and, yes, even suppress appetite in the overweight.

How does exercise work all these diverse wonders? Theories abound, but all have to do with the fact that moving your muscles triggers a number of chemical changes within the mind and body.

For one thing, exercise revs up circulation and delivers more oxygen to cells throughout the body, including, of course, the brain. Think of it this way. Increased oxygenation, even *without* exercise, can have a calming effect—one reason why actors and public speakers often take ten deep slow breaths before confronting an audience. It's also why many people, when they're emotionally overwrought and on the verge of saying or doing something they'll regret, feel an urge to step outside "for a breath of fresh air." They know instinctively that they'll be less tense, better able to deal with problem situations when they return.

Well, if deep breathing and fresh air, both of which help infuse the brain with more oxygen, are calming and ease edginess, imagine what the far greater reoxygenating effects of a few minutes of cycling, brisk walking, or swimming can do for mood and mind!

Perhaps even more significant in the context of mood enhancement is that sustained vigorous activity increases the brain's production of certain substances. One theory seeking to explain the positive influence of exercise on mood and behavior focuses on endorphins. Sometimes called the body's own "natural tranquilizers," these substances, produced by the brain, are similar to morphine in their chemical structure. And, like morphine, endorphins can lift gloomy moods, tranquilize feelings of stress, blunt physical pain and emotional distress. A boost in endorphin production may be one of the factors contributing to "runners' high." And endorphines produce feelings of well-being and reduced anxiety, without the horrendous side effects of addicting drugs.

Another theory is that exercise prompts the release of a natural stimulant, produced by the brain, called norepinephrine. Norepinephrine, it seems, is in shorter-than-normal supply in people who are feeling down—sad, draggy, disappointed, depressed. But with physical activity, many of these negative symptoms are ameliorated, or even disappear. Researchers speculate this is because exercise gets the brain to make more of this mood-altering chemical.

Regular vigorous exercise not only elevates norepinephrine and endorphin production, it also appears to increase reserve supplies of these substances, so that in times of emotional distress, they're ready and waiting to help us cope better and even think more clearly.

As for premenstrual headaches, edginess, and downs, regular exercisers report fewer and less intense symptoms than other women. How come? It could be the tranquilizing effects of pain-reducing, mood-mellowing beta-endorphins. Or the uplift that comes with increased supplies of norepinephrine. Maybe it's because physical activity helps to moderate production of female hormones estrogen and progesterone. It's even possible that by making us sweat, exercise relieves the premenstrual discomforts associated with water retention. Or it could be any combination of the above. The important point is, physical activity tends to make women feel better even on the most difficult days of the month.

Obviously, the ability to remain calm and "up" is an advantage regardless of whether a person is normal weight or overweight. But it's especially valuable to the female dieter.

Many of us, you see, are mood-motivated eaters. Our minds automatically turn to thoughts of greasy sweets or starches when things start to go wrong. The stress-easing effects of exercises can help us stay in control long enough to think twice about junking out. And second thoughts can make all the difference between being "good" and adhering to get-slim eating principles, and going off the deep end and into an eating orgy.

I know that's how it has been for many of the women I counsel. I program of regular vigorous exercise seems to "condition" them emotionally as well as physically. Instead of reaching for something to eat at the first sign of trouble, they're often able to remain in control long enough to remind themselves that food won't solve anything.

Physical activity is not a cure-all for the big and little emotional upsets each and every one of us encounters every day. But because of the chemical changes it stimulates within the body and brain—changes that can help us *cope more constructively*—it may be the next best thing.

Exercise is *so* important that one of the first questions I ask women who are feeling down or stressed out is "do you exercise?" If the answer is no (and your doctor gives you the go-ahead) my recommendation is always the same. "It's time you started." That's my advice to you as well.

Of course sustained low moods should be checked out by your doctor. But vigorous physical activity can set off a marvelous chain reaction: just going through the motions and sticking to an exercise routine will make you feel better about yourself. As you gain strength and as you meet your exercise goals, your self-esteem will increase and you'll feel more confident about accomplishing other goals in your life—including your goal of losing weight. Not only that, exercise will help you maintain a positive frame of mind. Little niggling problems won't get you down as much as they used to. And even when you're up against a big problem, you'll be better able to resist the urge to "comfort" yourself with self-destructive eating. You'll see.

Exploding the Muscle Myth

There are always a few women in my diet groups who are reluctant to start exercising in a major way because they're afraid of developing a muscular, mannish build.

If this is one of your concerns, forget it.

The male hormone testosterone is largely responsible for the shape and muscularity of a man's body—just as estrogen plays a major role in the development of our softer, weaker, less muscular, and yes, fatter figures. Lacking high levels of testosterone, you would have to exercise many times harder and longer than a normal male in order to build up bulging biceps, triceps, pecs, etc.

In other words, if your testosterone levels are in the normal range—and you don't make a fetish of weight lifting like the women you see in the bodybuilding magazines— exercise won't make you a muscle monster.

This is a mixed blessing. The calorie cost of maintaining muscles is much greater than that needed to maintain fat. (That's one reason men lose pounds faster.) If physical activity did give women hunking muscles—as it quickly can for men—weight control would be a lot easier for us. But as the childbearers of the species, nature made us fat prone, not muscle bound.

Exercise will produce muscles enough to strengthen and firm your body, reduce jiggle and flab, help define your waist, tone your hips, thighs, and rear, and slim your arms and calves.

It *won't* turn you into the Hulk.

Ahhh...the Afterglow

Okay. Now you're tuned in to the positive effects of increased physical activity on your metabolism, hormones, alpha and beta receptors, the enzyme LPL, brown fat, mood, etc. You're geared up and gung ho to get started.

But wait a minute. There are two more benefits you should know about. Both have to do with what happens *after* you exercise. For one, during the postworkout period, your metabolism stays revved up for a while. That means your body continues to burn calories at an accelerated rate . . . *extra* calories, expended in addition to the ones you used up during the time you were active! In effect, these are free calories. You don't have to lift a finger or toe to get rid of them.

Just how long does this afterburn last? Some experts say less than an hour. Others calculate that the effect can linger on for the rest of the day. But even just an hour's worth of increased calorie burning is a great little bonus. And as your body becomes more muscular, and less fat, you'll burn even more calories, since the muscle tissue is more "active" than fat. With activity, brown fat also fries off more calories.

Added to all the other exercise benefits, this calorie burn-off is the icing on the cake . . . or, maybe the luscious strawberry on top of the bowl of chilled blueberries.

And then—haven't you noticed?—when you exercise vigorously, your cheeks get pink and your whole body takes on a rosy hue. This blushing effect indicates that blood is being carried to your skin, and with it, needed nutrients, more oxygen, and more water. In exchange, more wastes are removed. With vigorous activity, skin is nourished, moisturized—and more collagen is produced. In fact, studies comparing women who don't exercise with those who do, find that exercisers have fewer wrinkles and bags!

Are you ready to get going?

11 How to Make Exercise Work for You

Estimates vary, at least for starters, say the experts, you should try to work up to twenty minutes of aerobic activity at least four times a week.

I can almost hear you groaning. "There's no time." "It's boring." "I look horrible in shorts (leotard, bathing suit, jogging clothes)."

But the only way to take full advantage of the whole spectrum of exercise benefits and improve health, your mood, and the shape of your shape is to get out there and aim for that twenty minutes four times a week. Think of it this way: Just ten minutes of brisk walking in one direction, and then you get to do an about-face. Come on . . . is that so grim?

Maybe you won't exercise for cardiovascular (heart/artery) fitness or to limit your risk of osteoporosis and other diseases. (For most women, I've found, health reasons are the least motivating.) But you do want to tone up your body, keep your mood upbeat, and increase calorie burn-off, don't you? All these benefits are yours for a mere twenty minutes four times a week. No shrink or beauty salon offers as much in return for so little. What a bargain!

We don't know how much physical activity it takes before some of the other fat-fighting effects kick in—

effects such as the rebalancing of the profat hormones, altering alpha/beta receptor ratios, deactivating fat-padding LPL, and stimulating fat-burning brown fat. But most educated guessers agree that four, twenty-minute aerobic sessions per week should do it.

Aerobics Defined

The word "aerobic" has been used so often and so loosely that I'm not surprised many women think it's a synonym for "vigorous." Aerobic exercise *is* vigorous, but all vigorous activity is not aerobic. Aerobic exercises are those that *increase your heart rate, make you breathe deeply, and keep large muscle groups in continuous motion for sustained periods of time*.

By that definition all of the following are aerobic:

Brisk walking	Swimming	Cross Country skiing
Jogging	Biking	Using a rowing machine
Running	Disco dancing	Jumping on a trampoline

Ice-skating, roller-skating, and fast ball sports such as handball and racquetball are aerobic, too, if done continuously, in nonstop motion. (I don't know about you, but when I skate, I spend most of the time in a panic, hanging on to the side of the rink for dear life. And that's not aerobic.)

"Stop and go" exercises and sports that require momentary bursts of effort, interspersed with periods of standing still or "waiting time" can be good for calorie burn-off and muscle tone, but they're *not* aerobic. For example, softball, golf, bowling, weight lifting, karate, and those stretch-and-bend calisthenics featured in women's magazines (the sort that tell you to tighten your tummy muscles while standing in the checkout lines), all fall into the nonaerobic category. They may strengthen certain muscle groups, but they don't turn on the body's antifat mechanisms.

If you're not sure whether an activity is aerobic or not ask yourself the following questions:

- Does it make my heart beat a little faster?
- Does it make me breathe more deeply?
- Does it require me to keep my leg and/or arm muscles moving continuously?

Three yes answers and you can be 99-percent positive that the exercise is aerobic and will give you the broadest range of fat-fighting advantages—but only if you do it for at least twenty minutes four times a week.

(Sorry to say, but even with a vigorous partner, sex is not aerobic. You may be huffing and puffing, your heart may beat faster, and large muscle groups may be moving about. But the actual *activity*, the thrusting, doesn't last twenty minutes. At least as far as I know from my experience, from what other women tell me, and from reports I've read.)

How to Plan a Personalized Workout Routine

Even some of the most super-motivated women—the ones who really *want* to get moving and start losing weight and fat—haven't the foggiest idea how to get started.

Many of them have been active with housework, "running" errands (which usually means driving), picking up after everyone, cooking, and working outside the home at paid work or volunteer activities. But they don't do any real "aerobic" activities, the kind that helps get the fat out. And they never did.

So, when these women want to start on an exercise program, they don't know what they're getting into. They don't know what they can or can't do. They don't know where to begin, what to begin with, or even how to begin.

If you've had a weight problem for more than a few years, or even if your problems are recent but you never thought about getting physical before, you might be in the same boat. Not to worry. I'll take you step-by-step through the how's of getting started.

1. *Most important, don't do anything out of the ordinary before you check with your doctor.* Tell her or him you want to start exercising and explain your goal: twenty minutes of aerobic activity at least four times a week. Your physician might want you to undergo a series of tests to make sure your heart, lungs, knees, ankles, etc. can "take it." There's always a possibility that physical problems will restrict your activities. DON'T IGNORE YOUR DOCTOR'S ADVICE. If you engage in the wrong type of exercise, you might end up flat on your back in bed for days.

2. *After you've been cleared to begin, start slowly.* This is crucial, no matter what activity you've chosen, and even if you are young and in tip-top condition except for your weight.

Doing too much too soon is the number-one reason for exercise burnout. Don't forget a body that hasn't been used for years is vulnerable to strains, sprains, aches, and fatigue, and these are surefire turnoffs. I've seen it happen all too often. Two or three days of overdoing and the would-be exerciser decides it's not worth it after all and lapses back into comfy, fat-coddling idleness. (I've done it with a Hula Hoop I bought to burn calories while also getting my rump and tummy into shape. With just three go-rounds, I threw my back out. Aloha, Hula Hoop.)

Don't let it happen to you. Forget about "no pain, no gain." Pain means cut it out this very minute.

3. *Warm up and cool down.* Just as easing into any new activity is important, so, too, is easing into the one you do well—each and every time. *Always* take a few minutes or so to warm up before, and cool down later. Ballet dancers, professional ball players, and gymnasts all do it. You should, too. Get a book on your chosen form of exercise, or ask an exercise coach how best to bend and stretch before your workout. After that, start your session slowly. If you're into stationary biking, begin with low tension. The same with the rowing machine. If you've chosen brisk walking, just amble along for the first few

minutes. Cool down and stretch out after exercise—this gets circulation gently back to normal and helps prevent postworkout stiffness or soreness. Of course, this extends your workout period, but it's an essential few minutes extra.

4. *Consider the best beginner activity of all—walking.* Walking is easy, requires no special equipment other than good sturdy shoes, and you're already an expert at it!

Start by walking an extra five minutes every couple of days. Keep the pace relaxed and comfortable at first. Every few days add a minute or two and increase your pace slightly. As you go farther and faster, get your arms into the act by swinging or pumping them as you stride along.

Your goal, remember, is to work up to a brisk twenty-minute walk four times a week, minimum. (Five or more times for forty-five minutes would be even better.) What's brisk? Some people try to get up to a certain heart rate, and check their pulse to see if they're into their "target range." (I get all mixed up trying to find, measure, and determine my proper pulse.) Some try to keep going until they're sweated up, or strap gizmos to their legs to determine their miles per hour. Let me give you an easier formula: Brisk walking should have you huffing and puffing, but not so much that you cannot carry on a normal conversation. Gasping is not the goal!

Some women buckle weights to their ankles, which burns a few more calories and helps tone legs, but be careful. I twisted my ankle when the five-pound weights I wore rotated my legs out over the sidewalk.

Go for the basics: a brisk walk. Brisk walking may be all you'll ever need or want to do. In fact, many exercise physiologists consider it the *ideal* aerobic activity; it conditions heart and lungs and helps prevent loss of bone density as well as any other exercise, but is less stressful to bones, joints, muscles, and tendons than jogging, aerobic dancing, jumping rope, etc.

But isn't walking *too* easy to burn off extra calories? I'm often asked. The answer is no. It costs the same number of calories to walk a mile as it does to run a mile, believe it or not, since energy expenditure is determined by moving your legs and covering a certain distance. In other words, it "costs" the same number of calories to walk a mile as to run a mile. (You would, of course, burn off more calories running for two minutes than walking for two minutes, since in running you'd cover more ground.)

Brisk walking has just about everything going for it, including the fact that it's an excellent preconditioner for other activities you might want to move on to.

5. *Vary your routine.* Next to taking on too much too soon, boredom is the most-often-cited reason for becoming a fitness dropout.

If you love walking and never tire of it, then keep it up. But if and when it becomes all work and no fun, why not consider a different route, walking with a partner or hiking group, or striding along with a "Walkman" buddy. Another possibility is choosing among the many other aerobic options open to you.

My own personal nominee for next best beginner exercise is swimming. It's even kinder to an underexercised body than walking, and it works all the muscle groups from head to toe, whereas in putting one foot in front of another on solid ground, legs get most of the benefit.

Now, you may be horrified at the thought of making a public appearance in a bathing suit. I was. In fact, I must have been the only woman to make a debut at the pool area of my gym bundled up in a voluminous long caftan. But I discovered right away that most of the other swimmers were not Miss Body Beautiful either. You'll see. Women of all shapes and sizes swim and work out at health clubs and gyms. It may not be flattering, but it is a comfort to realize that the ones who get ogled are the ones with the great figures; the rest of us may as well be invisible for all the attention anyone pays us.

Swimming does have its drawbacks. Because the body floats, you miss out on some of the bone-strengthening effects of "weight-bearing" exercise. But this minus can be a plus if your joints are weak and should not be overstressed. Swimming also requires some skill (though you actually burn off more calories if you're a lousy swimmer who flails away than if you're an expert who glides effortlessly through the water). And of course you must have access to a pool.

As in walking, easy does it at first. A few minutes of slow, gentle swimming is enough for the first week or so. Gradually increase your distance until you are regularly doing twenty minutes at least four times a week. And don't stick to the same stroke lap after lap, day after day. You'll be less bored and get a better workout if you do the crawl for a few minutes, then sidestroke, backstroke, breaststroke, etc. (Of course, don't hang on to the edge with each lap or change of stroke—keep going for that twenty minutes.)

And just as varying your swimming strokes can make time in the water more enjoyable, a whole repertoire of activities can make exercise more fun. You might, for example, walk one day, swim the next, take an aerobic class another day, and go biking with a friend the fourth. It's a way to beat the boredom factor, and it's even better for your body than performing the same exercise every day. Because different activities use different muscle groups in different ways, a varied regimen can add up to better all-over toning.

Mini-tip: In increasing your exercise options, look for at least one that gives you a change of pace and "neutralizes" the demands of what you do all day on the job.

Example: Since my work requires concentration and total focusing on other people, I look forward to swimming as an opportunity to zone out and let my mind wander. No talking, no phones. Just my own breathing and the gentle swooshing of the water.

Colleen, on the other hand, is a wife and mother who spends almost all day every day tending her two-year-old twin daughters. Early morning (5:00 A.M.!) walking/talking with a neighbor helps satisfy her need for adult female companionship.

Jessica is an ace secretary with two crotchety bosses.

"I have to take a lot of guff," she says. "They sometimes drive me *crazy*." Jessica vents her anger and frustration without jeopardizing her job with fast and furious games of racquetball that allow her to let off steam, slamming the ball, as she burns off calories.

A word of caution: Don't make the mistake of assuming that just because you are in condition for one type of activity you can plunge into vigorous sessions of another activity without adequate preparation. To do so might result in pulled muscles or worse. Take it from me. After swimming for months, I attempted a "slow stretch" class and did my darndest to keep up with the group. But the next day, I couldn't stretch slow, much less walk, without aches and pains. Much better is to start each new activity much as you did the first: slowly and gradually. And always warm up and cool down as well.

6. *Be patient and persistent.* It may take a few months before you have the endurance to jog, swim, bike, etc., for a full twenty minutes. So what? Every move you make along the way helps burn off extra calories, firm flab, and promote antifat changes within your body. In the meantime, try to add a minute, thirty seconds, even fifteen seconds to your time every few days without forcing yourself beyond your capabilities. Eventually you will achieve your goal.

7. *Recognize these danger signals.* I've emphasized the go-slow approach to physical activities, but it's especially important to take it easy at first if you're an exercise beginner. Even if your doctor says you're in good shape except for your weight, you should be alert to warning signs, such as breathing difficulty (deep breathing is fine, gasping means stop), rapid heartbeat, sharp pains. These aren't to be ignored. Maybe some super-fit young jock can "work through the pain," but for us, pain means trouble.

If you feel weak, nauseated, or dizzy, do not go for that one more round, hill, lap, rep, minute, or mile. Slow up or stop.

And, of course, don't exercise if you're sick. Your body needs a rest to heal itself. Besides, your body uses (and needs) its energy for fighting infections and healing. People who do exercise, however, seem to become ill less often. Why? One guess is that since exercise heats the body, it acts like a temperature, killing off invading bugs and germs!

How to Fit Fitness into Your Schedule

If time's a problem, join the club. Almost everyone— and I'm no exception—has trouble squeezing exercise into a life that's already overcrowded with commitments and obligations. However, I'm convinced that with enough motivation and creativity, you *can* beat the clock.

Kristy, for example, wanted to be more active but said she couldn't find a time slot for regular exercise. "Every hour of every day is already jammed," she sighed. "There's work, my night-school classes, and my boyfriend. I can't leave my job, obviously. It's important to get my degree. And I don't want to give up my boyfriend. So tell me, how can I exercise?"

I was stumped. Then I asked her what she did between 5:00 P.M. when she finished work and 7:30 when her classes started. Kristy caught my drift immediately. "No way! I'm not about to go jumping around during that time. I need that hour and a half to change gears from work, eat dinner, and study."

Kristy was a toughy. "How about getting off the bus one stop before the college?" I asked.

But Kristy had the "perfect problem"—she wanted to do something perfectly or not at all. "That's only a ten-minute walk. What's the good of that?"

"It's a start."

But from that start, Kristy really took off. She gradually increased the distance until she was walking all the way from the coffee shop where she had dinner to the library where she studied. Soon she discovered that the thirty-minute walk was actually more beneficial than lingering over a second cup of coffee. She tells me that on the evenings when she gets to school on foot, she arrives feeling less fatigued, better able to study before classes, and more alert and receptive during classes! Could be coincidence, of course, but I doubt it. She's convinced, and so am I, that brisk walking wakes up her body and her mind.

Michelle, thirty-five, has three schoolagers, a part-time job, and does Red Cross volunteer work several evenings a week. Like Kristy, she saw no easy way to integrate exercise into her life. But she was determined to make the time. Always an early riser, Michelle now sets her alarm clock to go off half an hour before her usual wake-up time, goes into the den, slips an aerobic exercise tape into the VCR, and gets in thirty minutes of exercise—including a five-minute warm-up and cool down—before kids and husband wake up!

Dara holds down a full-time job and is completing a college degree at the age of fifty. She combines studying with pedaling the stationary bike set up in a corner of her bedroom. Impossible? Not so. The handlebars of the bike are fitted with a book rest. Once she gets started, her legs do all the work, leaving her mind free to concentrate on French verbs.

See what I mean? Where there's a will, there's definitely a way. It may mean juggling your schedule around, slicing minutes off the time you used to spend on other things, even perhaps paring away nonessentials. For instance, Terry decided she could live without her favorite sitcoms and now spends three evenings a week doing laps at a nearby health club. "I can actually see my body shaping up. I like myself better for not being a couch potato . . . and then there's this fabulous man who swims the same nights I do. Was it worth becoming an ex–Cosby addict? You bet!"

The Anything-Goes Approach for Even Better Results

I've emphasized aerobics because they are the exercises that pay off with the widest range of antifat benefits. Concentrate your efforts on one or more aerobic activities. Move along at your own pace and in your own preferred way.

In the meantime, however, don't forget that anything and everything that gets you up and out of that chair and moving your muscles, "costs" calories. That includes nonaerobic exercises, like working out on machines, calisthenics, karate classes, volleyball, or touch football with the kids. Anything.

The possibilities are practically infinite for mixing aerobic with other activities and coming up with a routine that's fun, suits your present state of fitness, and rewards you with the fat-fighting advantages you want and need.

Even small exertions you probably never thought of as "exercise" count!

Instead of carrying four bags of groceries into the house at once, make four trips back and forth from the car to the side door. Instead of handing car keys to the valet, leave your car a few blocks away and walk to the restaurant. At the shopping mall, park as far away from the stores as you can. Instead of riding the elevator up two or three floors, take the stairs. When there's an escalator, climb it—some women get their calves in such great shape that they begin taking the steps two at a time!

When you're seeing a man, try to arrange it so that at least some of your dates are "active." (I hear you giggling out there. Well if sex is not aerobic, "active" sex is at least toning.) Instead of all movies and plays, suggest an occasional game of badminton, a bike ride, dancing . . . or a long, romantic walk along the beach at sunset.

As for me, sometimes, late at night when I feel too restless to sleep or work, I pace my room. Or I turn on the radio and shimmy like I'd never do at a disco. Or I play a tape of my favorite orchestral works and furiously conduct the allegro. Really! Try it! Conducting, even with a pencil, is great for firming upper arms. Even rocking in a rocking chair helps tone legs and stomach.

I could go on and on, but you've got the idea. Minor efforts such as these, along with regular "real exercise" can net you even faster, surer weight loss. The more you do, within reason, the greater the fat burn-off, and the sooner you'll see the results on the scale and in the mirror.

How Much Is Too Much?

Though I've been urging you onward and upward throughout this chapter, I don't agree with many exercise "authorities" that more and more, and harder and harder, is always better and better.

Exercise, because it helps reduce body fat, can result in decreased estrogen production—and with less fat-storing estrogen working against you, weight control becomes easier. However, too *much* exercise, too rapid a weight loss, too few calories, or an unbalanced diet can cause estrogen levels and/or body fat to drop low enough to interrupt the menstrual cycle. Ballerinas are the classic cases in point, as are female bodybuilders, and those women who crash-diet, even if they *don't* get skinny; among these groups cessation of periods is not uncommon.

I know a few women nowhere near the usual age for menopause who claim they'd love not to have to bother with periods. In fact, many women, given the choice, would probably prefer to live without the monthly hassle of menstruation.

What most of them don't understand is that super-low levels of estrogen, the hormone that governs the menstrual cycle, is risky with regard to the bone degeneration associated with osteoporosis.

Dry, old-looking skin, lacking in tone, and a drastic decrease in vaginal secretions, rendering lovemaking almost impossible without the use of a lubricant, are two other side effects of diminished estrogen production. And I know you don't want to put up with crepelike skin and painful sex.

The goal of the Bodyrhythm Diet is to beat bulges. Not to overexercise or drastically cut calories. The goal is to lose fat, get toned, but keep enough body fat—about 20 percent of your weight—to maintain normal estrogen production. Enough of this female hormone, in other words, to keep your body functioning normally and your skin moist and elastic.

Do your best to be more active. Work up to twenty to thirty minutes of aerobics at least four times a week—more if possible. Participate in sports, games, and other physical activities (like walking through museums, window-shopping, visiting the zoo) whenever you can.

Take every opportunity to burn off extra calories with mini-exercises, the extra efforts you make when you climb stairs or walk instead of driving to the post office, etc. If you stick to these simple guidelines when you plan your personal fitness program, you should reap all the antifat benefits of exercise, without the potential drawbacks of overdoing.

A Better Body...Plus

I'm still looking for the magic that will give me *really* streamlined hips and thighs. And if I could have my way, my bust would be a little more voluptuous. (Wouldn't it be great if we could figure out an easy way to take excess fat and use it to fill out our defects?)

All in all, though, I wouldn't trade my slimmer, better-shaped-up body for the shapeless, bulging blob that was me in my twenties.

Learning how to eat, and why, made a difference. Learning how to exercise and why was almost as important. They're complementary. Together, diet and exercise helped me get rid of the fat that made me miserable. Diet and exercise are keeping it off.

But that's not all. Diet and exercise have done other things for me and for other women as well. Losing fat and shaping up helped them generate a new body confidence that translates into more *self*-confidence. Self-confidence that carries over into work and relationships. After all, we beat the odds. We did what statistics tell us is almost impossible to do. We lost weight and are keeping it off.

Over the years, I've seen many woman go from fat and full of doubt to slim and self-confident. For some it took a few months. For others, longer. But physical re-formation, when it happens, is almost always accompanied by positive changes in the way a woman feels about herself, her potential, and her capabilities.

I'm no superwoman and neither are most of the women I've counseled, even the most successful ones. So how did we do what so many other women want to do but can't? I think it has to do with understanding and accepting the fact that compared with men, we tend to be fat-prone. And, after accepting this dismal fact, learning how to eat and exercise in ways that work with our female bodies. That, in a nutshell is what the Women's Bodyrhythm Diet is all about.

We did it. We re-formed our bodies. And in the process, we're enjoying better health, more energy, and greater self-confidence. If we did it, I think you can do it too.

12 | Maintenance Eating: A Better Body from Now On!

Bodyrhythm Diet principles will result in a new and improved body. Most of you may be amazed at how quickly and easily pounds disappear with simple Stage I/Stage II eating. On the other hand, if you are especially diet-resistant, success will take longer. Just hang in there and persist! With the Bodyrhythm Diet you *can* win the fight against fat.

Now here's a fact most dieters would rather not face up to so soon after achieving success: You can't just fix fat once and then forget about good eating habits—not if you want to stay sleek and shaped up. Remember, nature seems to prefer a well-padded female body and will always do her best to make you conform to her wishes. She'll try to plump you up again by upping your appetite for certain foods and making cravings hard to ignore.

It's maintenance eating to the rescue! I developed the Maintenance Phase of the Bodyrhythm Diet to help you consolidate your losses, defuse cravings, and stay as trim as the day you achieved your weight goal. With the Maintenance Phase, you should be able to outwit nature, keep cravings under better control, and help keep your mood and energy up where you want them.

Maintenance Basics

Maintenance breakfasts, lunches, and dinners are similar in format to the meals you ate on the Bodyrhythm Diet—and for the same reasons: starches (high-fiber are still best), proteins, and small amounts of fat that are the building blocks of every maintenance meal work together to help keep the pro-fat hormones estrogen, progesterone, and insulin in better balance; minimize cravings and mood swings; and, of course, supply you with the nutrients you need to feel and look your best.

But in the Maintenance Phase, you will have a wider variety of foods from which to choose.

For example, whereas on the diet your starch choices were limited to cereal, bread, or rolls, in the Maintenance Phase you can have any of these, OR favorites such as corn on the cob, baked potato, rice, or pasta, to name just a few. Your protein and fat options are similarly expanded. You can even have wine, ethnic foods, and desserts.

As for the all-important matter of cravings, when you feel vulnerable to nagging food urges, you will simply double up (or triple up) on starch portions, and, if necessary, choose a higher-fat protein.

For most women, after they lose weight, it's starch they want, and it's starch—in larger, but *controlled* portions— that usually satisfies the urge to junk out. Higher-fat proteins can help, too, but starch gives you more of what your body cries out for on craving days—enough, usually, to keep cravings manageable, but not enough to pile on unwanted pounds.

The Maintenance Formula

Extras can be added, and you can vary the Maintenance Plan from time to time according to your appetite, and for special occasions (more about how, why, and when, later). But on *most* days, adhere to the antifat Maintenance food plan that follows.

Breakfast

1-ounce portion cereal

8 ounces low-fat milk

Sound familiar? That's because maintenance breakfasts are identical to the ones you ate on the diet itself. However, for variety, you can create a breakfast consisting of:

1 portion of any Maintenance Starch

2-ounce portion of any Maintenance Protein (or, 1 egg, 2 egg whites, 1 ounce low-fat hard cheese, or ¼-cup low-fat soft cheese.)

1 portion of any Maintenance Fats

Lunch and Dinner

1 portion Maintenance Starch*

3-ounce portion Maintenance Protein* (or equivalent)

1 portion Maintenance Fats

Free Foods, as much as you like.

Remember, when cravings are a problem, doubling the starch portion and choosing a higher-fat protein should help bring them under control.

Snacks

Free foods: Low-cal vegetables are "allowed" whenever you feel the urge to munch. No need to keep tabs on how much you eat. But do restrict your choices to the "free" vegetables.

Fruit: As on the diet, limit yourself to two pieces of fruit per day. Choose one that is high in vitamin C. On craving-less days, select as your second fruit one of the lower-sugar varieties. When cravings are a problem, a fruit with a slightly higher sugar content should help satisfy your body's demands for more carbs.

Calcium-required foods: Don't skip them. Two servings of milk (or equivalent) are an important part of Maintenance Phase eating.

Maintenance Starch Choices

As you'll see, Maintenance Phase eating offers a much wider variety of starches than the diet itself. But it's definitely not anything goes.

Rice is fine, for example, but not if it's fried. A potato is terrific, and you can even top it with sour cream (if sour cream is your fat choice for the meal). But creamed potatoes and french fries are out as regulars. Plain rolls, crackers, bread, muffins, are in. But croissants, Danish pastry, cake, pie, doughnuts, and other fat-loaded baked goods should be saved for once-in-a-while special occasions.

Limit your choices to those listed below. If you select the starches listed, in the amounts specified, 90 percent of the time, you should be able to maintain your body beautiful.

NOTE: FOR EXTRA HELP ON CRAVING DAYS, DOUBLE UP ON THE STARCH PORTIONS LISTED BELOW.

Maintenance Starches

One serving equals one ounce of the following (double up—have two servings—if cravings become a problem):

Breads, cereals (hot or cold), crackers, muffins, rolls, or even tortillas; whole-grain always works best.

(Hint: Watch out for sweetened breads, rolls, or muffins, especially those with added dates, coconut, raisins, berries, nuts, etc. They are little cakes in muffin or bread disguises. Hint #2: Put a slice of bread, a roll, cracker, or tortilla to the scale test—some rolls weigh in at a hefty four ounces. Hint #3: Hold a slice of "regular" bread; this weighs about one ounce. Remember that weight as a way to judge the weight of other bread products.)

or,

One-half cup of the following (measured after cooking):

Dried beans, such as navy, lima, soy, garbanzo, red, white, or pinto. (Hint: In Mexican restaurants, refried beans are refried in gobs of lard—don't order them.)

Corn or peas. (Hint: If you use canned beans, corn, or peas, rinse well.)

Grains and pastas, including barley, bulgur, groats, grits, rice, noodles, spaghetti, macaroni, etc. (Hints: Remember, that's cooked measurement. Look for whole-grain, high-fiber pastas and brown rice or other whole-grain products.)

Root vegetables; beets, carrots, parsnips, rutabagas, sweet potatoes, turnips, leeks, onions, white potatoes, and yams are the most common root vegetables. (Hint: Think of two eggs fused together—that's about a half cup, or one serving root vegetable. Restaurants usually serve a "four-egg" potato—two servings in other words. Hint #2: A cup of mashed potatoes, with butter or cream, doesn't count or add up to keeping your weight off—a cup of mashed potatoes is 280 calories, *before* gravy or butter blob. A cup of fries is 450 plus calories—skip them, too.)

Winter squash: these are the squashes that are yellow or orange inside, such as acorn, butternut, hubbard—pumpkins too. (Hint: Summer squash, those with whitish flesh, such as zucchini and crookneck, are less starchy, and count as "free foods.")

or,

Four cups popcorn. (Hint: that's plain popcorn—no butter or salt added. Of course, I don't expect you to eat popcorn as a starch at meals, but you could. Rather, if you are a popcorn addict, *skip* your usual mealtime starch and plan to eat the popcorn for later.)

Maintenance Protein Choices

Too little protein might equal hunger or cravings, and the last thing you need when you are trying to maintain your weight is a stomach crying out for more food. Too much—especially of the wrong, fatty proteins—and you can activate your body's fat-storing mechanisms. A happy protein medium is important, and that's what Bodyrhythm Maintenance meals give you.

For maintaining your weight, you can add variety to breakfast by having a Maintenance Breakfast Protein Choice such as an egg, a small pork chop, or even two ounces of tuna. (Many women eat half a tuna sandwich for breakfast and say it seems to boost their energy all morning long!) You'll read more about Breakfast Maintenance Menus in later pages. As for lunch and dinner, you can have three ounces of Bodyrhythm Diet Protein or its equivalent at lunch and dinner.

Remember, stick to low-fat (Stage I) choices when you are craving less. When and if you feel threatened by nagging food urges, you can have lunch and dinner proteins that are slightly higher in fat (the Stage II proteins, in other words). These should help blunt cravings and prevent backsliding and binges.

A word to the wise: Some women assume that once down to their weight goal, they can eat any protein they like, in any amount. Don't do it. Too much of the higher-fat proteins when you don't need them to help prevent pigouts means more fat where you don't want it.

A few protein pointers:

Avoid fried, breaded, sauced, buttered, and sautéd dishes. If you want sauce, have it "on the side"; use one tablespoon and count it as a fat portion. Continue to remove the skin from poultry and any visible fat before cooking.

No duck, goose, beef, or pork ribs, the wings and backs of poultry—these are mostly fat. Steer clear of high-fat, high-salt processed meats, including bacon, ham, sausage, and cold cuts—all around 75-percent fat. If you really crave some smoked fish—lox, smoked cod, or finnan haddie—buy it at a fish market (less salty than canned or packaged), take it home, and rinse it. It'll taste about the same, but contain much less salt. A bonus: When rinsing, some of the fat also goes down the drain.

Weigh your protein portions now and then to make sure you haven't lost touch with "reality."

The complete protein list—low-fat and higher-fat choices—is in Chapter 8.

Breakfast Protein Choices

When you're bored with "standard" Bodyrhythm Breakfast (you remember it—one ounce of cereal with eight ounces low-fat milk), you can select one of the following proteins for breakfast, along with one Maintenance Starch and one Maintenance Fat choice.

Choose one:

¼ cup cottage, pot, hoop, or farmer cheese (low-fat is best)

1 ounce hard cheese (low-fat is best)

2 ounces fish, shellfish, chicken, or red meat

1 egg or 3 egg whites

Lunch or Dinner Proteins

For *craving-less* days, choose *one* of the following:

3 ounces low-fat fish (the "white" ones)

3 ounces skinless white meat poultry, or game hen

3 ounces shellfish

½ cup cottage, pot, or farmer cheese (low-fat is best)

6 egg whites

For *craving-more days*, when doubling up on starch isn't enough to tune out nagging food urges, you can try a higher-fat lunch protein, such as:

3 ounces higher-fat fish (the "darker" fish)

3 ounces skinless dark-meat poultry

2 eggs, or 1 whole egg and 3 egg whites

2 ounces hard cheese, preferably low-fat or made with skim milk.

Maintenance Fat Choices

Back in the diet section, I explained why a small amount of fat is an important part of every Bodyrhythm Diet meal. You still need some fat now, when you are trying to hold the line against weight gain, for the same reasons you needed it then: to help you feel comfortably full for longer periods after a meal, to facilitate vitamin absorption, and to minimize cravings.

But don't overdo the fats. Remember, fat calories are more fattening calories and they have a way of accumulating. Especially in areas where your particular body wants to pile on pounds. If you tend to be pear-shaped, consuming more fat will make you regain below. If you are apple-shaped, your core will spread out. If you are banana-shaped, you won't be chiquita anymore.

Better safe than sorry. Select one of the following fats, *in the amounts specified*, for every meal. As in the diet, you can use margarine or mayo as a spread for bread or rolls. Drizzle dressings on salads or over vegetables, as before. Or use two tablespoons of sour cream on your potato, or have a tablespoon of gravy or sauce on your meat or pasta. Just don't go over your fat allowance of *one* portion of any of the following per meal.

Maintenance Fats

Choose *one* for each meal:

1 teaspoon margarine, oil, or mayonnaise (or if you choose "diet" margarine or "diet" mayo, use 2 teaspoons)

2 teaspoons salad dressing

2 teaspoons peanut butter (Hint: Some think peanut butter is a protein, but since it's at least 75-percent fat, I consider it a fat. I can't have it around, since I *never* eat it by the teaspoon: I eat it by the jarful, fingerful by fingerful.)

1 tablespoon rich sauce (Hint: For a great saucy taste in every bite, try the "dip-prong" maneuver: Lightly dip the tines of your fork into sauce or dressing. Don't scoop, just dip enough so that a thin film of sauce adheres. Now fork up meat, pasta, salad, whatever. More flavor in every mouthful, but a minimal fat/calorie cost.)

1 tablespoon cream cheese (HInt: Cream cheese is *not* cheese. It's 90-percent fat.)

2 tablespoons sour cream (Hint: Nondairy or imitation sour cream is not low-cal. It's the same calories as the "real" thing, and it's often high in saturated fats. Use it if you like, but use the same allotment—two tablespoons.)

⅛ (4-inch diameter) avocado. "Biologically" a fruit, but
considered a fat. (Hint: An eighth is about two tablespoons.)

6 nuts. Good luck. If you can count out six nuts and not
finish off the bag, you're amazing! But if you eat the rest,
don't even think of using nuts as part of your fat allotment.

Maintenance Free Foods and Snacks

Be careful with "free foods." Some women, for example, consider popcorn a free food with no calories. Come
on. Popcorn *is* high in fiber and low in calories, but it's
not "free." Popcorn is corn—and it counts as a starch.

Others think of frozen yogurt as a "free" snack. But
yogurt, even the nonfat kind, is not calorie-free. Many
brands are loaded with sugar. Think of it this way: Jelly
beans and sugar cubes are also nonfat—and hardly qualify
as "diet," "free" foods, or "nonfattening." Nonfat yogurt is nutritious, but count it as part of your calcium
requirement, not as a free food.

For snacks, I suggest you limit yourself to fruit, a glass
of milk, nonfat yogurt, or free vegetables. For unlimited
munching, stick to those free veggies. Eat them raw or so
lightly steamed they are heated rather than cooked. That
way, more sugar stays trapped inside the fiber walls and
out of your body.

Free Foods (Low-carb Vegetables)

Go for the "greens": such as, asparagus, broccoli, green
beans, snow peas, to name a few—all the greens except
limas and green peas.

Go for "whites": Cabbage, summer squashes, cauliflower,
cucumbers, are some—all white veggies except the root
vegetables, such as potatoes, turnips, or onions. And do
not eat high-sodium celery as a free food.

A more specific and complete list of free foods appears in
Chapter 8.

Maintenance Fruit Choices

Two fruits a day are still the rule, even now when your goal is "simply" to keep your weight stable. Fruits offer antifat benefits galore: fiber, which moderates estrogen production; fructose for a slower, more gradual insulin response that helps keep blood sugar levels steady and minimizes hunger; energy; a deliciously sweet taste; plus lots of essential vitamins and minerals.

Fruits should be fresh, whole, and eaten with the peel whenever possible. Fiber is as important as ever—and peeled fruit, as well as canned fruit and fruit juices, just can't compare to whole in terms of fiber content. Eat your fruit fresh, not baked or steamed, since cooking breaks down the cellulose plant walls, freeing more sugar. However, a baked apple or other cooked fruit can be eaten as a special treat, but don't overcook the fruit, and eat the peel when possible.

Remember, fruit is *not* a "free" food. Fruit contains simple sugar, and too much eaten at once can cause a sugar "rush" that mobilizes insulin into more efficient fat-making mode.

Continue to eat one "high C" fruit each day. To avoid carbohydrate overload, save fruits as snacks. When you're relatively craving-free, choose lower-sugar fruits. When cravings mount, have a higher-sugar fruit; it should help appease nagging food urges. In fact, one higher-sugar fruit, plus doubling up on starches, could be enough to keep cravings under control.

Maintenance Fruits
Choose no more than two fruits each day.

High-C fruits: Eat one every day (both stages).

Such as: 1 orange, ½ grapefruit, 1 tangerine, ¼ cantaloupe, 1 cup strawberries, 1/3 papaya

Lower-sugar fruits: Eat one when cravings are low.

Such as: 2 apricots, 1 nectarine, 1 peach, 2 plums, wedge of melon, ½-cup berries, or any high-C fruit

Higher-sugar fruits: Eat one when cravings turn up.
Such as: 1 banana, pear, or apple, 1 cup grapes, 20 cherries, 1 cup watermelon, 1 cup pineapple.

Maintenance Calcium-Required Foods

On the diet, or while maintaining your weight, calcium-rich foods are crucial. As you know, adequate amounts of this important mineral, plus daily exercise, can help keep your bones strong and reduce your risk of osteoporosis. Two glasses of milk each day, or its equivalent, will help meet your needs.

If you are having cereal for breakfast, count the eight ounces of milk you pour over it (drink or use to lighten coffee, tea, or decaf) as half of your calcium requirement for that day. Milk consumed in beverages during the day should also be counted. (Cream or "creamers" do not count as *milk*. Skip them.) When eating out, ask for no- or low-fat milk with your coffee, tea, or decaf, or drink these beverages "straight."

If you prefer not to "drink" the rest of your calcium requirement, you can make up the difference by using skim or powdered milk or buttermilk as a recipe ingredient. Or you can take your milk in the form of nonfat yogurt. (Top it with sliced fresh fruit from the fruit list, and you have your own, fresh-fruit yogurt sundae.)

Have *two* of the following every day.

8 ounces nonfat milk
8 ounces low-fat milk (120 calories max.)
4 ounces canned skim milk (without sugar)
1/3 cup dry powdered nonfat milk
8-ounce cup buttermilk (no more than 120 calories per cup)
¾ cup plain yogurt (without fruit or sweeteners added; made with skim milk)
¾ cup nonfat frozen yogurt (no toppings other than fresh fruit)

Maintenance Seasonings

Sodium can play havoc with a woman's weight because it tends to increase water retention, so watch out! Limit all canned and bottled sauces (such as soy, cocktail sauce, hot sauce, salsa, tomato sauce) to one tablespoon per day. Limit yourself to one stalk celery, one tomato, one carrot, and/or one onion per day. These vegetables are high in natural sodium and/or sugar.

Menu Reminders

For information assembling Bodyrhythm Plan Maintenance basics—starch, protein, fat, milk requirements, and fruit snacks—into tasty, satisfying, and nutritious meals, refer to the menus below. Follow them or use them as "models" for creating menus featuring your own favorite foods.

A reminder: When cravings occur, it's time to double up on starches, switch to higher-fat proteins, and/or choose a higher-sugar fruit.

Often *just one* double-starch, higher-fat protein meal will be enough to moderate cravings and prevent a junkout. Sometimes, *just one* higher-sugar fruit will do the trick . . . a banana, a pear, and the craving, *poof,* is gone!

Menu Basics

MAINTENANCE BREAKFAST PLAN

1 ounce cereal with 8 ounces low-fat milk.
  (Note: If you use nonfat milk on hot cereal, add one fat
    portion.)
or,
Protein Portion: Choose one: ¼ cup soft cheese, 1 ounce hard cheese, 2 ounces fish, shellfish, poultry, or meat, 1 egg or 3 egg whites.

Starch Portion: Choose one, such as: 1 ounce cereal, 1 ounce bread product, ½ cup cooked grains

Fat Portion: Choose one: 1 teaspoon margarine, oil, or butter, 2 tablespoons sour cream, 1 tablespoon cream cheese, or 2 teaspoons peanut butter or diet margarine.

(Note: Breakfast is not a craving time for most women. If cravings do seem to be a problem, have a higher-sugar fruit as a snack between breakfast and lunch. Don't eat double starches early in the morning: it may trigger cravings and hunger. Carbo-overload can also make you feel drained out. Of course, extra fats in the A.M. also make you feel sluggish. Eat as the Maintenance Plan suggests, and cravings or that tired feeling shouldn't be a problem. Don't skip an ingredient. Don't add on.)

MAINTENANCE LUNCH AND DINNER PLANS

CRAVING-LESS DAYS

Protein Portion:
Choose One
½ cup spreadable cheese,
3 ounces low fat fish
3 ounces low-fat poultry
3 ounces shellfish
6 egg whites

Starch Portion:
Choose One
1 ounce bread product
½ cup pasta, beans, grains, corn, or root vegetable
4 cups popcorn

CRAVING-MORE DAYS

Protein Portion:
Choose One
2 ounces hard cheese (low-fat)
3 ounces higher-fat fish
3 ounces higher-fat poultry
3 ounces red meat
2 eggs (or 1 whole egg and 3 whites)

Starch Portion:
Choose One
2 ounces bread product
1 cup pasta, beans, grains, corn, or root vegetable
8 cups popcorn

Fat Portion (Both Stages):
Choose One at Each Meal

1 teaspoon margarine, oil, or mayo
2 teaspoons diet margarine, diet mayo,
  salad dressing, or peanut butter
2 tablespoons sour cream
1 tablespoon rich sauce or gravy
⅛ avocado
6 nuts

Free Foods
Unlimited amounts

Calcium Requirement
1 Cup Milk or Equivalent
(Note: Have two cups if none consumed
at breakfast.)

Fruits

1 high-C fruit   1 high-C fruit
1 lower-sugar fruit   1 higher-sugar fruit

Maintenance Menu Suggestions

Below are seven days of Sample Menus with ideas of what to eat on craving-less days or craving-more days.

Note: I've provided recipes for starred (*) items.

SAMPLE ONE

BREAKFAST

Cook in water:
  1 ounce whole-grain hot cereal
    (such as Wheatena or 7-Grain Cereal)
Stir in:
  2 teaspoons peanut butter
  dash of cinnamon
Pour on (drink, or use in coffee, decaf, or tea):
  8 ounces nonfat milk
(Hint: Since the milk is nonfat, you need to add one fat portion. Here it's two teaspoons of peanut butter.)

Craving-Less Days	Craving-More Days

SNACK

1 medium kiwi

SNACK

1 cup pineapple

LUNCH

(Brown-bagged)
Chicken-Stuffed Potato
Mix together:
3 ounces white-meat chicken,
⅛ avocado
1 teaspoon mustard
1 tablespoon salsa
Stuff into:
½ baked potato

LUNCH

(Brown-bagged)
Chicken-Stuffed Potato
Mix together:
3 ounces dark-meat chicken,
⅛ avocado
1 teaspoon mustard
1 tablespoon salsa
Stuff into:
1 baked potato

(Hint: Wrap the stuffed potato in a plastic bag and zap it *briefly* in the microwave. Don't wrap the potato in foil for the microwave or you'll have an electrified potato and oven.)

SNACK

1/3 papaya

SNACK

1/3 papaya

DINNER

(At home)
3 ounces broiled scallops
Hurried-Curried Rice*
    (using ½-cup rice)
Steamed broccoli,
    snow peas, bell peppers

DINNER

(At home)
3 ounces broiled swordfish,
Hurried-Curried Rice*
    (using 1-cup rice)
Steamed broccoli,
    snow peas, bell peppers

(Hint: Make extra fish and vegetables for lunch the next day as Seafood Salad.*)

SNACK

8 ounces low-fat milk
    heated with vanilla
    extract

SNACK

8 ounces low-fat milk
    heated with vanilla
    extract

SAMPLE TWO

BREAKFAST

Cheese Dietish*

SNACK	SNACK
1 tangerine	1 apple
LUNCH	LUNCH
Seafood Salad*	Seafood Salad*
(Using light fish with ½ cup rice)	(Using dark fish with 1 cup rice)
Seafood Salad Dressing*	Seafood Salad Dressing*
SNACK	SNACK
1 cup nonfat milk	1 cup nonfat milk
DINNER	DINNER
3 ounces broiled chicken breast	3 ounces broiled lean hamburger
Salsa*	Salsa*
Steamed broccoli, green pepper, and cauliflower	Steamed broccoli, green pepper, and cauliflower
Oven-Fried Chips* (Using ½ potato)	Oven-Fried Chips* (Using 1 whole potato)
SNACK	SNACK
1 peach, cut into: ¾ cup non-fat yogurt dusted with cinnamon	1/3 papaya, cut into: ¾ cup nonfat yogurt dusted with cinnamon

SAMPLE THREE

BREAKFAST

1 ounce cracker (such as 2 Wasa Sesame, or
3 ½ Bran-a-Crisps, or 12 Matzo Minis)
Spread with:
¼ cup pot cheese mixed with
2 teaspoons diet margarine and
no-sodium seasonings

SNACK

½ grapefruit

SNACK

½ grapefruit

LUNCH

(Indian Restaurant)
3 ounces Tandori Chicken
    (See recipe for
      Hunk-i-dori Chicken*)
½ cup nonfat yogurt
½ cup rice
steamed vegetables

LUNCH

(Indian Restaurant)
3 ounces Lamb Shish Kebob
    (See recipe for
      Lamb Sleek Kebobs*)
½ cup nonfat yogurt
1 cup rice
steamed vegetables

(Hint: Restaurants generally serve six-ounce protein portions. Ask for a "doggie bag," put in half the protein for another day's meal *before* you start to eat. Hint #2: Remember, for craving-more times, you need two servings of starch. Hint #3: Even while working on weight maintenance, it's still important to ask for dishes made without butter or oil, and sauce served "on the side." Don't use additional fat, however—restaurants generally use fat in cooking. In Indian restaurants, watch out for the word "ghee." It's means clearified butter!)

SNACK

1 peach topped with:
¼ cup nonfat yogurt

SNACK

1 banana topped with:
¼ cup nonfat yogurt

(Note: Since lunch included ½ cup of yogurt—part of your milk requirement—you only need ¼ cup yogurt now.)

DINNER

(Picked up at Takeout
    Mexican Chicken Bar-
    becue)
4 ounces chicken breast
Salsa
2 corn tortillas
1 teaspoon margarine

DINNER

(Picked up at Takeout
    Mexican Chicken Bar-
    becue)
4 ounces dark-meat chicken
Salsa
4 corn tortillas
1 teaspoon margarine

(Hint: You can mix starches. Just be sure you get the right amount for each stage. Here, two corn tortillas—one-ounce total weight for both—equals one serving starch. Since you need double starches during craving-more times, eat two additional tortillas, or have two tortillas with one ear of corn.)

SNACK

¾ cup nonfat
    frozen yogurt

SNACK

¾ cup nonfat
    frozen yogurt

SAMPLE FOUR

BREAKFAST

½ English muffin
1 teaspoon margarine
1 ounce low-fat cheese
1 glass nonfat milk

SNACK

¼ cantaloupe

SNACK

¼ cantaloupe

LUNCH

(From yesterday's lunch)
Doggie-Bag Chicken
Salad*

SNACK

2 apricots

LUNCH

(From yesterday's lunch)
Doggie-Bag Lamb Salad*

SNACK

1 small apple

DINNER

(At French Restaurant)
4 ounces steamed mussels,
    steamed asparagus
1 ounce French roll

(Hint: A one-ounce roll resembles a slice of bread folded in half, and folded in half again.)

1 teaspoon butter

(Hint: Try to avoid butter, but once in a while it's okay.)

DINNER

(At French Restaurant)
4 ounces broiled trout
    steamed asparagus
2 1-ounce French rolls

1 teaspoon butter

SNACK

8 ounces low-fat milk,
    heated with cinnamon

SNACK

8 ounces low-fat milk,
    heated with cinnamon

SAMPLE FIVE

BREAKFAST

(Breakfast meeting at a deli)
½ bagel
1 tablespoon cream cheese
2 ounces turkey meat
½ slice tomato

(Hint: While at the deli, buy sliced dark and light meat of roasted turkey. Ask the deli man to please wrap your order in three-ounce portions. Your order will be packaged by the time you are ready to leave. Put the turkey in the fridge at work, and freeze at home for quickie lunches or dinners such as Toss-Away Turkey Salad below.)

SNACK

1/3 cup powdered milk,
    stirred into hot coffee

SNACK

1/3 cup powdered milk,
    stirred into hot coffee

LUNCH

(Salad Bar)

LUNCH

(Salad Bar)

For both stages have all the assorted free vegetables you want.

Go for "greens," but not if they are "greased." Go for the "white" veggies, but skip gloppy pastas soaked in fat.

¼ cup garbanzo beans	½ cup garbanzo beans
¼ cup kidney beans	½ cup kidney beans
½ cup cottage cheese	3 tablespoons hard cheese, grated
	(Hint: three tablespoons of grated cheese equals about one ounce.)
	1 hard-boiled egg

(Hint: While at the cafeteria, buy an orange, put it in your purse to snack on later.)

SNACK	SNACK
1 orange	1 orange

DINNER	DINNER
(Fast-Food Place)	(Fast-Food Place)
½ hamburger bun	1 hamburger bun
4 ounces charbroiled chicken breast	4 ounces charbroiled hamburger (well done)
1 plastic-package mayo	1 plastic-package mayo
or,	*or,*
1 tablespoon "special sauce"	1 tablespoon "special sauce"

(Hint: What's so "special" about this sauce? It's mostly mayo, relish, and catsup—just like Mom made.)

lettuce	lettuce
slice of tomato	slice of tomato

SNACK	SNACK
¾ cup nonfat yogurt	¾ cup nonfat yogurt
½ cup frozen blueberries	1 cup frozen purple grapes

SAMPLE SIX

BREAKFAST

French Toasted*

(Late breakfast: No snack)

LUNCH	LUNCH
Soft Chicken Tacos*	Soft Beef Tacos*
with,	with,
3 ounces chicken	3 ounces lean beef
lettuce, onions	lettuce, onions
Salsa	Salsa
2 corn tortillas	2 corn tortillas
¾ cup nonfat milk	1 ear of corn
	¾ cup nonfat milk

(Hint: The fat? Assume that in cooking the chicken or beef, some fat was already added. Hint #2: "Soft" tacos are tacos that are *not* made with a fried tortillas. If there are no "soft tacos" on the menu, ask, *"por favor,"* for the "regular" tacos with a side order of heated corn tortillas. Then discard the lard-fried taco shells and wrap the contents in your soft, fresh tortillas. Hint #3: Milk helps dissolve the hot spicy taste. Hint #4: Since there is ¼-cup of milk used in French Toasted,* drink only ¾-cup milk now.)

SNACK	SNACK
1 orange	1 banana

DINNER	DINNER
(Italian Restaurant)	(Italian Restaurant)
Green Salad	Green Salad
no dressing—use	no dressing—use
lemon juice or	lemon juice or
champagne vinegar	champagne vinegar

(Hint: If this is a romantic evening, skip the onions in the salad.)

4 ounces broiled sea bass
1 tablespoon sauce
½ cup spaghetti
fresh steamed green beans

4 ounces broiled salmon
1 tablespoon sauce
1 cup spaghetti
fresh steamed green beans

(Hint: If you've decided on spaghetti for your starch, ask that the bread basket be removed. You know why.)

SNACK

¾ cup low-fat yogurt
1 cup sliced strawberries

SNACK

¾ cup low-fat yogurt
1 cup sliced strawberries

SAMPLE SEVEN

BREAKFAST

(family over)
Huevos Rancheros*
2 corn tortillas
1 cup low-fat milk,
    heated with 1 cup strong coffee
(You need something "strong" with all the family over.)

SNACK

1/4 cantaloupe

SNACK

¼ cantaloupe

LUNCH

Crabby Bagel*

LUNCH

Lox-a-Bagel*

SNACK

1 orange

SNACK

1 apple

DINNER

Toss-Away Turkey Salad*
    (made with light meat
    from deli)

DINNER

Toss-Away Turkey Salad*
    (made with dark meat
    from deli)

SNACK	SNACK
4 cups air-popped corn	8 cups air-popped corn
1 cup nonfat milk	1 cup nonfat milk

(Hint #1: Since there was no starch at dinner, you can eat the starch—the popcorn—now. Hint #2: If you go for oil-popped corn with butter added—so tempting at the movies—you'll jack up a four-cup serving for only 100 calories to four cups for a whopping 480 calories! And besides, much of the "butter" on movie popcorn is really saturated coconut oil with butter-flavoring added.)

How to Have Your Cake and Keep Your Shape, Too

Bodyrhythm Maintenance Phase eating is safe and sensible. It's healthful and well balanced. And it will work to keep you at your goal *if* you keep within the guidelines.

Many women find they continue to lose weight, even on the Maintenance Phase. If that's true for you, then triple your intake of starches. That means you could eat a potato *and* one slice of bread for dinner. Or one cup pasta with a small roll. I urge you not to increase protein servings beyond the three ounces or eat higher-fat proteins too often. That's because protein often comes with excess fat, the most fattening calories. Too much fat can be dangerous in terms of heart disease or cancer. Excess protein also may cause a loss of calcium from the bones. All in all, it's better to stick to extra starches if your weight continues to drop.

"But what about sweets?" I'm most often asked after I've explained maintenance principles. "Are cakes, ice cream, and other goodies off limits *forever*?"

Not exactly. In fact, there's built-in leeway for an occasional splurge—sugar or otherwise—on the Maintenance Plan. You *can* stay shaped up and have your cake. Not every day, or every week. But once in a while. However, you must control the circumstances and the amounts.

Plan ahead. Save sweets for special occasions—your birthday, for example, a major holiday (Secretaries' Day and Election Day are not major) or an important dinner (every Saturday night is not that important). You might find that planning ahead for a sweet treat in a sense doubles your pleasure: like other pleasures (you know what they are), the anticipation can be almost as enjoyable as the eating! However, keep in mind that special occasions should be just that. Don't go out of your way to look for excuses to "celebrate." Tough days at work aren't special. Days when you are feeling sick, down, bored, or mopey aren't special. If you don't use sweets to make yourself feel better, but instead enjoy them as part of a real *occasion*, they can be relatively harmless in terms of your weight.

Avoid sweets when you are over your goal weight. Maintenance eating should keep the pounds off. But if the scale does indicate an upward trend in your weight, stay away from sweets entirely until the needle on the scale goes back to where you want it to be. In the meantime, sugar is the enemy. It triggers insulin. Insulin will pack extra sugar calories into your fat cells and aggravate hunger. And sugary foods are often filled with fats. You don't want to have to deal with hunger, cravings, and fat when you are already a couple of pounds over your goal.

Don't eat "diet" sweets. I've seen it happen too many times: the woman who regularly uses artificial sugar or "diet" pastries and candies to feed a sweet tooth eventually develops cravings for more and more of "real" desserts or becomes candy-crazed. When she finally gives in, she's out of control. Much better to have the real thing in the first place—but have it rarely. When you do go for it, have the most sinfully rich *real* dessert you can find. If you settle for second best or opt for a dietetic version, you may feel cheated and pig out later. Choose the best. But have it on special occasions, when your weight is where you want it to be. And eat half portions of the dessert.

Practice quantity control. Half a piece of cake is better than none. And it's a lot better for your shape than a whole piece. The point, of course, is to limit yourself to half portions of dessert. You *can* do it. Whenever someone tells me a single scoop of ice cream or a half slice of pie won't satisfy her, I remind her that two scoops of ice cream or a whole piece of pie probably won't "satisfy" her either. Where sweets are concerned, there's *always* room for more. But the best "treat" you can have is a feel-good feeling about yourself. Remind yourself you *can* have more dessert—but not now. Another time. (Sweets won't become extinct while you shed those couple of excess pounds.) Think of sweets as an "extra." Something to enjoy, bite by bite, not to fill up on. The "more" you want to experience, if your weight is up, is more of a positive feeling about yourself. And you'll feel better if you skip the dessert and lose those few extra pounds.

Whenever possible, eat your sweet away from home. It's much easier to practice quantity control in the presence of others. If you order a slice of cake in a restaurant, you probably won't have the nerve to order a second slice. (I don't.) The same goes for seconds at a dinner party; most of us don't want to be piggy in public. But the cake you buy to eat at home is another matter. When guests leave and the rest of the family is in bed, the siren song of leftovers can be irresistible. Tip: When you celebrate special occasions at home, buy only as much dessert as you think you'll need. If there's any left, offer it to your guests. If they refuse, *throw it out* immediately. And I mean flush it down the garbage disposal or shove it down the trash chute. Don't just wrap it in neat little bag and let it lie in the trash can in the kitchen. You know why.

Tips for Special-Event Eating

Parties and dining out, especially at ethnic restaurants, can pose special problems when you are trying to hold the line against weight gainback. The trick is to indulge without overindulging. These pointers can help.

Keep track of your intake. It's important not to eat

large amounts at any time, in any circumstances. Restaurants and parties are no exceptions. Eating too much all at once causes an insulin increase, resulting in more calories stored as fat, fewer calories burned. Further, overeating one night makes it harder to cut back the next day because insulin is still at work dragging out sugar. You're hungry the next day—and it's nearly impossible to cut back when your body is driving you to eat more. (That's one reason why it's so hard to pay back calories just by saying, "I'll cut back and make up for it tomorrow." It's deficit spending—and the calories just keep getting charged up in fat deposits.) With insulin in high gear, it locks those calories away for a longer period of time. To prevent these diet disasters from happening, try to stay within the Maintenance Guidelines and limit yourself accordingly.

In an Italian restaurant, for example, if you are craving-less, have a half cup of pasta (one serving starch), three ounces of broiled fish or chicken breast (dinner portion of protein), and a tablespoon of sauce (one fat). If you are eating Mexican style, and you are in a craving-more mode, choose two corn tortillas (a one-ounce, single serving of starch) plus a half cup of rice (another serving of starch) and three ounces of beef or dark-meat chicken (higher-fat protein choices). You can assume that there is enough fat in the sautéd rice to cover your fat portion.

If you have no cravings, but a higher-fat protein (prime rib, salmon, eggs) is all that's offered to you, don't take it as a sign from the Fates that you were meant to overeat. Instead, cut off all visible beef blubber, scoop the cheese out of the omelet, or scrape away the blobs of butter, sauce, or gravy from your salmon and eat a three-ounce portion. Skip the fat portion with that meal—higher-fat proteins have more than enough fat when you are craving-free.

The method is not entirely precise, of course. In many cases you'll be over your quota for a meal. But if you steer by these rough estimates, you won't go too far astray.

Order sauces, gravies and dressing "on the side." It's the only way to be sure your food doesn't come drenched in fat. Measure out the appropriate amount and add it yourself. No need to carry a set of measuring spoons with you; you know what a tablespoon of sauce looks like. And after weighing portions at home, you should be able to judge three ounces of meat, chicken, or fish by the "eyeball" method.

Tell the waiter to hold the salt and MSG. It may not work, but it's worth mentioning. Sodium, remember, not only holds on to water, but can increase starch absorption within your body, which means that salted food can deliver more calories than the same food unsalted.

Try to avoid family-style restaurant situations. You know, those Chinese, Indian, and Thai places where food is wheeled in on heaping platters and everyone digs in. Free-for-all service can make it more difficult to practice quantity control. Just the sight of all that food can trigger an outpouring of fat-making insulin. In addition, you might get food-greedy in those situations, as I do. (I feel like chopsticking hands or dueling forks for more than my share.)

On the home front, serve dishes from the kitchen so you aren't tempted by the sight of all those platters and bowls of food making the go-round on the dining-room table.

Go back to the Bodyrhythm Diet if you overdo. Even a single major eating episode, if it includes too much salt, carbohydrate, and/or fat, can add a pound or two. The only way to know for sure is to step on the scale first thing the next day. Over your goal? Don't let it throw you and don't throw out the scale. And for heaven's sake, don't let extra pounds throw you off the track into a bag of cookies. Instead, go back to Stage II eating immediately. These meals, slightly higher-fat and higher-starch than Stage I food, will make you feel less deprived and pacify hunger that always occurs after overdoing. Once cravings and hunger are under control again, switch to Stage I and stay there until the extra pounds are gone. It's the best way to prevent a minor problem from ballooning into a major one.

Alcohol? Within Limits

Now that you're slimmed down, you can have a drink, *once in a while*. But keep in mind that with your smaller body mass, alcohol will affect you faster, and harder. At the very least, control over your eating will dissolve more readily. (Not to mention the effect it can have on your ability to function responsibly when you get behind the wheel.)

If you choose to have a drink now and then, abide by these guidelines:

Save drinks for special times . . . holidays, parties, romantic dinners. Every day is not special. Being alone is not special. Being sick is not special.

Limit yourself to three drinks a week, tops. Without exception, women who drink more than that have a harder time trying to keep the pounds from creeping back. By the way, one drink is a three-ounce glass of wine, six ounces of beer, or an ounce of the hard stuff.

Drink with your meals, not before. Alcohol lowers inhibitions and the sugar in some drinks can cause a drop in blood sugar, making you feel hungrier, especially if it has been a few hours since you last ate. The combination is somewhat less likely to result in major overeating if you sip your drink with your meal (or even afterward); the food in your stomach will soften the impact.

Keep a close watch on your weight. There is only one way to tell exactly how alcohol affects your body's fat-making mechanisms, and that is by taking the scale test. If you start to gain soon after you add an occasional drink to your diet, cut out the alcohol until your weight drops back down. Then limit yourself to two drinks a week.

Yes, You *Can* Keep It Off

No matter how careful you are, you can expect small ups and downs in your weight. The downs are no problem but the ups can be traumatic. Be prepared. Don't panic.

Don't try to comfort fears with food. *Do* have an antifat plan that includes a *daily* weigh-in and a return to Bodyrhythm Diet eating *immediately* if you gain even a single unwanted pound.

That's right. I want you to weigh yourself every day now, even though I suggested that you step on the scale only once a week when you were on the diet. That's because on the diet you were looking for weight *loss,* and weight loss is always interspersed with plateaus when—despite your best efforts—your body temporarily refuses to release more fat. By allowing several days to go by between weigh-ins, plateaus are less noticeable, less discouraging.

The situation is different now. You've lost pounds of fat and your main concern is keeping them off. With a daily weight readout, you'll know about small problems as they arise—and be in a better position to prevent them from becoming big problems. I don't have to tell you it's a lot easier to get rid of one or two pounds than it is to deal with five, ten, twenty!

If post-pig-out cravings are a problem, ease back to Stage II—double starches, higher-fat proteins, a sugar-dense fruit. When residual cravings have subsided, shift into Stage I.

Stay there until your weight is back where you want it. If cravings were nonexistent to begin with, you can turbocharge into Stage I immediately.

Don't wait until tomorrow to address those extra pounds. Don't put it off until the beginning of next week, or when you come back from vacation, or after the holidays, or when you feel more motivated. Do it *now*, while that small problem is still small.

By getting yourself back onto the diet proper—Stage II, if you need help in craving control, Stage I when cravings are not a hassle—you can use and reuse the Bodyrhythm Diet to get and keep the body you want. From now on.

Maintenance Recipes

BREAKFASTS — ANY DAY

Cheese Dietish

¼ cup cottage cheese
½ teaspoon vanilla
cinnamon
1 teaspoon margarine
½ English muffin

Measure out the cottage cheese with one of those measuring cups that holds exactly ½ cup. Don't just plop out spoonfuls without measuring. Put the cottage cheese into a coffee mug (easier to clean than a mixing bowl). Mash in cinnamon, margarine, and vanilla. Put muffin on foil. Spoon cottage cheese mix over muffin and pat down with a fork. Toast in toaster oven.

French Toasted

¼ cup skim milk
1 egg
1 teaspoon vanilla
cinnamon
1 slice of old bread (not moldy, just stale)
1 teaspoon margarine

Mix up the milk, egg, and vanilla in a bowl. Dunk the bread into the bowl. Start the coffee. Spray a frying pan with nonstick spray. Check the bread—it should be soggy. Slide the bread into the pan. Pour over any remaining egg mix. Turn once. Sprinkle with cinnamon. Top with margarine. (Hint: Subtract the ¼-cup milk from your daily milk requirement.)

Huevos Rancheros

1 egg
1 tablespoon salsa
⅛ avocado
pepper

Spray pan with nonstick coating. Beat up the egg in the pan. Turn on the burner. Add the salsa. Cut the avocado into the eggs. Use as much pepper as you like. Makes one serving. If you're serving family or guests, just multiply the recipe by the number of servings. (Note: Use prepared salsa instead of doing all that chopping and mincing of tomatoes, onions, and garlic that so many recipes call for in making Huevos Rancheros. I'd love to know how to get that onion-garlic smell off my fingers after chopping—I end up smelling like a walking deli. But maybe some men find Essence of Deli a real turn-on. Someone told me to roll deodorant onto my fingers before chopping. Not only did that not prevent the smell, but my breakfast tasted like Huevos Antiperspirantos.)

LUNCHES AND DINNERS

Crabby Bagel (for craving-less days)

⅛ avocado
¼ teaspoon mustard
½ of a 2-ounce bagel
1 slice tomato
3 ounces crab

Rinse the crab and pat dry. Mash up the avocado and the mustard. Smear onto bagel. Top with tomato slice and crab. Toast.

Doggie Bag Salad

3 ounces chicken breast (restaurant leftovers)
or,
3 ounces lamb (restaurant leftovers)

(Note: For craving-less days, use any low-fat protein, like chicken breast, halibut, or shellfish. For craving-more times, use a higher-fat protein, like lamb, beef, or higher-fat fish, such as swordfish or salmon.)

½ cup mushrooms
1 bell pepper
1 green onion
1 tomato
½ cup cooked rice (restaurant leftovers)
    (For craving-more times, use 1 cup rice.)
1 teaspoon sesame oil
1 tablespoon rice vinegar
lemon juice (as much or as little as you want)
a smidgen of crushed red pepper
paprika

Line up the chicken (or lamb), mushrooms, peppers, onion, and tomato on a cutting board. Chop away. (My chopping board is my "center for aggression-releasing therapy.") Put everything in the recipe into a plastic container. Close it *tightly*, then shake well. (Hint: If you want a hot lunch, just put the container in the microwave oven. Be sure the container is microwave safe, or you'll have salad with plastic drippings.)

Lox-a-Bagel (for craving-more days)

3 ounces lox
1 two-ounce bagel
1 tablespoon cream cheese
1 slice onion
1 slice tomato

Rinse the lox. Pat dry with dish towel. (Hint: Don't use paper towels for patting the lox; the paper fibers will stick to it.) Spread bagel with cream cheese, top with onion, tomato, and lox. Toast or not.

Seafood Salad

3 ounces leftover fish
(For craving-less days, use a low-fat fish—the "white" ones, like halibut, sole, cod, founder, or shellfish. For craving-more times, use a higher-fat fish—the "reddish" ones, like swordfish, salmon, tuna.)
any leftover steamed vegetables
fancy lettuce—like watercress, curly endive, radicchio
frozen peas and corn
(Note: For craving-less days, use ¼ cup peas and ¼ cup corn for a total of 1 serving starch. For craving-more times, use ½ cup each for 2 servings starch.)

Chop up the fish and steamed vegetables. Tear up the lettuce. Dump everything into a plastic container. Stir. Serve with Seafood Salad Dressing. (See "SAUCES.")

Soft Tacos, with Chicken or Beef

½ green jalapeño chili
¼ yellow onion
bunch of cilantro, snipped of stems
½ tomato
1 garlic clove
3 ounces chicken breast, cut into strips
(for craving-less days)
or,
3 ounces beef, cut into strips
(for craving-more days)
2 corn tortillas (4 tortillas for craving-more days)
salsa
2 tablespoons sour cream

Remove the seeds and membranes from chili. (Use gloves; don't wipe your eyes or touch your nose.) Chop up the chili, onion, cilantro, tomato, and garlic. (Hint: It takes you less time to chop these few ingredients then it does to haul out the blender and then wash it later.) In a nonstick pan, "fry" the chicken or beef in water. Drain. Add the tomato-chili mix. Heat the tortillas in the oven. When the meat is cooked, put the tomato-chicken mixture onto the tortillas, roll up. Serve with salsa and 2 tablespoons of sour cream.

Hunk-i-dori Chicken

1 tiny onion
1 clove garlic
4 ounces chicken breast (weighed without skin or bone)
   (Use dark meat for craving-more days)
¼ cup lemon juice
¼ teaspoon dried rosemary leaves
¼ teaspoon dried thyme leaves
⅛ teaspoon curry powder
⅛ teaspoon pepper
paprika
½ cup yogurt
½ cucumber
mint leaves

Chop up the onion and garlic. Put the chicken in a baking dish. Top with everything else in recipe except the yogurt, cucumber, and mint leaves. Cover and bake at 350° until the chicken is no longer pink inside, about 20 to 30 minutes. (Note: Real Tandori chicken is made in a clay pot and roasted in a super-hot oven. I don't have a clay pot or an oven that can be used to make pottery on its day off. But I've got the chicken and spices.) Chop up the cucumber and mint leaves, and stir into the yogurt. Serve the chicken with the yogurt on the side; include the yogurt as part of your milk portion. Serve with Hurried-Curried Rice.

Lamb Sleek Kebobs (for craving-more times)

4 ounces trimmed lamb
3 small onions
3 cherry tomatoes

　1 green bell pepper cut into slices
　1 tablespoon soy sauce
　⅛ teaspoon ground ginger

Cut lamb into chunks. Thread lamb, onions, tomatoes, and green pepper onto bamboo skewers or knitting needles. Mix soy and ginger and baste when you think about it. Broil until the meat is no longer red inside. (Hint: Instead of basting, I use the spray technique. Buy a spray bottle from the drugstore. Fill it with ½ cup water, the soy sauce, and ginger. Spray the lamb during cooking. Hint #2: Buy a new spray bottle; don't use one that had window cleaner in it.) Serve on a bed of 1 cup Hurried-Curried Rice.

Toss-Away Turkey Salad

　(Use any leftovers or hand-me-downs from the week's meals.)
　3 ounces turkey
　　(Use any leftover light meat for craving-less days; use
　　any leftover dark meat for craving-more days.)
　½ tomato
　½ cucumber
　½ onion
　any green vegetables: lettuce, broccoli, chard, spinach, green
　　beans, or any leftover veggies.
　1 teaspoon mayonnaise
　pinch curry powder
　pinch ginger
　juice of 1 lemon

Find a large salad bowl. Cut the turkey into slices. While you're at the cutting board, cut up the tomato, cucumber, onion, and any green vegetables into chunks. Throw all of it in the bowl. Mix the mayonnaise, curry powder, ginger, and lemon juice together. Stir into salad. Eat out of the bowl.

STARCHES

Hurried-Curried Rice

handful of cilantro
1 stalk celery
2 green onions
1 tablespoon lemon juice
1 teaspoon soy sauce
1 teaspoon curry powder
pinch ground ginger
2 teaspoons herbed salad dressing
½ cup cooked rice

With scissors, snip off the stems from the cilantro. Lay the celery, onions, and cilantro side by side on a cutting board. Chop away. Dump chopped vegetables into hot rice. Stir in the everything else. Heat up. (Hint: This recipe makes 1 serving starch. If you want to use this recipe for craving-more times, use 1 cup of rice for a double serving of starch. You may also want to add more soy sauce, lemon juice, curry powder, and ginger. But watch out, too much ginger and curry and you could be sitting at the dining table wiping your nose or mopping your brow. . . not romantic.)

Oven-Fried Chips

½ potato
1 teaspoon oil
chili powder

Turn oven on to 500°. Cut the potato into thick slices—about ¼ inch. Smear oil around a strip of foil. Sprinkle chili powder over foil. Flip the potatoes over the oil/chili powder. Bake for 15 to 20 minutes; toss them around if you remember to do so. (Hint: Don't bother peeling the potatoes. It's just one extra step and everyone I know loves the chewy peel. Hint #2: For craving-more times, use 1 whole potato.)

SAUCES

Seafood Salad Dressing

>   1 tablespoon catsup
>   ½ teaspoon chili sauce
>   1 tablespoon tomato sauce
>   1 teaspoon oil
>   juice of 1 lime
>   1 teaspoon or so of capers

Mix it all together. (Hint: Save those containers that you get at the drugstore with your prescription pills. The larger the container the better. Spoon the salad dressing into these. It won't leak, and by keeping the salad dressing separate from the salad, you won't end up with droopy lettuce at lunchtime. One woman told me the containers used for urine specimens work the best as portable salad-dressing containers—but be prepared for stares when you pour the contents of a urine container over your salad.)

De-oiled Tomato Basil Sauce

>   ¼ cup boiling water
>   ½ cup fresh basil
>   1 clove garlic
>   1 tablespoon tomato sauce
>   1 teaspoon "poultry seasoning"

Drop everything in the blender or food processor. Blend. If it gets clogged, add more water, spoonful by spoonful. (Hint: Do not try to unclog the blades by sticking your fingers into blender.)

Preferred Brand Name Products

Note: This is a partial list. But it contains brand-name foods generally available in your local supermarket. Check for similar products. But read all labels.

Seasonings and Sauces

SEASONINGS: Gaylor Houser's Vegit, Mrs. Dash (any variety), Shilling, Spice Islands

(*Warning:* Beware of trick advertising. Some labels claim "no salt." But the product may contain *sodium*, technically not salt. However, it's the sodium part of salt that holds water and can make you feel bloated and sluggish. Sodium also comes disguised under such names as "sodium benzoate," "monosodium glutamate (MSG)", and "calcium disodium". Then there are gibberish additives like "hydrolyzed vegetable protein" and "soy isolates," other sources of sodium. To be on the safe sodium side, use herbs, spices and seasonings without salt, sodium, sugar or other additives.)

SAUCES: Pritikin (all varieties), Enrico's No-Salt-Or-Sugar-Spaghetti Sauce, Del Monte (no salt) Sauces, Hunt's

No Salt Sauces, Ortega Green Chili Salsa, McIlheny Tobasco Sauce.

(*Hint:* Look for other sauces made without oil, salt sugar, or meat. Or make your own sauce: Chop tomatoes, garlic, fresh basil, oregano and onions. Stuff in a blender. Whirl away. Add a bit of chili for a hot sauce. Serve on chicken or fish.)

Milk Products

NONFAT DRY MILK: Carnation

(*Note:* Look for other brands. But be careful. Some brands of powdered milk have whole milk or cream "solids" added. Avoid those. And don't use "non-dairy creamers," often full of corn syrup (sugar) and coconut oil—far more saturated than butterfat. Use nonfat powdered milk or evaporated skim milk to lighten your coffee, decaf or tea.)

EVAPORATED NONFAT OR SKIMMED MILK: Carnation, Pet

(*Note:* Don't use regular evaporated milk—high in fat—or "sweetened condensed milk"—not only high-fat, but high in sugar as well.)

NONFAT (NO FRUIT) YOGURT: Alta Dena, Continental, Dannon

(*Note:* Use nonfat plain yogurt without fruit or sweeteners. If you want a sweet taste, add your own fresh fruit. Why pay to have jam added that's labeled "fruit"?)

Cereals and Breads

COLD CEREALS: Kolln's Oat Bran Crunch, Uncle Sam, Nabisco Shredded Wheat (biscuit or spoon sized, regular or with added bran), Kellogg's Nutri-Grain Nuggets

(*Hints:* Cereals lead the way in supermarket confusion. Here are a few pointers: 1) Since you eat more than cereal in a day, there's no reason to select a costly vitamin-fortified brand. 2) Look for cereals that are "whole" grain. Just because a cereal says it's made from "wheat" or any grain doesn't mean it hasn't been processed down to the pulp—literally. 3) Puffed cereals are more air than cereal. But "whole grain" puffed cereals—wheat, corn, rice, oats—are nutritious, fiber-rich, low in salt and sugar. 4) At one time, the amount of sugar in any product was easy to spot—the closer to the front of the list of ingredients, the more the sugar. Not so now. Under attack, cereal manufacturers cut back on white sugar. But they added other sugary sweeteners that add up to the same thing. These include brown sugar, honey, sucrose, fructose, corn syrup, etc. Then, to satisfy savvy eaters who knew there wasn't much difference among various sweeteners, the cereal folk started pumping in fake sugars. Skip those. Stick to basics in cereal—whole grains, with little if any sugar or salt.)

HOT CEREALS: Wheatena, Quaker Oat Bran, Old Fashioned Quaker Oats, Nabisco Wholesome 'n Hearty Oat Bran

(*Note:* Look for other brands as well. Select whole grains—many "wheat" or "rice" cereals are processed to remove the tough, high-fiber, outer bran. But they lack natural nutrients and fiber. Check for cereals without added sugar or salt. Avoid "instant" cereals—they're almost always loaded with sugar and salt.)

BREAD: Pritikin Whole Wheat Bread, Pritikin English Muffins

(*Note:* Look for 100% whole grain breads, rolls, muffins and pita. Just because a bread is labeled "wheat" or even "whole wheat" doesn't mean it's 100% whole wheat. The label should read "100% whole wheat." Tricky, tricky. Avoid "diet" bread, so processed it feels like you're chomping cotton. Whole grain bread with natural fiber makes you chew. And chewing stimulates the fullness center of your brain.)

Canned Tuna and Chicken

TUNA: Chicken of the Sea, Star-Kist, Featherweight

(*Note:* Use "water packed" tuna to reduce fat. To cut down on sodium, use "dietetic," "no salt added" or rinse "low-sodium tuna." If you use regular water-packed tuna, rinse it for a full minute and you remove 75% of excess sodium.)

CHICKEN: Featherweight, Swanson Chunk White Chicken (rinse well)

Fats

OILS: Puritan Oil

(*Hint:* Generally, an oil that's clear when refrigerated—like corn, safflower, or the new canola oil—contains less saturated fat. Olive oil, although cloudy when chilled, is a "mono-saturated" fat, still a good, tasty choice.)

MARGARINES: Fleischmann's (unsalted) or Parkay (unsalted), Mayzola (unsalted).

(*Note:* The softer the margarine, the less the saturated fat. Tub margarines have less saturated fat than stick. And liquid bottled margarines, such as Fleischmann's and Parkay, have less saturated fat than tub margarines. Use salad oil for even less saturated fat.)

MAYONNAISE: Best Foods (Cholesterol Free), Kraft Miracle Whip (Cholesterol Free), Weight Watcher's (No Cholesterol Mayonnaise).

(*Hint:* Instead of gobs of mayonnaise in tuna or chicken, use nonfat yogurt with a dash of dry mustard.)